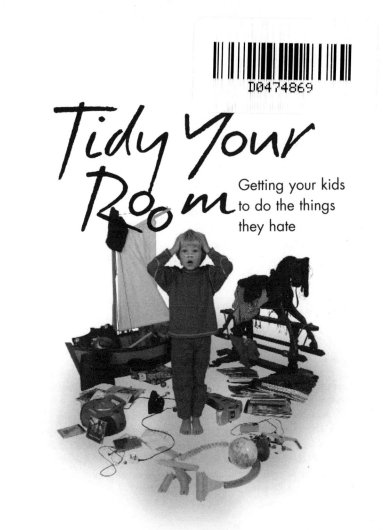

Tidy Your Room

Getting your kids to do the things they hate

Jane Bidder

Editors: Richard Craze, Roni Jay

new tricks for old dogs

Published by White Ladder Press Ltd

Great Ambrook, Near Ipplepen, Devon TQ12 5UL

01803 813343

www.whiteladderpress.com

First published in Great Britain in 2006

10 9 8 7 6 5 4 3 2

© Jane Bidder 2006

The right of Jane Bidder to be identified as author of this work has been asserted by her in accordance with the Copyright, Designs and Patents Act 1988.

ISBN 1 905410 04 2

ISBN 978 1 905410 04 0

British Library Cataloguing in Publication Data

A CIP record for this book can be obtained from the British Library.

Designed and typeset by Julie Martin Ltd
Cover design by Julie Martin Ltd
Cover photograph by Jonathon Bosley
Printed and bound by TJ International Ltd, Padstow, Cornwall

The paper used for the text pages of this book is FSC certified.
FSC (The Forest Stewardship Council) is an international network to promote responsible management of the world's forests.

FSC
Mixed Sources
Product group from well-managed forests and other controlled sources

Cert no. SGS-COC-2482
www.fsc.org
© 1996 Forest Stewardship Council

White Ladder Press
Great Ambrook, Near Ipplepen, Devon TQ12 5UL
01803 813343
www.whiteladderpress.com

DEDICATION

This book is dedicated to Giles (who doesn't lift a finger); to Lucy (who could run the house); and to William (who has just employed a cleaner for his student pad).

Acknowledgements

Grateful thanks to Oliver Shuster for his painstaking analysis of our *Tidy Your Room* survey.

I would also like to thank my agent Phil Patterson of Marjacq Scripts as well as Roni Jay and Richard Craze for their unfailing good humour and professional attitude.

Finally, I'm extremely grateful to all the parents who were cajoled into filling in our survey when they could have been spending their precious time in nagging their children to tidy their rooms.

Contents

Introduction

"Go and tidy your room!" How often have you said that to your kids without any effect? Face it. You might as well save your breath because even as you're instructing them (all right, yelling at them) to clean the offending bedsit area, they're already doing something much more interesting, like logging on to MSN. And if they do make an attempt to tidy the piles of books, CDs and chewing gum off the floor, they probably won't do it the way you want.

Now all that's about to change. This book holds the secret to getting your kids to do what they don't want to do. Well, maybe that's a bit of an exaggeration but it will definitely help. And as every despairing parent knows, that's a start.

We've divided the first part of this book into age groups because although it would be nice if our five year old learned to change the duvet cover, even the most demanding of us parents needs to recognise that their arms probably aren't long enough. On the other hand, an eight year old might well be more conscientious about washing up than an 18 year old, so if you want to swap ages and chapters, please feel free.

Mind you, however old your kids are, there's one trick that can be applied to all ages. And that's this: *If you learn how to make them WANT to do that job, you've cracked it.*

Now there are all kinds of ways to do this, ranging from bribery to shame, depending on your child's personality and possibly star sign. There's also the winning (or losing) combination of your own personality and theirs. Some parents definitely rub their kids up the wrong way. My 14 year old is constantly telling me I should give him more slack. So part of the trick in getting them to do those jobs they hate, is to change the way you ask them to do it.

Yes, it does sound a bit like politics, doesn't it? But hang on in there, and we'll explain how. Just one more thing before we go on. When your kids refuse to lift a finger, remind them that in the good – sorry, bad – old days, children had to do really tough jobs like plough the land, go up chimneys and sell things in the street. So they've got it easy, now, haven't they?

Chapter one

How to get toddlers to do the things they hate

OK, this might sound a bit like child slavery, but what's wrong with that? Start as you mean to go on and you might just, hormones permitting, have a fairly passable teenager on your hands. Your future daughter-in-law (or son-in-law) will thank you, presuming your untidy little offspring ever finds anyone to take them on.

WHAT YOUR CHILD CAN DO AT THIS AGE

Isn't a toddler too young to enter the work market? Not at all. Under fives can do more than you think. The trouble is that we assume toddlers need us. In fact, they can be a very useful support for adults too. After all, parenting should be give and take, rather like a marriage except that (sadly) you can't divorce the kids.

Here are some examples.

Passing things

'Please can you pass me the remote control?' is a perfectly reasonable request when you've collapsed on the sofa in front of the telly after the school run, cooking dinner, a day in the office and toddler bath time.

Rather like someone learning a foreign language, toddlers can understand more than they can say. So if you point to the remote control and repeat the request, they will eventually get the hang of it. It is, however, vital to remember your own pleases and thank yous. If we don't say it, how can we expect them to reciprocate?

A word of warning, however. Don't criticise them if they drop the control and the batteries fall out, rolling under the sofa to places where you and the vacuum cleaner have never ventured. If you tell them how stupid they are, they won't be very keen to repeat the performance which means that next time, you'll have to get up and get that remote control yourself. Instead, praise them for toddling across the room and tell them how helpful they've been.

There are other things they can pass too. One of the most essential, I have learned over the years, is another roll of loo paper from the cupboard when you are marooned on the seat with one remaining square. Passing the loo roll, however, also requires another skill. You need to make sure they know where such necessities are kept in your house. It's not a bad idea to inform older members of the household at the same time, including any resident husbands or wives and teenagers who presume that new rolls of loo paper arrive like magic.

Collect their own coat/socks/gloves

Yes of course it's quicker to nip up the stairs and get the above items yourself. But if we encourage them at this early age to get their own stuff, they're more likely to carry on when they're older.

Again, this requires a bit of skilful planning on your part. Keep essentials such as coats, socks, gloves, wellies, and slippers close to hand so they don't have to stumble up the stairs and fall down again when retrieving them. This is particularly useful during the panic school run slot when every second counts. I keep a wicker basket of gloves and hats in the hall so they can play lucky dip. They might not end up with matching garments but that's not the point.

Get themselves dressed

Save this one for weekends at first until they improve, as this particular skill can be time consuming – especially if they throw a strop at the same time about what they will and won't wear. One trick is to leave out a choice of gear but always put it in the same place as close to the bed as possible. Start off by making it a game. Isn't it fun? You're going to get out of bed and dress yourself! Yes of course they'll need help with some things but you'll be surprised at how fast they learn.

OK, maybe they won't. So if they need a bit of extra encouragement, try the sing song game. This involves singing out the name of the garment (sock, t-shirt, shorts) as they put it on. It's time consuming which is why we suggest you save this one for weekends but it might just work. And let's face it, even if they only put on some of their clothes, it's a start.

Put their training cup/mug on the table when it's time to eat

Yes, you will need to keep the cup/mug in a place where they can easily reach it. Otherwise you might well be delayed by a trip to casualty. But if they can get into the habit of going to a floor level cupboard and getting their cup, plate and cutlery every time you say 'Please help me lay the table', you're almost there.

It also works in reverse. Don't be so relieved when meal time is over that you allow them to escape, leaving you with all the mess. All right, so they might be a bit young to wash up but they can still pick up their mug and take it to the sink. We agree it's unfortunate if the mug is still full and they spill the contents en route but hey, what's a bit of mess if we're training these kids up for the future?

Put away their toys

This is the first basic step to our ultimate goal of tidying a teenager's tip – sorry, bedroom. The great thing about toddler toys is that they don't usually stick to the floor like gum or other unmentionables to be found in older siblings' dens. So it shouldn't be difficult for a smallish child to pick up a couple of toys and put them somewhere else.

It's the 'somewhere else' that can be the key phrase in the Putting Away Their Toys skill. If you have a bright toy box, kids might be keener to put them in. I have a crafty minded friend who makes her own out of large cardboard boxes. Because her kids have helped her make them, they're keen to use them. She even has one box for puzzles, another for pull along toys and another for little figures. Yes, it *does* sound a bit obsessive but she says it's good for their sorting skills and it keeps them quiet for a while.

Washing up

You have to be a brave parent to do this one as it might involve a certain amount of mess. But that's one of the main points we want to get across. It might be quicker and less messy in the short term if you do it yourself, but if you don't delegate, they won't ever learn. So give them a pinny and maybe a little stool to stand on at the sink and off you go. Alternatively, if you prefer washing, give them a drying up cloth but get them to stick to safe cutlery and avoid glasses.

Clap hands to amuse a younger baby

If you've been brave (careless?) enough to have another baby after your toddler, you might as well make the use of the latter. When mine were little, my eldest son was invaluable in amusing his baby sister with games like Pat a Cake and Funny Faces.

Jobs outside the house

Strapping themselves into the car. Clunk, click. Make it a game. If the little darlings fight the belt, refuse to drive until they put it on. Alternatively, get older children to do this job for the younger ones. (Always make sure it's done up properly before you drive off.)

Holding shopping. Nothing heavy, you understand, or someone will be onto ChildLine. But they could carry the odd tin for you.

Paying up

Most children love playing shop. So let older pre-schoolers help you find the right change if your shopping isn't big enough to warrant a credit card. It also teaches them the difference between coins.

WARNING *Do not, on any account, let them find out what your pin number is. A certain child of my acquaintance (not my own – honestly) topped up his mobile phone credit courtesy of his father's plastic. And he wasn't even nine years old.*

Look for a car parking space

My lot used to love this 'job' when they were small. First one to call out 'There's one' got loads of praise.

On the job thinking

When you're doing jobs yourself, ask yourself if your children are old enough or capable enough to help you with whatever you're doing at the time. It might give you some ideas.

HOW TO GET THEM TO DO IT

This is where we enter the heavy psychology bit. Actually, it's not that heavy – we're just trying to sound knowledgeable. In fact, it's common sense with a very large dash of parental cunning.

Explain why it needs to be done

I have a friend who has always logically explained to her children why they should wash their hands after the loo, clean their teeth, and not run across the road. She's very calm and will quietly point out what will happen if they do and don't do these things.

She also does the same with jobs that they're not keen on. For example, if they don't want to put away their toys, she will tell them that someone might trip over them and hurt themselves. Or that they won't be able to find them the next day. Personally this never worked on my children because they're too strong minded but it's worth starting off with the logical approach before you try other tactics.

Praise them/thank them so they want to do it again

If you're sitting marooned on the loo seat and your toddler actually manages to get off their backside to pass you another roll of paper, believe me you'll be grateful. Toddlers are vain people. If someone praises them, they'll want to do it again. So make sure they know how grateful you are. And tell them what clever little sausages they are, as well.

Also sing their praises in front of other people – when the kids can hear you. It will make them feel good and make them want to repeat the performance.

Give them their own equipment

Embroider/write their name on a drying up cloth which can then be their very own. In fact, we think this is such a good idea that we might just start manufacturing our own White Ladder for Kids drying up cloths.

Make it into a game

Who can tidy their bedroom faster? Who can clear up their pile of toys before someone else? You could even offer small rewards. Another idea is to hide little treats round the room which they can find as they clean or tidy up. A kind of treasure hunt with ulterior motives.

Water play

Water games usually go down well so use this in conjunction with jobs. Put a bowl of soapy water in the garden, if it's a nice day, or on a sheet of paper on the kitchen floor. Get them to scrub down bath toys or anything else that's washable.

Stage your own musical

Put on the radio or get them to sing while they're doing jobs. I know a mum – honestly – who will stand in the middle of her children's room and point out areas that need tidying while at the same time, singing Do, Ray, Me etc. from the Sound of Music. And it works even though she does look a bit like a musical conductor.

Bribery

This one's a bit tricky as you don't want to start too young or you could be paying out thousands by the time they're teenagers. You also need to follow through your bribe so if you promise them an ice cream if they get themselves dressed all on their own, you mustn't fulfil your side of the bargain if they haven't fulfilled theirs. And don't even contemplate 'forgetting' to keep your promise when they have done all they can to keep their side of the bargain.

Bribes don't have to be based on money. They could be treats like a trip to the park or the ice cream van.

Stick to a routine

Children feel comforted by routine – as do many adults. So incorporate certain jobs into your daily family routine. Explain to your children from as early an age as possible that after they have finished eating and it's gone down, they help you clear the table. After they've got dressed, they fold their pyjamas and pull up the duvet. After their bath, they clean their teeth and hang up their towel to dry.

WHAT TO DO WHEN THEY WON'T CO-OPERATE

We think this section is very important. We personally hate parenting books that presume readers have children who will do what they are told. This only happens in fairy tales or very boring families. My three all have minds of their own, which is why White Ladder asked me to write this book. So here's what to do if, or when, they won't play ball.

Empathise, empathise, empathise

"Tell them you understand how they feel," says psychologist Gaynor Sbuttoni who is also a mother of three. "Say 'Yes, I know it's boring to tidy your room and I can understand that you don't know where to start because it is a bit of a mess, isn't it? But if you do this pile first and then this one…' That way, you're keying into their wavelength by showing them you're on their side. You're also providing a practical way out of their dilemma by suggesting a strategy."

Provide an incentive

They might be too young for bonuses (that comes in another section) but you can encourage them with a little handout on the quiet. Keep a bag of stickers or sweets or whatever that they can dip their sticky little hands into when they've performed that job. No, only one!

Show them the consequences

Oh dear, has someone trodden on your favourite toy and broken it? That's because you didn't put it away safely. We're not suggesting you break a toy on purpose but if it happens, it happens. And of course, if you happen to stumble over a toy and break your ankle, someone else is going to have to look after the kids, aren't they? Actually, that's one way to get a break (all puns intended).

Appeal to their desire to be grown-up

Say 'That's a shame, I thought you'd be big enough to do that.' Most toddlers want to be grown-up unless they're reverting to babyhood, thanks to a new brother or sister. If that's the case, tell them you'll ask the baby to do it. That should get them going. (It will make all the child psychologists write into us too.)

IT WORKED FOR US! PARENTS' TIPS

A problem shared is a problem halved. If we all confided in other parents about difficulties, we might get some more ideas on how to tackle them. So we've spent several months interviewing parents all over the country on how they get their kids to tidy up. Here are some of their suggestions.

"My son is now eight but since he was two and a half, he has loved helping with 'a job'. I had to try and do the washing up quietly so he didn't join in because there would be too much water to clear up afterwards. And he likes nothing better than to empty my cupboards so he can tidy them. I think he liked it because it was something we could do together and actually, it was preferable for me to do this than sit on the floor playing cars. To get kids to help with house-work, I'd suggest turning it into a competition such as who can make their room the tidiest and who would like a turn with my broom?"

Jane

"I have a two year old daughter who has started taking an interest in helping me clean. It is really hard to get it done but one thing I have done is give her a duster and then I have one and she helps me pol-ish. It's all about involvement and making things fun. She is also starting to take an interest in what we are cooking and likes to watch things cook. For Christmas, I plan to buy her a toy vacuum cleaner which I hope she will want to use whilst I use mine."

Helen

"I got my children, aged seven and three, to start helping when they were three but it wasn't slave labour. I presented it as 'helping me' or making it into a game. If they don't want to help, I operate a quid pro quo scheme. So I'll say that if they don't tidy up after themselves, I won't take them to the park or let them play Playstation etc."

Louisa

"We have a system of counting to encourage our three year old to focus on something. For example, she tidies the room while I count to ten. I'll count to five while she gets her shoes on. It works very well. If we're out and she doesn't want to go home, she knows that if

I start to count, I'm serious and she always comes. It also works for stopping unwanted behaviour. Stop before I count to three." (*Author's note: Wonder how long this will last...*)

Anne

Top tip

When the novelty wears off, count in a different language.

"I was widowed two years ago and afterwards, I didn't care about rules and discipline because I was too depressed. Now I'm trying to claw back some structure in the house and it's very hard. It's also difficult as a single parent because you have no one to back you up. And if you're extremely tired, there comes a point where you just give in and say 'All right then, don't bother.'"

Caroline

"I get my children, aged 10, seven and three to put their pyjamas under their pillows. It's only a small job but it's something the little one can do."

Sarah

Sarah Beeny, television presenter, says: "I ask my 18 month old son Billy to put things in the rubbish bin, in an excited voice. He's usually willing to do this. The only trouble is that he puts lots of other things – which I haven't asked him to – into the bin as well and then expects a similar amount of praise!"

Key points

● *Start young* The sooner you do, the less they are likely to question. And they'll be used to helping as they grow up. Make the most of this impressionable age

● *Make it fun* Try to make jobs a nice thing to do and not a boring chore. You can do this with music and imaginative games

- *Remember you're helping their brain develop* This isn't just a book on child slave labour. Doing jobs can help their minds grow

- *Be imaginative* There are all kinds of jobs that even small children can do

Chapter two

How to get four to eight year olds to do the things they hate

The good news about this age group is that they can usually understand what you're asking them to do. The bad news is that they've learned to say 'no'. Our mission is to find an in between route so that you win but they think it's a compromise.

WHAT YOUR CHILD CAN DO AT THIS AGE

Fit the batteries into the remote control and other electrical apparatus*

The great thing about having small children is that they have small hands which can get into places that bigger hands can't – like that fiddly bit at the back of the remote control. Kids are also often more technically wired up than we are so as well as fitting the batteries, they can also tell us how to work the remote control if we're still at the manual stage. I know one parent who actually woke up one of his sleeping children to help him out with a DVD that he couldn't operate. That's going a bit far but, as he said, it made his son feel good about himself because he could do something his dad couldn't.

Lay the table

The trick about this one is that they learn to do it as a habit. Don't just save it to impress your mother/sister/visitors and then feel embarrassed when the kids say they don't know where the cutlery is

*WARNING *Please make sure it is safe for them to do this.*

kept. Teach them where to find things and make it routine for them to get the table ready before you eat.

Clear their own plate after a meal

Again, schedule this into the general dos and don'ts of eating like not eating with your mouth open. Make sure they know where the bin is and try to get them to aim straight so you don't have to do the floor again. Ideally, then get them to head for the dishwasher if you have one. And yes, to put the plate in and not on it…

Hang up their clothes

Start now and you might just instill the habit. One of my friends colour codes her kids' clothes on a hanging rail. Her children actually enjoy finding the right section to hang their clothes in.

Top tips

- Get or make novelty hangers so the kids want to use them

- Make sure that wardrobes and drawers are within their reach. If they're inaccessible, it's too easy for them to say 'I can't do that'. Those slide-under-the-bed drawers are great for kids because they're easy to pull in and out. Buy the kind that don't require runners. You can get them from John Lewis and other stores

- Put up low level clothes hooks so they can hang up their own coats. Write their name on a wooden clothes peg so they can 'peg' together their Wellington boots

Put their clothes in the dirty linen bin

Sounds obvious but make sure they know where it is. Make it part of their bath routine. When they get out, they put their discarded dirties in the right place. Don't just bend down and do it yourself because it's quicker or they'll never learn. Teach younger children to tuck one sock into the other so they don't go missing.

Load the dishwasher – and unload it too

All right. This might be a bit tricky for a four year old but you can start off with plastic cups and cutlery that won't hurt them. This does, however, require a bit of teaching first. Everyone has their own idea of how to put in plates and knives so train your kids up in your way of thinking.

Top tip

Don't let them get away with it if they claim they didn't load the dishwasher because they didn't know if it was clean or dirty. Get them to open up and see which one it is. It's not difficult.

Tidy their room

You're going to find this in all the age group sections because it's an essential skill – right through to adulthood. Four to eight year olds are still, hopefully, a bit more biddable than teens so make the most of it. Buy brightly coloured plastic crates for them to store toys/CDs/other stuff in. Every few weeks, encourage them to have a purge and throw out/give away things they don't want.

Top tips

- Get them to make labels like CDs/Musical toys/games to stick on the boxes

- Be specific. Don't just say 'tidy your room'. Point out certain things which need to be put away such as clothes or toys. Alternatively, divide the room into sections and get them to tidy one at a time. Don't make them do it all at once or it will seem too daunting. See chapter Five for how to teach your child tidying skills.

Take down the Christmas decorations and store them in boxes

Get them to write labels on the side.

Moving house?

Help them get used to the idea by giving them a box and getting them to pack some of their own things. Again, label and even decorate the label.

Use a wipe on/wipe off board

Or you could use a magnetic calendar to remind them what jobs they have agreed to. Reminding them to do something doesn't mean they're forgetful or naughty. It's natural. As parents, we need to keep reminding them again and again.

Jobs outside the house

Cleaning their bikes

Give them a sponge and an old washing up bowl. Show them how to get round the spokes.

Sweeping up leaves

Give them the right tools and show them where to put them. Use the opportunity to show them the different kind of trees.

Picking up apples from the ground

Sort out the baddies. Get them to help you cook an apple pie with the good ones, as an incentive. Get them to put the bad ones on the compost.

Picking flowers for the house

Get them to pick flowers for the table or guest room when you have visitors.

Cleaning out your car

Provide them with two old carrier bags. One for rubbish and another for things that belong inside the house. Check both afterwards to make sure they haven't thrown important things away.

Top tip _____

Encourage them to do this by allowing them to keep any small change they find.

HOW TO GET THEM TO DO IT

We've already given you some ideas in the previous section for toddlers. These can be expanded for this age group.

Explain why it needs to be done

If you don't unload the dishwasher, we won't have any clean cups next time you want a drink.

Praise and thank them when they do it

If you don't, why should they do it again?

Give them their own equipment

Instead of the family dirty linen bin, give them a string bag and get them to put their own dirties in it.

Bribery

By the age of five, it's a good idea to start giving them pocket money so they learn the value of money. It's also a great incentive for jobs round the house. Link the jobs with the pocket money. If they don't do certain jobs, they don't get the money. If they do, they get a bit extra. We'll leave the details up to you, depending on your parenting style and budget (and see chapter 15).

Pocket money isn't the only way to bribe them. Is there something they really want? If so, use that to their (and your) advantage. For example, if they want to redecorate their bedroom, they can choose a new duvet if they promise to keep their bedroom tidy for the rest of the school term. But they have to stick to their side of the bargain.

Non-financial incentives

Draw up a list of privileges that they can earn if they do certain jobs. For example, if they lay the table, they don't have to help load the dishwasher.

Make it into a game

Who can lay one side of the table faster than the other?

Crack a few jokes

I don't know about you but I generally fail to see the funny side when my kids don't listen. So recently, I've introduced a new rule: make a joke every day. However, as my kids say my jokes are pathetic, this doesn't always work. Instead, I've resorted to a wry sense of humour which often comes out of my mouth before I've analysed it. The other day, my 14 year old tore into the house wearing very muddy trainers. "Take your feet off," I yelled without thinking. He thought that was quite funny and now I use that instruction instead of the much more boring 'Take off your shoes'.

Ask them in another language

This is not, by any means, guaranteed to get the job done but it might be enough for them to turn round and say 'Wot are you on?' Hopefully, younger children will be more impressed and it might even help their French or German. I often insert the odd French word so they get the rough idea. Try these phrases for size. 'Will you get out of le lit?' Or 'Tidy your chambre, s'il vous plait.'

Star charts

Put it on the wall and fill it in daily. Make a list of the jobs you want them to do and whether or not they've done them. Give them rewards at the end of the week. Use a wipe on/wipe off board or magnetic board to list chores they have agreed to do. It's natural for children to need to be reminded about a job.

WHAT TO DO WHEN THEY WON'T CO-OPERATE

Get the punishment to fit the crime

If they won't lay the table, they won't have a place to sit at. Sounds a bit tough? Maybe. But how difficult is it to put out a mat?

Teach them the consequences

If they won't tidy their bedroom, they won't be able to find that toy they've been looking for.

Ask why they won't do it

If they hate that job so much, maybe they could trade it for another. If it's a 'Can't be bothered' attitude, explain we all have to do things we don't like at times. Get them to think what would happen if you went on strike and never cooked/washed/ironed/unloaded the dishwasher. Even better, try this for a day and see what happens.

Show them up

If your child won't help, persuade a visiting child to hand you that nappy/pass the trainer mug. Then praise them and give them a small reward. There's nothing like the green eyed monster to gain co-operation and next time, your child might come up trumps. Naughty but it works.

Put them down for a legal career

They can make money by arguing against logic.

IT WORKED FOR US! PARENTS' TIPS

"I tell my six and seven year olds that the more they do to help me, the more time we will have to do fun things together. I also show them that some chores can be quick."

Mandy

"Our eight and six year olds tidy their rooms and make their own beds. If they won't, we say we'll take something away or they'll lose a treat."

Sally

"I have a 'Wonka Bar' chart named after Roald Dahl's Charlie and the Chocolate Factory. It works a dream round the house. There are four columns on the chart: one for me, one for my husband and one each for the children. Then there's a list of all the things I do round the house that they could help with. Ten ticks on the chart earn you a chocolate bar if you're an adult. For children, it works according to age. For example, my son is six so he just needs six ticks. Alternatively, if they don't want a chocolate bar they can have £1 pocket money. My family soon sussed out the easy ticks and so making beds and laying the table are done like a dream. My husband takes the recycling down the garden and has made the bed for the first time in 13 years of marriage! My daughter now has a tick for practising the piano which I always hate nagging about. I, of course, end up with hundreds of ticks but psychologically, this has worked well for me as everyone can see all the jobs I do every day."

Giselle

"My four year old dusts as a game. She also 'plays' at gardening and enjoys helping her dad make dinner sometimes."

Hollie

"I get our six and four year olds to tidy their rooms and load the dishwasher by bribing them with television or letting them stay up later. Mine are still small enough that if I stand there looking menacing for long enough, they eventually give in and do it. I think mothers who work (and I'm one) feel guilty about being away from their children and when they're with them, they don't want to upset their kids or cause tension or fights so the kids get away with far more. You have to remember who's the boss. I also try and remember my mother getting me to do things. Stand firm and think of a suitable sanction if they don't do it. One of my friends brings all the clean washing into her girls' room and they put it all away. That's their job and if they do it, they get their pocket money. If not, they don't."

Anon

"Our children are aged seven and five. They tidy their rooms, help with younger children, water houseplants and garden. If they won't help, we threaten them with 'No TV'. Threats and praise also help."

Anon

"I insist my children do jobs and explain they need to know how to look after themselves when they leave home. I expect boys to do the same as girls as I think so many relationships are ruined by men who expect everything done for them. I also use a system of rewards. For example, I think of something they want and only give it if they do what I've asked. I also make them use the washing machine for their own clothes. I suppose I see them as equal to me but needing training to do things and explaining why. I also try to help them see the positive side of their failures – such as showing them that something shrank because they put it on the wrong setting but that they can do it better the next time."

Lynne

"When my children were this age, I used to encourage them to match odd socks in the laundry basket by buying them a pile of Pokemon cards and handing over one card for every pair of socks they matched up. Being boys, they were quite competitive and I could sit and drink coffee while they turned the house upside down. As a keen but lazy gardener, I also offered a 5p bounty for every slug they found and disposed of, for me. This one worked best when they could hear the ice cream van a few streets away. When they got older, of course, this didn't work. Then I would give them a choice. Do you want to wash the car or the dog? Do you want to do the dishes or hang out the washing? This last one worked particularly well. As I have three boys, they could not allow their friends to see them hanging out the washing so they would always choose the other option, whatever that was. My children, unlike my friends' kids, never said they were bored. That's because the first time they said it at the start of the school holidays, I found them something to do like weeding, cleaning, putting the laundry away. If they protested, I pointed out that they had just complained they had nothing to do."

Jacqui

"I expect my sons to do as much as my daughters as I think too many men expect their wives to run after them."

Anon

"My daughter has a tick list for piano practice. When she gets to seven ticks, she gets a small present."

Helen

"My four year old granddaughter refused to carry her baby sister's soiled nappy downstairs from the bathroom to the outside bin, even though it was sealed in a plastic bag. I got round this by saying 'Oh please help granny. I can't manage the baby unless you do.' It worked because she could see I needed a hand."

Susan

"Our eight year old is borderline special needs and genuinely finds being organised or tidy an enormous problem. So we don't set an objective level of tidiness for all the kids to achieve but set him a 'target' that stretches *him* while still being attainable. So if he tidies the floor, we'll tidy the rest of the room. This has led us to think more generally in terms of individual standards that are challenging but not unreasonable for all tasks. For example, our six year old is helpful but lazy so he's expected to achieve quite a lot but is allowed to tackle tasks in short bursts."

Maddie

"Our eight and six year old regularly lay and clear the table for meals, get drinks for the family before meals and tidy their bedrooms. I expect them to do it because it's the way the household works. You also have to be specific. 'Tidy your room' is too vague. You need to give instructions like putting your clothes in the cupboard; putting books on the bookshelf; putting toys in a box. Decide on boundaries and compromise. Plates have to be put in the dishwasher by everyone, but if it's not your room and not your mess, it's not your problem if it's not tidied to your standards. Only have a few rules for the things that are really important to you."

Sue

"We introduce a bit of competition between siblings – mean but effective – such as who can tidy their room the best? Of course, they are both winners in the end but the thought of winning keeps them going. I also make jobs into a challenge, for example 'I bet you can't finish tidying by the time the timer goes off' or 'When you've finished, there'll be a surprise treat for everyone'. It might just be one sweet but the suspense keeps them going. We never *ever* pay for jobs round the house. This is a slippery slope. We generally work on incentives like 'When you've done that, we can go to the park'."

Jenny

" My eight year old picks up her clothes but as I work full time and don't get home until 6.30, I don't feel it's appropriate to expect too much. I would far rather she has some playtime and then time for a story. I also think it's important to look at what needs to done across the week, rather than expecting to get everything done on the day. Children like to know what's planned. I believe in reward charts and goals. Also saving up stickers for a treat."

Laura

(For more about reward charts see page 26.)

"I never give up with my children aged six and two, because then they'd never do anything. I tend to join in so we do it together. I find it helps if the children choose their own jobs. For example, my daughter likes dusting the television and sees it as 'her' job so she's quite keen to do it. This also gives a child more of a sense of control and independence. As a last resort, I will sometimes say that if things are left on the floor, then I'll assume she doesn't want them and throw them away. Then they get picked up fairly fast. I've never actually followed through on this one although their dad has. At school, they play fast music during 'tidy up' time. I'm also a NeuroLinguistic Programming Practioner, so I'm very aware of the language I use and its effects. In practice, I am more likely to tell them what I want them to do, rather than telling them off for doing the wrong things. I generally focus on praising good behaviour. At the end of the day, children want your undivided attention and they will do whatever it takes to get this. They don't judge by what is naughty and what isn't. We do that instead."

Joanne

"Over Christmas we got fed up with family who descend, enjoy our hospitality and then leave without even putting so much as a plate in the sink. Especially those with no kids and no responsibilities – in other words the ones for whom Christmas is relaxing rather than exhausting. We decided we didn't want our kids to grow up behaving like that towards other people. So the new rule is that whenever we have a proper family meal together (in our case probably three or four times a week) no one leaves the kitchen after the meal until all the clearing up is done. It doesn't matter what job everyone does, but it isn't fair for one person to put their feet up while someone else is still working. So the children, being little, can do fun or easy jobs like loading the dishwasher (which they seem to enjoy for some reason), putting away the condiments or wiping the table, while we break our wrists scrubbing at the burnt pots and pans (as they get older this may change), but the principle is that we all start together and we all finish together. They have yet to find any way of arguing against the fairness of this, and so far it's working well."

Richard

Radio 1 DJ *Judge Jules*, aka Julius O'Riordan, has a six year old son, Jake. He says:

"Jake cleans his bedroom but that's about the long and the short of it. We persuade him to do it by threatening to cancel whatever fun activity is planned for that forthcoming weekend. When I was a child, I did loads of jobs. I swept up leaves, washed up, tidied up, ironed and put washing on the line."

REWARD CHARTS

Some parents believe in these and others don't. Although they can encourage some children, they can also demoralise others if they don't get the results. And it can damage their self-esteem if someone else gets more points than them every time.

Dr Jill Curtis, child expert and psychotherapist, says "Star charts can be most effective *for some children*. If this reward doesn't seem to work for your child – and for many it does not – don't worry, but try to work out another way of marking success. It could be as simple as praise from you. Words do count."
www.familyonwards.com

Key points

- *Keep going* and don't give up. If you let them off something, they'll refuse to do it next time

- *Build on the jobs* they've already been doing

- *Praise, praise them* Every child and adult is encouraged by this

- *Remind, remind, remind* Don't expect your children to remember every time that they're meant to be doing something. But don't nag them so they're turned off

Chapter three

How to get eight to 12 year olds to do the things they hate

Uh, oh. We're getting into the almost-teens territory here. Which is why it's even more important to get them into the habit of doing some work for their living. The trick is emotional intelligence. Get them to want to do those jobs – even if it's for money.

JOBS THEY CAN DO

Vacuum the carpet (not the cat)

They could start off with vacuuming their own bedrooms and then move onto others. However, a few driving lessons might be necessary first or you could find them slicing off part of the woodwork in their enthusiasm or reluctance to do it properly.

Some clever toy companies actually make mini vacuum cleaners. You can even purchase toy vacuum cleaners. However, it's cheaper to buy them a dustpan and brush. In fact, their nimble little fingers are probably far better at getting into spaces you can't reach.

Dust their bedroom

This might sound a bit tough but if they don't start now, they might not ever. Present them with a duster and, if they're the kind of child who might abuse solvents, put some polish on it for them. Suggest they move objects round on their dressing tables or desks in the process.

Clean their own shoes

Well, you didn't get them dirty, did you? Make it easy for them with those packets of shoe shine polishes. Allocate one day of the week, like Sunday, for them to do it.

Match socks

Isn't it amazing how socks come apart in the wash? But now you've got your little helper to put it right. So the next time they say they're bored, suggest a sock matching game. And when they've finished their own underwear drawer, they can do everyone else's too.

Clean the car

Not just the inside but the outside too. Get them togged up in clothes that you don't mind getting dirty and wet. Provide them with a bowl of water or a hosepipe and leave them to it.

Make their own packed lunches

Help them, if necessary by putting out the right ingredients.

Put the kettle on

This is a bit of a grey area as you also need to warn them about boiling water. But they've got to start somewhere. And once they've got the hang of it, you can then teach them to make tea although we'd recommend you save this for the 10 year age group upwards. They'll probably like this job as it will make them feel grown-up.

Other basic culinary skills

Make toast. But do teach them basic safety rules first such as only toasting ready sliced bread in case they try to stick in bread that's too thick. Never, ever try to get the toast out with a knife or they could get electrocuted. They could also learn to make their own school sandwiches although you might regret this in the early morning rush when they're deliberating between peanut butter and jam, or both.

Change the ringer on your mobile phone

Explain how to retrieve missed calls etc. In fact, they'll love this job and we have to throw in the odd perk so they want to do some of the jobs they hate.

Top tip ——————————————————————

Look out for some great cookery cassettes called Cooking For Kids. They were actually thought up by a former war correspondent who changed careers. In our book, kids can be as challenging as war zones so maybe he's on the right track.

Teach them how to fold napkins into fancy shapes

Not a vital job, we admit, but they might enjoy it and it would raise your street cred at dinner parties.

Change their bedlinen

This might be a bit of a tough one at this age but you can start by getting them to replace their pillow cases. In the next age range, they can move on to duvets.

Amuse younger children

When my eldest was this age, he was brilliant at this. In fact, I don't think I could have managed without him. The great thing about older children being entertainers/substitute nannies, is that they don't have to do much. They simply have to make silly faces or be cool or play the odd game. Younger kids normally think they're so wonderful that they take it all in.

WARNING *Never leave a child of this age unattended with younger children for obvious reasons. If you're in the house but not in the same room, keep a regular check on them.*

Help carry the shopping

Don't assume it's all too heavy. Give them a couple of things in a carrier bag. Encourage them to help you pack at the supermarket by giving them their own plastic bags to fill, and let them pack their favourite foods.

Take visitors' coats

Preferably not to sell on eBay but to save them until going home time.

Unload the dishwasher

But teach them to avoid sharp knives etc. A trip to Casualty will only make you late for the next job.

Sort out the rubbish

And understand how the recycling bin works.

And don't forget jobs from previous sections which are still applicable to this age group.

HOW TO SELL IT TO THEM SO THEY AGREE TO DO IT

Start off with the basics.

Why they need to do it

If they don't change their pillow cases, their bed gets smelly.

Praise them for the things they do

It will make them keener to do other jobs.

Give them their own equipment

How about a pair of rubber gloves with their name on a clothes peg to keep them together? Or a pinny with their name on it?

Bribe

But don't give away money for small favours. The little-by-little approach makes them try hard more consistently. You can do this in different ways. Put a price tag on each job, for example making the bed every day gets 10 pence. Give them a set amount of pocket money every week but only if they do the list of jobs you've both agreed.

Allow them to change their room around

Or give it a makeover. It might encourage them to keep it tidy, or at least sort out the rubbish before they change it.

Permit them to tidy out your briefcase

And/or handbag in return for tidying up their own school bag. Agree they can keep loose change that they find, as payment.

Give them a choice of jobs

This usually works best when it's written down rather than agreed verbally. That way, they can see what they've agreed to do. A list is the obvious way to do this. But you could also try a 'lucky dip' jam jar filled with pieces of paper, each of which has a job on. Every day, every member of the family has to pull out a 'job ticket'. They might loathe the job – or they might like it. That's part of the fun.

Banking bonuses

Sit down as a family and work out which jobs can be done by which members of the family. Write down a core list of important jobs under each individual's name. These jobs 'have' to be done or else their salary (in other words, pocket money) doesn't get paid. If extra jobs are done willingly on top of this, you agree to pay a bonus.

Crack better jokes

Or you could say things in a funny voice. Try holding your nose and coming out with a squeaky command. They'll think you're mad but it might grab their attention for a few seconds. Use that time fast to connect their ears to their brains.

WHAT TO DO IF THEY WON'T CO-OPERATE

Don't give in and do it yourself

The next time they ask you to do something, explain you can't agree because they didn't do the job you asked them to do. Stick to it.

Explain the consequences

If they won't help amuse the younger children, it means you'll take longer getting out and then they'll be late for something they want to get to.

Work shamelessly on their consciences

They helped to make the car dirty by chucking all that rubbish in the back so they ought to help clean it out.

IT WORKED FOR US! PARENTS' TIPS

"It was a horrible rainy day so I got the kids to tidy out the kitchen drawers. I've got one which is full of miscellaneous things that don't seem to belong anywhere, like rubber bands and loose change. They actually enjoyed sorting it out and I let them keep the change as a reward."

Michelle

"Mine are still quite small – eight and five – but they do have a responsibility to keep their rooms tidy. It's usually prompted by me saying 'Look, I can't see the floor and I need to vacuum the carpet. You have a choice. Tidy your stuff away or it goes in a big black bag and in the dustbin. They also know they're expected to help clear the table after meals and put their own dirty laundry in the laundry basket. However, this sometimes needs a reminder. Other than that, because I'm a writer, I believe deadlines come before dusting. So they probably don't have a good example of doing jobs round the house!"

Kate

"We drew up a loyalty chart, based on the supermarket loyalty card schemes. Every time the children do a job, we give them so many points. After a certain number of points, they get a free gift. But I do think that girls are better at doing jobs round the house than boys."

Laura

"Our children are aged eight, 10 and 12 and they do lots of jobs round the house. But they differ. One enjoys tidying her room; one hates it. They all hate scraping leftovers off the plate to load the dishwasher. We link jobs with pocket money but sometimes they turn down some jobs and go without the money. We also warn children when they'll be expected to do a task. Don't expect them to drop what they're doing. Star charts and reward systems work, but need commitments. Lots of praise and helping with the task is important as young children need to know how to do things more than we realise. So show them how to tidy a room without just shoving everything into the wardrobe. Make tasks into a family occasion; the children have enjoyed clearing up the garden together or cleaning the house when we are expecting visitors, if we all work together. Don't expect to achieve these ideals all the time. All families nag and grumble sometimes."

Carole

"Ours are nine and five. We get them to do jobs by linking it to a reward or punishment. For example, we either promise some form of treat or threaten a prohibition of a favoured pastime/thing until the job is complete. We also tend to put time limits and deadlines on the activities."

Brian

"My nine and 12 year olds tidy their rooms, sometimes load the dishwasher, make their own beds, dust, vacuum and do the ironing even though it often needs doing again. Praise helps and so do threats. If they really refuse, I don't give them pocket money."

Anon

"The only way to get my 13,11 and eight year olds to do jobs is to stand over them and threaten them with a smack! Seriously, try making it fun and light-hearted. Also try timing them for a bit of healthy competition and barter with them too. If they'll do this for you, you'll do that for them."

Anon

"Our nine year old tidies his bedroom, empties wastepaper bins and lays the table. He has to do seven chores each week to earn his pocket money. Some parents might say that offering money for household chores will lead to an expectation for all housework to be paid. But by defining which chores are eligible to count towards the pocket money requirement, we've been able to avoid this problem."

Susie

"It's all about communicating with your children as burgeoning people – not as inferior beings who have to be kept in line. They need to grasp the connection between having a nice lifestyle and doing certain things in order to achieve it. That's best taught by example. I also only give them pocket money and time out when jobs are completed satisfactorily."

Caroline

"Sometimes, we just have to stand there until our seven and ten year olds do the jobs we've asked them to."

Anon

"Try to instill a sense of the benefits of a clean and tidy house e.g. if you don't trip over things, you can find things. By making these things a family activity, a sense of responsibility will hopefully grow.

A friend also gave us a great idea. Each member of the family has a box which is kept in the same place, like under the stairs. As you go about your daily business and you find something that is somewhere it shouldn't be, you just put it into the relevant box. At the end of the week, empty the box into a pile on the bed so the person is forced to clear it away. Works like a dream on my wife!"

Brian

"We've only just started getting our seven and 10 year olds to do jobs in the last few months so we've been building up slowly. I pick my battles and only get them to do jobs I really want them to do. I say 'I'm your guide, not your slave'. I also tell them that if they don't tidy up their toys, they will go into a big black bag. I also highlight choice and consequence. If their toys get broken when someone stands on them, it's because they should have put them away. At the same time, I tell myself that the world won't end if their rooms aren't tidy every night. I also think you have to tailor tactics to each child. My two are like chalk and cheese; what motivates one, will often antagonise the other. I'm a great believer in sticking to your guns: once you've said they have to do something, don't let them off until they do it. Lead by example, be fair and consistent especially when they're not. And keep your sense of humour nearby."

Cass

Anthea Turner, stepmother of three girls aged nine, 12 and 13 and presenter of *The Perfect Housewife* on BBC3, says: "Leadership is the main key. As the saying goes: 'A fish rots from the head down.' In other words, if they don't see you doing it, they won't do it either. So the standards have to be set by the head of the household. If you leave wet towels on the bathroom floor, so will they. If your bedroom is a mess, why should they clear theirs up?

"I've also learned that children won't fold things up and put them in drawers. But they will put things in baskets especially if they're nice baskets. I love those picnic baskets with lids and have different ones for different things like dolls' clothes and socks. I label each one clearly so the girls know what goes in which. All they have to do then is pick up and drop. Even a four year old can do that because it's like a sorting game.

"The same goes with toys. Each child can have a basket with their own name on it, clearly labelled, in the lounge. At the end of the day, they put their own toys in their own basket. You can do the same with shoes by the front door.

"Another key word is repetition. Keep saying it. Put your toys in the basket. Put your shoes in the basket. Eventually it gets through. Also remind them that everything has a place and show them where that is.

"Praise and reward is another important phrase in our house. When the girls were little, we had a star chart and everyone was on it, even the dogs. At the end of the month, the winner got something really nice.

"Frankly, we've never had trouble with homework because the girls know that school would discipline them if they didn't do it.

"When I was a child, I did very little to be honest. It wasn't until I moved out to a place on my own, that I started to be tidy. Now when I go to my mother's house, I'll start tidying up. It makes her laugh. So the good news is that even if your children are messy now, there's plenty of time for them to change."

Key points

- *Now they're really getting to a stage where they can help out.* But make sure you thank them and know they're appreciated

- *Consider linking jobs to pocket money if you haven't already.* Decide which jobs should be paid for and which ones they should do anyway

- *Write jobs down on a noticeboard or list.* Children of this age have a lot to think about

- *Use jobs to develop their personalities* Fit the job to the child. Allow them to choose jobs. It might even lead to a skill or future job if they prove dab hands at cooking/ironing/tidying up

Chapter 4

How to get 12 to 18 year olds to do the things they hate

JOBS THEY CAN DO

Still short of ideas on how they could help? Here are some jobs they should be able to do.

Cleaning shoes

Give them their own shoe cleaning kit and show them how to use it. You can make one up cheaply with a shoe box and essentials inside. Or you can buy one of those sachets like moistened tissues which don't need much elbow grease. Set aside one day of the week and a time when everyone in the family cleans their shoes. Sunday night is a good one.

Definitely get them to do their own trainers. Teach them to knock them against each other (the shoes, not the kids), *outside* the house and not in, so all the dirt is outside.

Shopping

If you're worried about them going shopping on their own, or if their little hands can't cope with heavy bags, set them up on the computer and get them to do a home shop for you. Arm them with a list first so they more or less buy the right things. And always check they've ordered before keying in your credit card details. We suggest you do the latter yourself otherwise they might just be tempted to use your card for other things.

Put it in the microwave

This is a job that any streetwise kid worth their salt should know how to perform. So next time they moan that they're hungry (even though you've just cooked them a four course meal), teach them to read the microwave instructions and press the right buttons.

Work the washing machine

And the tumble drier. Also check your guarantee in case they break it in the process. Teach them to empty the filter which is usually located at the bottom of the machine. Many an adult doesn't know how to do this until the repair man says 'Didn't you read the instruction booklet?'

Dishwasher

Don't just teach how to load it or put it on. Also explain how to put dishwasher powder in and salt.

Empty the vacuum cleaner

Preferably into the bin and not on the floor.

Move furniture to vacuum underneath

This one's for older children.

Read bedtime stories to younger children

Get them to enjoy it by putting on funny faces. Demonstrate first of all.

Help them to amuse younger children by:

- Putting on puppet shows
- Making puppets out of gloves
- Playing board games
- Playing hide and seek
- Dancing to music

WARNING *Never leave younger children in the care of older children unless an adult is nearby.*

Clean out kitchen cupboards

Demonstrate first. Tell them they might find something interesting. Ask if they will rearrange things such as tins in one place and packets in another.

Empty your bin

Give each of them their own bin for their bedrooms. Try a different colour for each child. Make one day a week the 'bin cleaning' day. Ideally, make it the same day as your dustmen come. Then get them to put out the family bin at the same time.

Wash the bath out

Give them a pinny and make it fun. Give them the right cleaning materials and don't expect a brilliant job. But it will be a start. Next time, you can start them on the taps. Show them how to wrap a flannel round them and give them a buff.

Tidy the linen cupboard

If necessary, just get them to do one shelf. It's better than nothing.

Top tip

One friend got her kids to design shelf labels on sticky labels, for example 'towels', 'sheets' and so on.

Dusting

Give them a bright feather duster to make it more fun.

Tidying up other people's bedrooms

Get them to sort out your own dressing table or bedroom. Other people's rooms are always more interesting than your own. But make sure you hide any incriminating evidence first.

Give each child a 'tidy tray' or drawer

Get them to put things in it that they come across – they can do this for others in the family too. Set aside a certain time every week for putting these things back in the right place.

Use the stairs

I have a friend who has taught her children to put stray items at the bottom of the stairs. Every time someone goes up, they take something and put it away.

WARNING *You can fall over stair items and break an ankle, so make sure they're stacked right by the edge.*

Go through your old make up/tool box/whatever

This involves a certain amount of trust as they might throw away things you really want. So check the rubbish bin after they've finished.

Under the bed

Isn't it funny how kids often love the things you hate? One of my worst jobs is crawling under the bed to vacuum, only to find things that have been left there for years. But ask the kids to clean under the bed and explain what a great opportunity it is to wriggle around in the dark, and they'll jump at it.

Top tip

Allow them to keep any 'finds' they come across like coins or other treasures.

Answering the telephone nicely

Even well brought up children can let you down on the phone with a 'Yes' or 'What?' when they pick up the receiver. This one can only be achieved through constant nagging and also – it has to be said – setting the right example. Try writing down an agreed phrase and getting them to repeat it, parrot fashion.

You could encourage them or give them practice by allowing them to record a message on the answer phone. But do make sure it's clear and to the point. What might seem cute to adoring parents can actually be very yuk to callers.

When they ring someone else, enforce the importance of not just saying 'Can I speak to Peter?' but talking to whichever adult picks up the phone first. I learned this the hard way when the mother of a boyfriend complained I treated her like a telephone operator. Ever since then, I have always made a point of making polite conversation with whoever picks up the phone. And I also try to get my kids to do the same.

...and taking messages

'Someone rang,' is a favourite message via my son. Not who – he often can't even remember if it's male or female – but someone. So leave a pad of paper by the phone; preferably one that's big enough for them to see with an extra large jumbo pen or pencil firmly attached. Divide into columns with a heading for the caller, one for the time of call, another for the message, and one for the caller's phone number. With any luck, you'll get at least one of them.

Pick up their bathroom towel

Otherwise they have a wet one the next day. And no, *don't* pick it up yourself.

Clearing away old newspapers

Do this the day before the refuse collectors come. Make it a routine and they should (one day, before they leave home) do it automatically.

Cleaning out the fridge

A great way of teaching them how to spot sell-by dates. You can also use the opportunity to explain basic food rules like not storing raw meat next to cooked meat. Then, with any luck, they'll remember how not to give themselves food poisoning when they move into a student house.

Cleaning the loo

Another one that will come in handy when they have homes of their own. Someone will thank you for it one day.

Tidy up

Give them funny folders to put stuff in.

Basic cooking

Teach them how to bake a potato, make an omelette, and so on.

WARNING *Also show them how to use a fire blanket/extinguisher.*

Turn out lights

Stick Post-it notes next to the switch, reminding them how much electricity costs.

Bring down mugs from their bedrooms

If/when they don't, refuse to make them another cup of tea or coffee until they comply.

Learn to drive

So they can do the school run.

Mix cocktails for guests

They'll love this one. Buy them a fancy mixing recipe book and let them get on with it. Of course, they'll have to taste it first of all, just to make sure they've got it right.

Make your bed as well as theirs

Tell them that as they've done theirs so well, they can do yours too.

WHAT TO DO IF THEY DON'T CO-OPERATE

This is where we get tough. Refuse to do things for them. If they won't clear the table or make the bed, you won't have time to drive them into town.

Explain that as a working parent, you need help

If you don't work outside the home, point out that a family needs to be run on team effort. Everyone has to do their bit.

Reduce their pocket money

Or you could tell them they can't go to that concert on Saturday night. You need to be a toughie for this and it does rather depend on how bolshie they've been. But consider it.

Try positive discipline

Fill a jam jar with one pound coins and tell them they can have the lot at the end of the week if they do all their jobs. Every time they refuse to do a job, take a pound out and put it in your own purse. You'll either end up with more spending power or compliant children. Either way, you win.

Top tip _____

I do this myself with my nearly 15 year old and it works like a treat. You must use a jam jar however, or a see-through container so they can see the cash. For some reason, it's an important incentive.

_____

Shame them

You can do this by asking their friends what jobs they do round the house. Your child might then admit they do zilch. If you really want to put your child down, you can do it for them. Researching this book has definitely shamed my lot into doing more because I interviewed every one of their friends who visited.

Don't do any jobs for them

This idea was suggested by many parents who filled in our survey. If they won't make their bed, leave it unmade. If they won't clear their plate, leave it on the table. Sooner or later, the mess will force you to have a discussion (i.e. argument). It might just clear the air and get something done about it.

Give up

This idea was also suggested by some parents in our survey. We all do it from time to time. And there is a case for picking your battles and only making a fuss about certain jobs. On the other hand, if you let them get away with doing nothing, you're not helping them to become responsible adults.

IT WORKED FOR US! PARENTS' TIPS

"I didn't push my daughter to do much around the house when she was young. But when she got to 14 or 15, she automatically started helping. It just came naturally and I think that's better than nagging. It shows that sometimes it pays to wait until they're old enough to want to do it or understand why you need help. I also encourage them to do the jobs they like. My son is building a garden shed with his father at the moment and he likes that. My daughter really enjoys cooking. We concentrate on the positive. It's never too late."

Bev

"My two youngest are 14 and 15. They both cook a meal a week and clean the kitchen afterwards. This is to help their cooking skills and also to help me. I was one of those mums who made the first two start doing their own washing and ironing and cooking one meal a week when they were 15. My oldest son is now very grateful for the grounding it's given him. At other times, I make a list of all the jobs that need doing. Then we work as a team, crossing off each job as it's done. This way, it's seen as fair as the time spent is the same and the number of jobs doesn't count. When they were little, I used to get them to tidy their toys away by putting my hands in front of my eyes and counting to 10. Then when I uncovered my eyes, they froze. If they hadn't finished, I'd do it again – and I always acted flabbergasted that they could have done such a good job. I pretended to think they had used magic to tidy up. Ah for the days when fantasy was believable."

Elaine

"If your kids won't help, go on strike. It doesn't always work but they do learn to appreciate the things you do for them. No more washing, ironing, cooking, waking them for school, giving them lifts, giving them money. Let them cope for a month or two. It's murder and will reduce you to tears but once everything is back to normal, they appreciate the things they once took for granted."

Anon.

"We use a mixture of nagging, threatening to hide the Playstation and not allowing the 18 year old the use of the car. Sometimes, if things have got into a mess, my 13 year old son and I have weekend projects like having a blitz on all the bedrooms. He's also responsible for packing his own games kit three times a week. When he was little, he would tidy up shoes. He's meant to give me his lunchbox at the end of the day but sometimes, on Monday mornings, I find it all smelly at the bottom of his bag. I also have three older children and I was stricter with them about doing jobs. When you have only one left at home, you tend to do more for them because there isn't the pressure of family life. That's not always a good thing."

Maggie

"My two children, aged 11 and 14, don't do nearly as much as my sister's but they do make their beds, take out their rubbish from their bins and bring down their washing from their rooms. They are also very good at laying the table, helping in the garden and bringing me things if I ask them to. They do get pocket money at the end of each week (£3 each) but seem to be only too happy to help anyway. I think it could be because they are also at their father's house on Wednesday and Saturday nights and he is very strict."

Eileen

"My sister's children who are 15 and 18 do dishes (something she and I always did as children) and vacuum the house. They also wrap all the Christmas presents for her and peel potatoes. She pays them small amounts to do jobs. My stepson does the dishes at his mother's house and she pays him 70p a week."

Deborah

"Negotiate. But be prepared to find a different negotiating tactic every time."

Anne

"My children aged 13 and 15 clean the goldfish bowl every two months and make their own beds. They hate tidying their rooms even though I nag them. The best advice I can give is that they have to see a benefit to a job before they will do it willingly."

Pat

"My children are grown-up now so my memories are a bit vague. But I do know that the key is to start early. You can't say 'Now you're 13, I think it's time you started cleaning your room.' These routines have to be established very young and then they're never questioned."

Paul

"Keep pestering. Bargain as in, 'I'll do this for you if you do that for me'. Start early."

Gill

"My advice is to send them to their grandparents or better still, move out and bring the grandparents in. Our children, age 15, five and four are as good as gold for their grandparents. They do lots of jobs and know that it means they receive lots of presents. We also negoti-ate, negotiate, negotiate to get jobs done."

Anon

"My kids have left home but when they were younger, I found the sheer effort of getting them to do anything was more effort than it was worth, especially with boys. My daughter liked to cook and would sometimes clean the entire kitchen while I was out, as a treat. But most of them are resistant to anything that suggests it's 'their' job. Also, they have so much schoolwork that it seems harsh to put other things on them."

Liz

"I've paid my kids for years to do chores. I have fixed rates per job: vacuuming the house is £3; dusting £5; mowing the lawn £4. They do, however, get very low pocket money compared with their friends – £20 a month."

Jan

"I worked on the principle that if you want your shirt ironed/packed lunch made, then DIY."

Bernadine

"The trick is to start them young, make it fun and as they get older, make them think it's a privilege to be allowed to do certain things. When they get to their early teens, explain how tired you get, espe-cially if you work, and tell them that for the sake of your health and the protection of their lifestyle, it's important that all family mem-bers play their part."

Margaret Morrissey, spokesman for the Parents Teachers Association

"This is what helps us with our boys, aged 15 and 17. Compromis-ing. Showing how much you appreciate their help when they turn their hand to something. Letting them know you really need a hand, particularly if you are to have enough time to be able to give them lifts etc."

Sandra

"We have twins of 19 and an older daughter in her twenties. When the twins use the car, they have to clean it in return."

Sally

"I pay my 17 year old son to clean windows. But he does other jobs like getting the rubbish ready for collection day because it's expected of him. I persuade him through emotional blackmail, I'm afraid. For example, I might look tired and tearful. Sometimes I start to do it myself and he feels guilty and takes over. However, I don't think it's easy for children to help out round the house as they have so much homework. When my eldest daughter turned 16, I told her I would no longer iron her clothes as she was old enough to be responsible. But what happened? She didn't iron them at all and wore all her clothes crumpled and creased until I eventually gave in after six months."

Alison

"Our children, aged 14 and 12, get £7 a week if they clean the kitchen every day. They're expected to do their bedrooms for nothing. They also have to do their own washing if their clothes aren't in the basket on Friday night. We also agreed that a task should be time limited so they didn't feel too daunted."

Fiona

"We get our children aged 14 and 16 to do jobs by paying them a small amount, depending on the task, or imposing some sort of ban on the computer or television or Playstation. If they really won't do something, we might ban it all together, depending on the circumstances. Actually, I think my children probably help more than most, according to what they tell me. It's important to value your children and be positive about the things they do, especially the things they do well. This builds up confidence. We all have to do things we hate and it's best to help children to understand this at an early age."

Sheila

"We have three children, aged 14, 13 and nine. When we're together, we discuss chores and see how we can make things easier on everyone. It's like a group family meeting but not so formal."

Victoria

"My 12 year old son tidies his bedroom under duress, loads the dishwasher, takes rubbish out when asked, makes the odd cup of tea and occasionally helps me with paperwork like addressing envelopes, sorting receipts into piles and doing some filing. I nag to get the tidying done and pay for things like office filing or sweeping up leaves. I also threaten him with my not helping *him* next time he asks. Or I say he can't go somewhere/watch Eastenders. A friend of mine takes the controller for the Playstation and television away. I've tried this and it's very effective. However, I also think it depends on how many children you have. My son is an only so I have got used to doing too much for him. If I had four of them, they would have to do more. I also bore him rigid by telling him, in an old bag voice, about all the things I had to do as a child. I explain that life is full of having to do things you don't want to do and that this is good training for when they have to go out to work and have horrid kids of their own. With any luck, he goes off and does the jobs he should do just to get away from me. The ultimate threat is that I tell my son that if he won't do a job with good grace, I will turn up at his school, wearing flowery jeans and lots of lipstick, call him 'my little soldier' and kiss him in front of all his mates."

Jane

"Instead of threatening to limit their television time if they don't do jobs, we give them extra television time when they *do* do them."

Anon

"Our 15 year old puts washing in the washing machine and tumble drier. I also take away Playstations, iPods and television in his room as a sanction. And I look very disappointed if something isn't done."

Anon

"We don't have to nag our 13 and 15 year olds because they learned the habit of doing jobs round the house from a young age. They do things like tidying their bedrooms, washing up, loading the dishwasher and making their beds as soon as they get home from school. It's the norm for them."

Suzanne

"My 13 year old son does the vacuuming as his main 'pocket money' chore. He actually enjoys dusting and started at about five because he used to enjoy spraying the cleaning products. I've tried to encourage him to tidy his room from an early age but my own isn't very tidy so that's a hard one to set an example for. However, he hates the washing up. So if I need to discipline him, instead of grounding him, I get him to do the pots every night for a week. Sometimes I give him the old 'We're a team' spiel. I'll also tell him he's not allowed to go out with his friends until the job has been done. I think you need to let go, as they get older, rather than mollycoddle them. Shut the door on their room if you can't stand the mess. It's their space and as long as they help to keep the communal space tidy, don't nag. Once they're older and able to take care of their own chores, don't do it for them. Let them go out scruffy and as soon as their friends start poking fun at them, they'll learn."

Andrea

"Our children, aged 11 and 16, wash and dry up, load the dishwasher, iron, help with younger children, take out the milk bottles and cook. We waited until they were 10 before we got them to do jobs but then we persuaded them by paying them for big jobs like ironing. They can also be encouraged to cook if they take care of the whole project, like doing the shopping and planning. Parents often let children get away with not doing jobs round the house because they don't have enough time to stick to their guns. We also try to make jobs fun and when we're on holiday, we all do the washing up together."

Katy

"I find that a list or rota is useful to remind both me and them that certain tasks should be delegated. I've also found that sending children to boarding school makes them much lazier as everything is done for them. One of their biggest faults is leaving towels on the bathroom floor as at school there's underfloor heating. Ouch!"

Nicki

"My kids are in their twenties now but when they were teens, the best way to get them to do jobs they hated was to beg."

Anon

Novelist and mother Katie Fforde says: "I feel I was hopeless in this department but now they're in their twenties, they're fine at doing chores. So it shows all is not lost…"

Key points

- *Your kids are growing up* They need to do jobs at home to prepare themselves for the wide world and university

- *So if you let them off* you're not doing them any favours

- *Encourage team work* if you've got more than one child

- *Show them the benefits of helping out* e.g. being able to find their homework easily

Chapter five

Tidy your room!

Well, after all, this is what the book is about. The funny thing about tidying up is that we expect ourselves and others to be able to do it automatically, a bit like breathing. No one sits down and tells us how to do it. There aren't any lessons like there are for reading or driving or any other skills.

So although it might sound a bit simplistic and possibly patronising, this chapter is about how to tidy up and how to impart these skills to your children, however old they are. Some of the following sections will apply to younger children as well as older ones. But often it depends on your child's ability and willingness. So instead of dividing them into ages, we've divided them into strategies and tactics.

When you're explaining how to tidy up, do the job yourself first of all, talking about what you're doing while your children watch. After that, you can do the job together. Then your children can do the job on their own while you watch and encourage them and gently explain how they might do something differently. And then your children can do it on their own.

IN THE BAG

Tell them to start with the floor. Get down on your hands and knees with them and start picking up any rubbish. If their room is like my son's, you'll find old crisp packets, tin rings, loose chains and lost homework in all kinds of unexpected places.

If necessary change the bag. Don't say 'Look at all this rubbish. Aren't you awful.' Try 'That's fantastic. We've got one bag full and now we're going onto another.'

You'll be amazed at the results. Simply tidying the floor will give an instant feeling of space and, dare we say it, tidiness.

Take another bag and tell your kids that this one is for things that they don't want to throw away but need to put in a different place. When the bag is full, go through each item in the bag and find a place for it. For example, if it's a lost sock, put it in the sock basket or drawer.

ON THE SURFACE

Then move on to surfaces. Put rubbish into the bags from the top of desks, units, beds and so on.

DIVIDE IT UP

If your kids have a big room or there's a huge amount of mess, we suggest you divide the room up into quarters. This can actually be a good mathematical exercise. Help them tackle one quarter of the room one day and another the next and so on. You can use furniture in the room to help you make the divisions. For example, say 'We'll do this side of the bed today and that side tomorrow.'

Alternatively, you could do the floor one day and the surfaces on another.

WIPE IT UP

Now they've moved all that rubbish from their desk or dressing table or whatever, it might be a bit mucky underneath. Give them a damp cloth and show them how to rub off ring stains etc. Then find them a duster and polish. Don't just say 'Dust' but show them how to spray enough polish and not too much. Make a game out of rubbing the duster in different movements.

If you're feeling really strict or you want to get your kids truly house trained, show them how to wipe down skirting boards with the cloth. This might sound obvious to us but it won't be to them and sometimes it's worth remembering that.

SWEEP IT UP

Show your children how to use the vacuum cleaner. Obvious? Not always. My then 13 year old son almost managed to decapitate my vacuum cleaner and if it hadn't been for the lovely woman on the other end of the phone at Customer Services, I would have been distraught.

Also show them how to use the dustpan and brush. This is a much forgotten item but is very easy for young children to use. If they can be trusted on the stairs, show them how to kneel on the top step, sweep it and then go down one step at a time.

PUT IT IN ITS PLACE

One reason why rooms get so untidy is that children don't know where to put things. So make sure everything has its place in life. Socks go in the third drawer down. Books go on the table by the bed or on the bookshelf. CDs go in the rack.

- This might mean buying containers or other things to store these items in. But that doesn't have to be expensive. Shop around for inexpensive plastic crates and label them so everyone knows what's inside.

- Keep shoe boxes when buying new shoes and store the shoes in these. It's cheaper than those shoe tidiers.

- Also hang on to old containers for storing things. Pringle tubes make great containers for rubbers and pencils.

EASY TO GET TO

Children are more likely to put things in their right place if that place is easy to get to. It's unrealistic and dangerous to expect a small child to reach up to a top drawer or one that is always sticking. In fact, any kind of effort – such as finding the right drawer – can be enough to put them off the task altogether. So try open baskets where they can see at a glance what's inside.

- Hanging rails can also be handy because children can see what's there at a glance. But make sure they're not too high for them to reach. And only buy sturdy makes which won't fall over on your child.

- Save ice cream containers for storing hair scrunches, loose coins, paper clips, bits of Lego etc. Use sticky labels to put on the lid so you know what's inside.

- Buy see-through plastic envelopes or folders for important information that they want to keep themselves.

- Put a noticeboard on their wall so they can pin up notices and any other bits of paper which they want to keep safely.

- Get a blackboard or whiteboard and prop it against their wall. They can use it to write things down so they don't forget. And you can use it to remind them of what they're meant to be doing when you say 'tidy up'.

COLOUR CO-ORDINATE

Grouping clothes together according to colour isn't just an adult thing. It also makes it easier to find children's clothes. And it makes it easier for them to put away a pink jumper or a blue one because they know where they go.

We also have a separate drawer for sports kit which, in theory, saves us from looking in different places for football shirts, socks etc.

DO YOU REALLY, REALLY WANT THIS?

Decluttering is becoming increasingly popular for adults. And amazingly, kids can feel better too when they get rid of their rubbish. Go through their wardrobe and drawers and anything else and ask if they still want something. Get them to try on clothes and see if they still fit. At the rate kids grow, you'll be amazed at how much storage space you're giving to stuff that doesn't even fit any more.

Bag it all up and get them to help you take it to the charity shop or friends whose children will still enjoy it. My kids get a lot of pleasure out of this. Recently, we gave some things to a neighbour's son who wrote us a thank you letter. I thought that was lovely – and surprisingly, my children were touched too.

Key points

- *Tidying up* is a skill that often needs to be taught. Don't assume they know what to do when you tell them to sort out their room or school bag.

- *Go through each stage* Show them how to do it even if it seems obvious.

- *Make sure* there's a place and home for every major item in your child's room so they know where it goes.

Chapter six

Kids' backchat

Of course, to find out what *really* makes kids do the jobs they hate, who better to ask than the culprits themselves? We spent several months researching the answers. With the teenagers, we had to wait until the morning after the night before, in order to get a sensible answer.

"I cook, clean, wash clothes, vacuum, do the dishes, load and unload the dishwasher, drown squirrels (sic), tidy my room, garden, iron, make beds, clean bins, water plants. My mum's a slave driver."

James, 19

"I do the dishes, tidy my room and wash the car. We just do it."

Andrew, 19

"I tidy my room, do the dishes and help garden. I have to."

James, 19

"I vacuum and can even change the hoover bag. I taught myself, I think. I learned to vacuum when I was about nine because I was made to for pocket money. I definitely hoover round corners although they're the most annoying things to do. I wash up and dry up without being asked because otherwise my mum would ask me so it's better to get it out of the way before she nags me. We're redecorating at the moment so I paint and strip walls. I'm quite good at taking the paint off windows. My mum taught me how to do this. In return, I get paid money which goes into the rugby tour fund; I'm hoping to go with school later this year. I can do washing as well. I can put it in the machine on the right number, depending on what clothes they are, and put in detergent. I've never shrunk anything. I do so much because my mum makes me."

Kieran, 15

"I walk the dog all the time. I got a dog when I was 13 so I knew not to cross the road at dangerous times. I also give the dog a bath sometimes but he hates it. I do vacuuming sometimes when I'm asked. I haven't broken the vacuum cleaner yet but my mum has. I can change the bag; it's quite easy because it's a clip on. I mow the lawn but it's hard because it's on a hill. I don't have to be nagged but I do it when I need money and my parents realise the house needs cleaning. I don't really tidy my room because I share it with my brother and he messes it up so there's not much point. I also wash the family car about once a month. I get extra money for that – about £10 depending on how well I wash it."

Matt, 15

"I clean the car when I'm desperate for money. I get £10 max if I do a good job. I hoover round the house occasionally if my mum really nags me. I sometimes use my dad's sit-on mower. I like doing this and he pays me £5 if I mow the lawn. Occasionally I tidy my room if my mum nags me a lot. I lay the table when my mum is cooking for me. I put all my own stuff in the dishwasher when I've finished. I've hung out the washing for my mum in the summer. I sometimes cook breakfast in the morning. My mum taught me how to make scrambled egg."

Will, 15

"Bribery is the only thing that works. Just give us money."

William, 22 (author's son)

"We've always had to make our beds and tidy our bedrooms. My mum writes a list of jobs and puts our name down next to them, like emptying the dishwasher and vacuuming and doing the ironing –

that kind of thing. If you don't do it, she gets pretty stressed out and you get shouted at. We water the garden and do the chemicals for the swimming pool as well as vacuuming it and putting the pool covers on at night. We rake the leaves in the autumn and mow the lawn. I've made dinner for everyone every night since I was 11. My friend says I make great quiches. As I got older, my younger brother Sam would help me do pasta. We have a cleaner who comes in twice a week as well so there isn't that much to do. But we would always wash up after dinner before dad gets back from work. When my brother and I were in the same class at school, I'd have to help him with his homework."

Laura, 19

"I wash up and dry up and do a bit of ironing. I also tidy up and stuff. Round mealtimes, I help in the house. I also do loads of gardening for my mum; digging the vegetable garden and walking the dogs every day. Mum tells me to do this. She used to pay me for doing the car but that stopped because I stopped washing the car. I got bored with it. If I don't do the jobs mum asks me to do, she throws a tantrum."

Sam, 15

"I don't hate doing any jobs. I just can't be arsed to do them. Also, we weren't brought up having to do jobs, so we don't do them. The best way to get us to do jobs is to treat us like adults. Don't nag or get cross or make us feel guilty if we don't do it. Then we will do it, if you see what I mean."

Charlie, 14

"I tidy out kitchen cupboards for mum. I like it because I put all the pots and pans inside each other."

Mary, eight

"I like using the vacuum cleaner because it makes me feel grown-up."

Lizzie, seven

"I hate tidying my room but mum gives me a Tesco bag on Sunday nights and makes me pick up rubbish from the floor. I get 30p a bag."

Matthew, nine

"My mum can't see very well so my five brothers and I all have different jobs. My job is to put all the newspapers in a pile by the back door and then one of my brothers puts the bin out."

Jason, five

"My dad's always moaning that he doesn't have time to watch television since mum went. So I thought of circling the programmes I think he'd like in the paper and getting him to sit down sometimes. He says it's my new job."

Melissa, 10

"I put knives and forks on the table before meals. Sometimes I put them the wrong way round."

Kerry, five

"I like making paper decorations for the table when it's Christmas or someone's birthday."

Susan, six

"I like vacuuming mum's cutlery drawers with the end of the vacuum cleaner. I take all the knives and forks and spoons out first and then get the mess out. It's amazing what you find. Bits of dirt, crumbs and fluff. I'm always telling her she should be tidier. When I have my own home, it's not going to be like this."

Andrea, 12

"My job is to put my shoes and my younger brother's shoes in a tidy row every Sunday night in the hall."

Mandie, six

Chapter seven

What the experts say

If we really want to get kids to do jobs they hate, we need to employ some psychological cunning. And sometimes, as we parents know all too well, it's time to call in the professionals. We asked experts who are parents too, for some tips and general advice.

WORK OUT WHAT KIND OF JOB YOU WANT THEM TO DO

"There are two types of jobs," says psychologist and mother Gaynor Sbuttoni. "One is the kind of job your child needs to do to help himself. And the other is the kind of job your child can do to help others.

"The trick is to concentrate on the first and work up to the second. If you can help your child to learn to make his own bed, or pack her homework for the next day, or empty their own wastepaper bin, you are teaching them to be self-sufficient. When they've mastered that, it's nice to get them to help others so they learn how good that feels."

DON'T BE VAGUE – BE SPECIFIC

Don't just say 'tidy your room' or 'clear up your toys', says Gaynor. "With my children, I've found it's essential to talk them through the basic stages such as where to put the toys or what to do with those magazines that are lying on the floor. Sometimes a job seems so vast and overwhelming that they don't know where to start and that's when they give up. But if you've given them definite instructions, they know what they're doing and they're more likely to do it."

Editor's note — see chapter 5.

BIN IT

Penny Palmano, writer, mother, stepmother and author of *Yes, Please. Whatever! (Thorsons Element £7.99)*, has also solved the 'Put away your clothes' problem by buying her children a big plastic bin each for them to chuck clean clothes into. "When I just told them to hang up their clothes, they either did it sloppily or not at all." Bins are easy and also specific which is what this section is about. If you say 'Put it in the bin', that's pretty clear. And as Penny says, it's better than clothes lying on the floor. "The other great thing is that they don't have to fold them. I also give them plastic trays to put their make up on."

Top tip —————————————————————————

Buy storage containers or baskets for young children to put away their toys.

—————————————————————————

ROLE MODELLING

"Show them how to do things by getting down on your hands and knees (if necessary) and demonstrating," says Gaynor. "So if they are having trouble tidying their room, show them how you tidy the kitchen and get them to help you. Say 'You do that bit there and I'll do this and we'll see what we're left with'."

Gaynor suggests talking out loud while you're doing this to encourage them and to give them ideas. "Try something like 'Oh dear, I need to find a new place for this. Now let's see, where can it go'. Then they can think about whether they would do the same to their bedroom."

Penny Palmano agrees. "Don't just say 'Please can you vacuum the carpet'. Explain how to go into corners. And show them how the different attachments to the vacuum cleaner go on and off."

"In fact, explaining how to do something is crucial," adds Dr Pat Spungin, psychologist, mother and founder of **www.raisingkids. co.uk**. "Otherwise it can stop children wanting to do it again if they get it wrong – and cause family arguments. My husband once offered one of our daughters money to paint the garden furniture. But he didn't explain how to do it and she got paint all over the patio."

WHAT TO DO IF THEY WON'T CO-OPERATE

Keep reminding them

This tip is from me. Unless your child is a natural home maker (and there are a few which we'll come onto later), you'll need to remind, remind, remind. In fact, there's nothing wrong with reminding them to do something, so don't start berating your kids for never listening. It takes time for the tidying up gene to kick in – especially if you've started a little late in their lives.

However, it is a bit boring to be the baddy reminder, so here are some things that might help them remember for themselves.

- *Make a checklist of jobs they have to do* Write out a small list of tasks and get them to tick them off when they've finished. Don't put too many on the sheet or they'll feel overwhelmed. Just seeing it written down, will jolt their memory and remind them. Put the list somewhere they will see it. Try anywhere near their computer/ music/mobile for starters. Or stick it to the back of their bedroom door so that when they slam it after a row with you, they'll see what they really should be doing.

- *Tie it into a day* If it's Tuesday, it must be the day to empty bedroom wastepaper bins. Mark it on the kitchen calendar. Then say something like 'It's Tuesday. What do we do on Tuesdays?'

(*Warning:* We can't accept responsibility for inappropriate answers)

- *Have house rules which are set in stone* "Draw up a list of house rules which includes jobs that certain people have agreed to do," suggests Dorit Braun, chief executive of ParentLine Plus. "It might be things like putting your dirty washing in the bin – and if you don't, it won't get washed".

Write it down

"I wrote out a code of behaviour for my son and gave it to him," says Heather Summers, communications and language expert and the author of *The Book of Luck, (John Wiley £12.99)*. "It included being polite and saying things like 'Good morning' and 'Good night'. Sometimes teenagers need things to be written down to make it go in."

Start young

This tip was repeated again and again by all the experts we asked. So if you've just had a new baby, it's time to read this. Within a year, you'll be able to send your newborn off to work. Only half joking. "Even toddlers can pull up their own duvet in the morning," says Dr Pat Spungin. "The sooner you start, the more used they will be to helping round the house or doing things for you. They won't question; they'll just get on with it."

Penny Palmano points out that the great thing about young children is that they actually think it's fun to help clean up the kitchen and dust. "Give toddlers their own special cleaning box with their name on it. Don't ask if they will do something. Tell them but in a nice way. 'Today, we're going to wipe down the cupboards in the kitchen.'"

Sue Firth, a psychologist, is a great believer in the starting young theory. "My seven year old daughter does jobs like clearing up her own toys. I've taught her that if she gets something out, she has to put it back. To get them going, I also advise finding a job your child enjoys and then working on it. My daughter loves setting the table and playing 'waitresses'. Recently, she's started to take our orders, which can be a bit annoying after a while but we go along with it. My son likes tidying up the playroom. We also link jobs with pocket money. Georgina, who's seven, gets £3 a week and Ben, five, gets £2.

"Ben also enjoys doing the polishing and I give him his own pinny and duster. I try not to be controlling and I don't point out the bits he's missed. Sometimes I say 'Here are the top five jobs for the day. Which ones would you like to do?' Then they pick one and can earn extra pocket money."

But it's never too late

If you've allowed your teenager to get away with it, you can still get him or her to make a start. Use a birthday as a starting point. 'Now you're 15, you can cook and clear away a meal.' Or 'Now you're 11, you can wash the basins.'

Top Tip

"I find it hard to clean my bathroom because I'm arthritic," says Granny B from Buckinghamshire. "So I suggested to my 12 year old grandson that he does all the 'white stuff' in the bathroom, including the toilet, for £10 a week. He comes on Saturday mornings and afterwards we have a cup of tea together. I make sure he washes his hands first."

Turn it up

This is another of my own tips. Jobs don't have to be done in silence. Put on the radio. It will take away the tension. If they're tidying their own bedrooms, suggest they put on some of their terrible music. I actually dance with one of my children when we're doing the housework together. I won't tell you which one because it will embarrass them. But it's fun and it makes us laugh instead of getting tetchy.

You help me and I'll help you

A tit for tat – in the nicest possible way – can work wonders when it comes to getting kids to do things they hate, says Gaynor. "'If you help me set the video timer, I'll help you tidy your wardrobe.' It helps them feel valued. Often kids are the ones who feel thick or inadequate because an adult is always telling them they are doing something the wrong way. But if they've got talents that the adult hasn't got, it makes them feel great about themselves. And it also shows them the pleasure of helping others. Presenting a job as part of a bargain makes them see the sense of doing jobs. Children are usually very fair underneath. They can see that if someone does you a favour, it needs to be returned."

Penny Palmano agrees. "Next time your teenager wants a lift, agree – providing he does something for you so you have time to give him that lift. It might be tidying your home office or washing up."

Bribery

Should you or shouldn't you bribe your kids to do jobs? The experts and parents we interviewed were divided on this one. After all, if your kids expect something every time they do something for you, where do you stop? But our experts also had some other interesting ideas.

- *If you are going to bribe them* keep rewards small, advises Gaynor. Or you lose the value of rewards for something more important. Children also need to learn that it's nice to do jobs to help others and not just to earn money.

- *Keep the rewards in perspective* advises Dr Spungin. "Don't promise them a fortnight's holiday if they keep their room tidy for ever. Be realistic. Make sure the reward is attainable and that it's not overindulgent".

- *Link pocket money to certain jobs*, says Penny Palmano. "There's a time when this can definitely get them going. After all, it's earning money for fair labour. We pay cash if it's a really tricky job like gardening. They get £4 an hour for weeding or cleaning the car. But be careful not to do this with all jobs or they'll expect cash in hand for everything."

- *Employ them like you would a cleaning lady*, suggests Masha Bell, teacher, mother, grandmother and writer. "When my daughter got to the age of 14, I employed her as my cleaning lady. She wanted to get an outside job to earn money but it would have interfered with her interest in music. So I paid her the going rate as a cleaner and she did the house for me three hours a week. She took it seriously because we both saw it as a real job."

Professor Cary Cooper, expert in time management says "In my view, the only thing that works is bribery, otherwise known as 'incentive based parenting'. We already gave them an allowance but if we promised them extra, they did things. One thing I did learn was to ask them to do jobs on a Friday. They were so keen to earn money for going out at the weekend with their friends, that they were more likely to agree".

Top Tip

Paying by the hour also helps them get into a 'work' frame of mind for when they do holiday jobs or the real thing. It also shows them that an hour can be a long time to do something boring. So when they do go into the real world of work, they need to do something interesting. That can be an incentive for passing exams.

- *Show them how to earn money for jobs.* What's that old saying about there being plenty of money to be made out of rubbish? One of my children's friends, who's only 12, cleans out his room twice a year and sells the things he doesn't want on eBay using his older brother's account. He also goes down with his mother to the local car boot fair and sells other discarded items there. Last year, he made enough to buy a new computer.

● *Offer them an on-the-spot reward for the job.* As one parent says, "If I ask one of my teenagers to get some shopping for me in town, I'll give them some extra money to buy a pie at the baker's to make the walk home more interesting".

Praise them

We all know that no one does a job better than we can do ourselves, but if you say as much, you're not likely to get more help from that quarter. "Never say 'That's awful – call that tidying your room?'" says Penny Palmano. "Or they won't want to do it again. Give them plenty of praise. Say 'that's *such* a help' even if it hasn't been. Tell them how grown-up they are. After that, you can say 'Another way of tidying your room might be to pick up the towels that are still lying in the corner'. Don't yell if they put on so much furniture polish that it creates scum on top of the table. Instead, show them how to do it properly. Be positive about the things they haven't done, instead of being negative."

Encourage team work

Office psychologists know what they're talking about when it comes to encouraging team work. If we all feel we're working towards one cause, we might be more likely to enter into the spirit. "If you've got more than one child, get them to work as a team," advises Penny who has a 17 year old son, a 17 year old stepdaughter and an 18 year old daughter at home. "They often do jobs together like cleaning the kitchen. It's also nice because it gives them time to chat about things they might not otherwise have had time to talk about."

Dr Pat Spungin agrees. "Get your family to see themselves as a team. You can do this by encouraging everyone to pitch in. Don't assume you have to do it all yourself or they'll take the same attitude."

Top Tips

- Like Penny, I get my kids to do jobs together but I listen in to their chat. You can learn all kinds of things this way.

- Use peer pressure to your advantage. Show younger children how helpful older children can be; these might be siblings or neighbours' children etc. It gives them a goal to work towards.

Work with distractions

"If your children find it boring to do jobs round the house, let them do jobs in front of the television," says Penny. "My stepdaughter likes sorting odd socks this way. And small children can do the same with boxes of toys. That's why so many people do the ironing or use an exercise bike in front of the screen."

Top Tips

- "My children like polishing/vacuuming etc. when they have their iPods in. If they don't own an iPod, tell them that they need to do more jobs round the house to earn one. (See section on bribery.)

- "Get them to make a party out of a job. If they moan about washing up, set up the radio in the kitchen and get them all doing it. Young children, in particular, love this," says Dr Pat Spungin.

If you can't beat them

If you can't beat them, join them, says Penny. "Do jobs with them and use the time to share confidences. If you're both cleaning the kitchen, it's a great opportunity for some deep, meaningful chat. Changing the duvet cover in tandem is another example."

Appeal to their better natures....

"Tell them you could really do with some help because you're running out of time," says Penny. "This attitude works much better than

'You're so lazy; you never do anything for me.'" Penny also admits that the odd bit of emotional blackmail can come in handy. "If my lot are reluctant to walk the dog, I'll point out that he could be ill/have an accident/will have to live somewhere else unless they pull their weight."

Writer Masha Bell goes one further. "Don't be afraid to show them how you feel. If I was tired, I'd get cross and they'd usually respond to reason."

And don't let them get away with it

"When you come home from work and your big teenager is sprawled out over the sofa, asking what's for dinner, say 'Hang on a minute…,'" advises Dr Pat Spungin. "Once you start saying 'All right, don't you get up; I'll do it,' you're in trouble because they'll think they can get away with it next time too. However, it's worth picking your fights and deciding what you're going to get tough over and what you can afford to let slip. You can't win every argument so it's more important to fight for the ones which mean most. We personally have a rule that they help to tidy public spaces that everyone uses like the kitchen and sitting room. How they keep their own room is their own business. Compromise is also important. If they're really busy with their homework, let them off the washing up that night. Say 'I'll do it for you' but make sure they know it's still their job."

Let them get adventurous

Allow them to do jobs they might make a mess off – within reason. "Our teenagers have been ironing for years," says Penny. "But I don't give them my husband's shirts to iron. Instead, they've ruined their own t-shirts by ironing the motif. But if they don't make mistakes, they don't learn."

Dr Pat Spungin warns that we shouldn't assume our children are too young to do something. "A time always comes in a child's life when they are old enough to be taught how to operate the digital camera/washing machine/house alarm/answer phone. In fact, children are often better at technical things like digital cameras than adults because they're not frightened of them."

Top Tip

I know one mum who allowed her eight and 10 year olds to paint their own bedrooms. The effect was interesting.

Find them jobs that develop their creative instincts

"When my son was about 13, he filed our extensive collection of CDs and really enjoyed it because it appealed to his kind of brain," says Dr Pat Spungin. "Some children naturally enjoy ordering things – so they could sort out cookery books too. If they make a face when you ask them to peel vegetables, get a fancy shaped cutter. They might enjoy making a picture out of the food."

Life coach Jackie Arnold says "My children enjoyed gardening if they could do something creative like making up their own pots of plants."

Ask them nicely

No one likes being told what to do and even if you think your children *should* do something, they're more likely to respond if you ask them nicely, says Penny.

This also applies in front of outsiders. "If visitors arrive, don't automatically expect your children to take their coats or make polite conversation. Talk to them beforehand and discuss how they could help you."

Heather Summers suggests using your voice to get what you want. "Sound firm and go down in tone at the end, in a command. Don't shout. Use positive language. Instead of saying 'Your room is a mess,' try 'You know your bedroom needs tidying and today's the day for doing it so will you do it now.'"

Teach them skills that they'll remember for ever

Cooking is an obvious one, says Penny. "But keep it simple like how to warm up pasta sauce. If it's too complicated, they might switch off or think they can't do it."

Other skills could include:
- *Ironing*
- *Making beds properly* e.g. tucking in the corners
- *Putting on a duvet*
- *Peeling potatoes*

Top Tip

To change the duvet cover, turn it inside out and, while still holding the two top corners, grab hold of the two top corners of the duvet. Invert, rather like tipping out a steam pudding, and shake the duvet cover down. My friend's son learned to do this at boarding school and has been teaching the rest of us.

Your child's personality will dictate what jobs they will and won't do

"Certain ten year olds are capable of loading the dishwasher correctly and others aren't," reminds Masha Bell. "We need to accept their limitations. Tidying up was a problem for my son. Sometimes there's not a lot you can do to change them. But there may be other jobs that they are good at and other children aren't. The trick is to experiment until you find their niche."

Life coach Jackie Arnold agrees. "My children weren't good at tidying up. I also used to nag them to polish but they wouldn't do that either. However, they *did* enjoy ironing because they could see the results. Psychologically, for them, seeing the results is really important. You don't always get that when you tidy a room because it gets untidied fast. But an ironed shirt is proof that you've done something. Other children might be different. It's like nagging. Some respond to it and others don't. I've also learned the hard way that some children are more willing to do jobs than others. It depends on their personality. And there's not a lot you can do to change it."

Professor Cary Cooper suggests linking the job with your child's personality. "My son liked being praised. So if you've got a kid like that, give them a task they can do well and then tell them what a great job they've done."

"My son worked best when he had a choice of jobs," says Heather Summers. "I'd say 'Would you like to empty the dishwasher or cook breakfast?'. Creating a regular pattern of jobs also helps. He would empty the bins every Tuesday and he would always clear up after himself. I started when he was 14 by saying 'This is the deal; these are the rules in this house.' At first, he wasn't very good at some jobs but I made sure I didn't criticise him too much."

Give them time

You might have to wait a few years but they'll get there in the end… "My kids never tidied their rooms – not even when they went to uni," confesses Professor Cary Cooper. "But when they started to own their own homes, they got much fussier. So there is light at the end of the tunnel even if you have to wait 30 years."

Key points

- *Be consistent* If you give them a job, make them stick at it. Otherwise, they lose privileges.

- *Praise them* This can be verbally, financially or both.

- *Be imaginative* when giving them jobs. You need to make them interested.

- *Some kids will be keener on helping out than others* If yours is a reluctant helper, try and find a job he likes.

Chapter eight

The best way to ask your kids in order to get results...and other strategies

We warned you there was some psychology involved in this. Well, you've got to be a bit devious, haven't you?

FAMILY DIY AND OTHER EMOTIONAL INTELLIGENCE TIPS

There are some jobs which help to bond a family – and some that make families fall out for ever. We'd rather concentrate on the former. If you have a kid that's *very* bad at doing jobs, set them up with a partner, even if that has to be you. Choose jobs that genuinely require two people such as folding sheets, putting on a duvet etc. It might just provide that kick up the proverbial that they need.

Don't be afraid to cry

Some children respond best to direct payment for specific jobs. Others react better to emotional blackmail. For example 'Can't you see how tired mummy is?' It sounds obvious but each child is different. You know what will motivate yours in other areas so apply the same logic to housework.

Shameful ways to make them help out

OK, so this isn't really ethical. Let's hope no one from the child protection agencies are reading this. But bitter experience with three lazy kids has taught me that the best way to make them help out is to shame them in front of their friends.

There are various ways of doing this.

You can wait until one of their mates comes round and then ask them to help clear the table/wash up/polish their shoes. When they moan and say 'Get a life, mum, I've got a friend round', you then ask the friend if they help out at home. With any luck, the reply will be in the affirmative. You then say to your child: 'Well if your friend helps out, I think you should do the same.'

If the reply happens to be in the negative, by the way, do not ask that child round to tea again. He/she clearly isn't a suitable friend for your offspring.

Alternatively, you could ask the friends to help. If you say 'Would you lot mind putting your dishes in the dishwasher/wiping the mats?', chances are that they will be so much in awe of you that they will. After all, you're not their mum so they'll do what you say.

If you're clever, you'll wait until your kids' friends come round, before getting them to tackle some really dastardly jobs such as digging the garden/cleaning out the rabbit.

Pretend you can't do it yourself

There's nothing like a little woman to bring out the maternal side in kids. So mothers who are really desperate (and deceitful) they could pretend you simply can't lift up something without their help. We're sure you can think of some other examples.

Fit the child to the job

Some of our experts have already touched on this but we feel it's so important that we're saying it again. Some kids (if they've got any character) prefer certain jobs to others. So foster that. If they're great at washing up, hand over the Fairy Liquid. If they loathe washing up but quite fancy the idea of grooming the dog, make that their job instead.

Playing consequences

This is one of those home truths that you can't instill into your children early enough. If they make a mess, they have to clear it up. If they want to cook, they have to wash up afterwards. If they want to play with their toys, they clear them away. And if they won't, they can't do it again.

Sometimes you have to be tough as a parent. Maybe that's why I'm such a lousy one but *you* can still try.

TIME IT RIGHT

Every good politician and parent knows that it's not *what* they say – it's when they say it.

Asking the children to do jobs they hate, can succeed or fail depending on your timing. If you demand that they empty the bins/tidy their rooms when they're deep in conversation on MSN or vacant eyed in front of the television, you're on a losing wicket. So here are some tips:

Wait until they aren't doing something important and then make your request.

- Speak slowly and clearly, pretending that you're talking to someone whose native language isn't English. This might sound condescending but it's not intended to be. It's merely that children don't usually listen to adults so the clearer you can be, the more chance you have of getting through.

- Sometimes it helps to pretend that these children are not your own. Now I know this sounds awful but if you close your eyes and imagine they're your neighbour's kids, you might speak more pleasantly to them and then you'll probably get better results than if you yelled. Trust me. This one works.

- Another weird tip, which has been tried and tested in our house by yours truly, is to speak with your eyes closed. For some reason, this stops you getting uptight about the fact that the job in question hasn't been done. You seem to concentrate on the words more than the feelings that are racing round your head. As a result, you speak in a calmer fashion. Well, just give it a go.

- Never yell instructions up the stairs. They won't hear you or they'll pretend not to hear you. If they do, they'll say 'What did you say?' or just 'Wot'. Then you'll have to run up the stairs and repeat the whole thing all over again. By then, you'll be feeling impatient and you probably won't ask them nicely enough for them to agree.

- Use new beginnings as new excuse for making them do jobs that they didn't do before.

Here are some examples.

- New year. Let's make helping out one of your new resolutions.

- New term. New leaf. Let's see if we can get a better report.

- New school. As above.

- New house. Now you've got a new bedroom, I want you to keep it tidy. Now we're moving house, you can pack your own things and throw away the bits you don't want.

- New baby. Now you've got a new brother/sister, I'm going to need more help. You can show him/her how grown-up you are because you can vacuum etc.

- Say 'Now it's a new year/term etc, we're going to do x,y,z'.

Jobs for each occasion

Use timelines and/or special occasions during the year to think up new jobs or encourage them to do old ones. Here are some examples.

- Christmas. Ask them to help write or design cards/envelopes/place mats. If necessary bribe them or just tell them that if they don't, Santa won't pay his usual visit.

- Easter. Instead of organising an Easter hunt for them, get them to do one for you. Ask them to hide small eggs round the house for you to find them. The reward is that they can help themselves as you go. It will keep them quiet while they're thinking you're doing them a favour. They could also organise an Easter hunt for visiting children.

- Summer holiday. Put one of them in charge of the calculator if you're going abroad, and get them to work out the exchange rate. Fantastic for maths. Yours, not theirs.

IT'S NOT WHAT YOU ASK THEM TO DO – IT'S THE WAY YOU SAY IT

Getting kids to do things they hate is often a matter of asking them in the right way. After all, if someone barked at you and told you to make supper now, you'd be less likely to do so than if that person asked you nicely.

Here are some ideas to get you going.

- Look them in the face. Direct your questions to their eyes and if they're not listening, do something to attract their attention. If necessary, do something really embarrassing. It usually works. This looking in the face bit is vital. It doesn't work if you yell an instruction down the stairs or call it out. It's far too easy then for them to ignore it.

- Another child ploy is to answer 'Yes' if you're asking whether they're doing their chores. As any child knows, a 'Yes' when an adult is out of earshot/eyeshot is just a ploy to put off the evil deed. So track them down and check they are actually doing it.

- If looking at them in the face doesn't work, try using your voice in a different way. This doesn't mean yelling or shouting although you're perfectly justified in doing that sometimes. Instead, try saying the instruction in French or Japanese or a made up language. If you're not fluent enough, just put on a foreign accent. They'll understandably look at you with a 'What is mum up to now?' look but it will get their attention. Then you can jump in and tell them normally, just what it is that you want them to do.

- Whisper. This is an alternative to the above. Of course they might not hear you with all the din they're making, but a whisper can be far more effective than a yell just because it takes them by surprise.

- Talk in a silly voice. The Dalek one seems to go down well.

- Sing. The same logic (or lack of it) applies.

- Ask them to do something in a poem. This does mean you have to be reasonably good at making up poems or limericks. But here's an example. Feel free to plagiarise.

  There was a young lady from Weitz
  Whose room was not very nice.
  Tidy up, said her mum
  Or it won't be much fun
  When your bedroom's infested with mice.

- Remember your pleases and thank yous. We think we've said this somewhere else in the book but it doesn't do any harm to repeat it. If we don't thank our kids for doing something or ask them nicely, why should they bother?

AIDES MEMOIRES

Sometimes, they need a little prod to help them remember what they have promised to do. Just like asking them to do something, you need to remind them nicely in order to get the most out of them. So try:

- Lists

- Wall charts

- Text messages on mobile phones. I do this every Wednesday to remind my son to go to his guitar lesson.

- Nagging

- If it's Tuesday, it must be ....

WHO'S A BIG BOY THEN?

Make them feel grown-up with big jobs. Children are often keener to do jobs if it makes them feel grown-up. Try these out for size and make them responsible for :

- Checking the smoke alarm batteries

- Doing the checking last thing at night

- Cooking supper. This includes planning the meal and shopping for it as well as washing up.

- Turning off the television

- Setting the house alarm

- Setting alarm clocks

- Putting the clocks forward and backwards at the right time of year

FLATTERY, BARTERING AND OTHER RUSES

We all know how nice it is to be praised and how soul destroying it is to be criticised. But it's easy to forget that in the day-to-day grind of constant nagging when it comes to the kids.

You're far more likely to get them to do jobs they hate if you tell them how good they are at something. All right, so there's still egg all over the plate while they're drying it up but at least they're trying.

The trick is to find something they really are good at and then plug it for all you're worth. My daughter is very good at tidying up kitchen shelves.

If they're not good at something, lie. Suppose you've asked your toddler to put away his toys and he's only put two in the toy box. The rest lie strewn over the floor as a booby trap for any sober adult. Do you say 'Why didn't you do what I asked?' No of course you don't. Instead, you cross your fingers and say 'Gosh, you've done a fantastic job with some of those toys. Now can you help me put the rest of them in the toy box?'

Another ruse is to make them into monitors for different jobs. My children's schools don't seem to have a monitor system but when I was at school, we had monitors in charge of different things like cleaning the blackboard. So do the same with your own brood. Make one the washing up monitor. Another could be the tidying up monitor. And if you've only got one child, you'll have to be a monitor yourself.

BARTER

In the old days, if we wanted a loaf of bread, we might barter a jar of honey for it. It's not a bad idea. Use it to give your kids a history lesson and get them to do things for you at the same time. Yes of course you will give them a fiver to go out with their friends or buy that comic. But only if they do something for you in return such as wash the car.

The trick is to explain this quid pro quo tactic in a nice and not nasty way. It's also essential for both parties to stick to the agreement. If you fulfil your side of the agreement even when they don't fulfil theirs, why should they do it next time?

DOING JOBS FOR EACH OTHER

One of the reasons why it's good for kids to do things they hate, is not just to lighten our own daily lengthy list of jobs. It's also to teach them how to be caring. If you have more than one child, you can take this a step further and get them to do jobs for each other. Always ask them nicely however. My 19 year old daughter often complains that I just expect her to do something for her younger brother even though he does very little for her. (She actually expresses this in a far less polite way which I can't elaborate on since this is a family book.)

Here are some examples of things older children could do:

- Help younger ones with homework
- Assist them with tidying up
- Show them how to do things like wash up/clear their room
- Wash younger children's hair

Younger children could:

- Help fold washing for older children
- Help make beds/change duvets
- Help carry things in from the car

TIDY UP INTERESTING PLACES

If you had a choice between tidying your room and tidying the attic or spare room, which would you rather do?

It's no contest, is it? Tidying a place which isn't yours and which offers interesting possibilities is much more appealing. It can also be very helpful. We've just moved house and it took me weeks to sort through all the rubbish we'd accumulated over the years. My husband and I agreed we should have done this years ago – and not just because of moving.

Clearing the house of stuff you don't need is actually very cathartic – and gives you more room to live in afterwards. So get the kids going. Send them up into the attic (supervised) or into the spare room where you've stored things you couldn't be bothered to chuck. Get an older child in charge – maybe a cousin or pay a neighbour's child – and ask them to sort things out in piles. For example, clothes, games etc.

Invite older children to make piles such as one for charity, one to keep, or one to give to friends. Get them to come with you down to the charity shop. It might be an eye opener for them to see what other people need.

Even better, allow them to hold a garage sale or take them to a car boot sale. They can keep the proceeds but only if they've done their fair share of sorting out first.

Top tip

If you don't have an attic or spare room, send them under their beds or yours. There's bound to be some rubbish there that needs sorting out.

COMPETITION TIME

If your kids are like mine, there's plenty of hot competition between them plus a large dollop of sibling rivalry. So keep it going by seeing who can be the tidiest or do the most jobs. Here are some ideas:

- Who can bring down the biggest number of dirty mugs from their bedrooms without spilling the contents on the carpet?

- Who can finish the drying up first?

- Who can make their bed first?

You get the idea....

GIVE ME FIVE – OTHERWISE KNOWN AS THE THREE LINE WHIP

Tell them what you want them to do. When they quibble, tell them they can have five/10/15 minutes to finish what they're doing now and then they have to do whatever it is you want. You stand a better chance of succeeding if you give them notice.

WHY BOTHER?

Let's face it. Getting kids to do jobs they hate can be more trouble than the jobs themselves. 36 per cent of the parents we surveyed, said they let kids off jobs because they couldn't be bothered to push it.

Psychologically, it's good for them

"If you let them get away with it," says psychologist Gaynor Sbuttoni, "it's not teaching them anything in the long term. If anything, it's telling them that if they make enough fuss about something, they won't have to do it. And that's dangerous, especially when it comes to school work. Instead, make it part of the routine. Agree the list of jobs in advance. Say 'This is going to be your job. Every Wednesday, I expect you to empty your bedroom bin/tidy your school bag out etc.'"

American research shows that children who help to sort laundry, water plants and dust, exhibit high levels of self-esteem, commitment and responsibility according to a recent feature in *Junior* magazine.

Children also take pride in earning money for jobs. And, as we remember ourselves, they'll value things that they bought with their own wages. "Children need to do jobs to learn the value of hard work and also responsibility," says Dr Pat Spungin, founder of **www.raisingkids.co.uk**. "It will also help them to become responsible partners when they settle down."

Even if they get in your way...

We all know the saying about too many cooks. This applies to kids too. It's very tempting to ask them to get out if they're under your feet, even if they're trying to help. But if you do, how will they learn? My mother was a great cook but had a small kitchen. Understandably, she didn't like anyone else in it. The result? I'm still learning to cook, at my age...

...or don't do it your way

No one will ever do things the way you would do them yourself. So what are you? A control freak? Loosen up and let them do it even if their way isn't as good as yours. You might even learn a few tips.

Here are some more advantages to getting kids to do jobs round the house

- Encourages manual dexterity

- Shows you mean what you say

- Helps you work as a team. Kids learn to realise that a whole family has to contribute if it's going to run smoothly.

- Can bring you closer if you do jobs together

- Makes them independent

- Increases their self-esteem especially if you praise them

- Teaches them to be kind

- Prepares them for being part of a partnership if they ever get married/live with someone

- Children who earn money for jobs, learn financial responsibility.

So why do we give up?

One mum who filled in her survey said it was because parents don't want to fall out with their kids. We can understand that. But on the other hand, we can't give in just to have an easy life, can we?

Key points

- *Use psychology* to get them interested. Explain why it's in their interest to help you. Tell them you're tired and need help. Flatter them and tell them how good they are at doing something.

- *Don't be afraid to barter* It's how the rest of the world works. If they do something for you, you'll do something for them.

- *If they won't do it*, there have to be consequences.

- *You're not nagging* You're helping them to become responsible adults even if you lose your voice and sanity into the bargain.

- *Choose your timing carefully* Ask them to do something at the right time and in the right place.

- *Don't give up* It won't really lead to an easier life in the long run because you'll still be the only one putting out the bins. Besides, they need to learn to be self-sufficient adults. Just like us. (Only half joking.)

Chapter nine

Work, work, work

There are so many jobs that a kid could do, that it's hard to know where to start. We've given you some tasters but here are a few more things to think about.

PRACTICAL JOBS THEY'LL THANK YOU (ONE DAY) FOR TEACHING THEM

How often have you wished you'd learned something a little earlier in life? Maybe you've blamed your own parents for not teaching you how to do something. Well, now's the time to take responsibility for passing that lesson on. There are certain practical jobs that all adults need to know. And they can start learning them when they're still kids.

Changing a light bulb
But teach them to check the electricity is off first.

Showing them where the fuse box is
Very useful if you happen to be out when the trip switch goes.

Teaching them how to sew on name tapes
Give them their own sewing box and explain that the eye of a needle isn't as impossible as it looks. If this is a success, start giving them their own little mending pile. If you're like me and can't sew for tof-

fee yourself, a child who *can*, is a little blessing. Many people iron on name tapes nowadays. If your child is safe with an iron, show them how to do it.

Teach them how to read a railway timetable

Keep a spare one in the house so next time you need to know when the train goes, they can look it up for you. Saves a second or two if you're rushing to get out.

Show them how to look up names in the phone book and/or Yellow Pages

It's amazing how many adults don't realise that office names are in the front of the phone book first.

Go over some First Aid basics

For example, running a finger under water for several minutes if they burn it on the cooker. Even better, send them on a first aid course.

Show them how to clean garden furniture properly

Give them the right tools e.g. scrubbing brush, pail and garden hose. Make it fun by suggesting they do it in swimsuits and get their friends round to help.

Cooking

We've mentioned this briefly in the teenage section but even young children can learn how to cook providing they're supervised. Start off with making sandwiches and then toast. My daughter learned how to make a cake at the age of eight.

How to use the washing machine and tumble drier and other white goods

It's amazing how many teenagers go away to university, never having done this.

JOBS YOU MIGHT NOT HAVE THOUGHT OF

We've gone through quite a lot of possible jobs already but if your lot don't fancy them or you need some mental stimulation, here are some other suggestions.

- Plump up the cushions. A doddle but it might wet their appetite for something tougher.

- Sweep the front path.

- Pull out the weeds in between the cracks.

- Clean the kitchen floor. Make it fun by getting them to 'skate' on it with cloths below their feet to dry it. I do it myself when I'm feeling energetic or just plain sad. Even better when done to Radio 2.

- Change fuses in plugs. Obviously this is only for older children who aren't likely to electrocute themselves.

- Sharpen their own pencils at the beginning of term. And while they're at it, they could sharpen yours too.

- Shake crumbs out of the toaster. Again, make sure they're old enough not to electrocute themselves. You'll also need to show them where the broom and dustpan and brush are kept to clear up the mess.

- Get them to make a kitchen noticeboard so they can write down food you're about to run out of. If they've finished the marmalade, they write marmalade on it. Everyone in the family should do this and even tinies can participate. It all helps team-work.

- Water pot plants. Get them to carry them to the sink first otherwise you'll have water dribbling down the walls. Alternatively, provide them with a posh spray.

- Arrange flowers nicely. No, it's not wet. Tell your sons that future girlfriends will be very impressed.

- Sort out all those loose photographs that you haven't got round to putting in an album. Buy a couple of cheapies and get the kids to stick them in, instead. Make it fun for them by allowing them to write rude comments underneath e.g. 'Here's dad in the shorts he shouldn't have bought.' Ask/bribe/encourage them to file the other photographs in envelopes with the relevant date and location on it e.g. Brighton 2006.

- Make it *their* job to answer your mobile when you're driving. Not only will it teach them a few skills in telephone manners, it will also mean you won't be breaking the law. And it will set them a good example on how to be a law abiding driver.

- Get them to navigate when you're driving the car. Even middle sized kids can do this. Younger children could help print out a map from the computer before you go. Then they could follow the road while you're driving. It might also help their map reading skills. In fact, it won't be them who's saying 'Where are we?', it will be you…

- Ask them to wash hair brushes once a week. Show them how to let them soak in a washbasin of shampoo and then shake them dry.

- Make up a present/Christmas bag. You know all those rolls of left-over wrapping paper and stray greetings cards that you bought and never got round to sending? Now's your chance to get the children to gather them together and put them in a big carrier bag labelled 'Presents'.

- Make up a stationery bag. Providing they're not too young to swallow things they shouldn't, suggest they gather stray paper clips, elastic bands, writing paper, stamps etc. and put them all in a box or bag, marked stationery. Then get them to spell the word and make sure they know the difference between that and 'stationary'.

As my mother always used to say, the paper stationery variety has an 'e' in it, for 'envelope'. Well there's no reason why you can't teach them to spell at the same time as tidying up, is there?

- Sort out your small change. If, like me, you tend to have a pot full of pennies and other small change, it's a great opportunity for little hands making light work. Get some of those change bags from the bank and encourage them to sort them out. The prize is obvious. They get to keep the proceeds – providing there's not too much.

- Arrange books in alphabetical order. They might only get to 'D' before they're bored but it's a start.

- Write out your shopping list. They could decorate it too. And it will help practise their handwriting, however old they are.

- Clean windows. Ground floor ones only. For older children and dormant teenagers.

- Sort out clothes they won't wear or have grown out of.

- Encourage them to hang things up by buying plain wooden coat hangers and getting them to paint their names on them.

SPECIFIC JOB TECHNIQUES. IN OTHER WORDS, ARM TWISTERS TO MAKE THEM DO SOMETHING

Music practice

Routine is the key to this one. Get them to practise at the same time every day, just as they clean their teeth. It doesn't matter if they only do it for a few minutes. At least it's a start. Also encourage them by listening to other children playing. My niece was really encouraged in her flute playing by my eldest daughter.

On the other hand, is it really worth it? Gaynor Sbuttoni isn't sure. "Music is meant to be for them. If they really don't want to practise, maybe we should accept that they're not interested."

Getting games kit ready

This is a killer in our house. My trick is to have second hand spares of everything and keep them in the bottom drawer of my son's chest of drawers. At least, that's the theory. Again, it's so much easier if I get it ready for him but as I keep telling myself, that's not going to make him a very good husband. That reminds me. Giles – it's sport tomorrow so pack your bag.

Flushing the loo

This puts a difference complexion on the word 'job' if you'll pardon the crudity but it's definitely an important one. Again, try a Post-it sign on the door saying 'Have You Flushed the Loo?' This is one that's definitely worth calling them back for so it eventually becomes a habit.

Thank you notes

Give them nice paper to write on. If necessary, write them a 'master' thank you letter that they can adapt to suit whoever they're writing to (though ideally they should compose the master version). Make compromises. If they have written the letter, you might have to write the envelope. Well they can't do *everything* can they?

Packing their own suitcases

This is a tricky one because they are bound to leave out vital items. Still, if they don't start, they won't learn.

You could always pull a fast one by allowing them to pack and then secretly putting vital things they've left out (like swimming costumes) in your own bag to produce when they panic.

 Top Tip

- "I keep a packing list for each child on the computer and print it off for them. I customise it as they get older. For example, when they stop needing nappies. And I remove irrelevant items like swimwear if it's a winter break. That way they can tick off as they go and can do most of it themselves." *Roni,* mother of three

● "When my children were younger, I got them to pack their underwear in a backpack which they carried and were responsible for. It meant that it was easy for them to find clean pants etc. in a hotel room even if everything else was all over the place." *Author*

Unpacking their school bag and packing it again

How many times have you missed a school trip/parents' evening/ charity fair because your child has failed to give you a crucial note at the bottom of their school bag?

Now you need never have that problem again. Make unpacking and packing the school bag part of their routine, just like cleaning teeth. Every time they've finished their homework, give them a short break and then get them to empty the bag and put in it what they need for the next day.

My 14 year old son used to do this as a habit every night before going to bed. But during the last term, we both got lazy and exhausted after moving house. So I allowed him to leave it until the next morning. Big mistake! It only added to the pre-school chaotic rush and invariably meant he left things out. Sometimes he wouldn't discover that he had failed to pack homework until he was at school and being told off for leaving it behind. This meant he would ring me in a panic and I would have to bring it in. After a couple of occasions like this, I got tough and made him pack his bag the night before.

Top Tip ───────────────────────────────

They still won't do it? Put a little surprise at the bottom of the bag like a 10p piece or a small chocolate bar. Suggest that if they unpack their bag and pack it again, they might find something to their advantage…

IS YOUR CHILD UP TO IT?

Sometimes it's much easier to do something for our kids than nag them into doing it themselves. And sometimes, we just do things for them through habit when they're quite capable of taking on the responsibility.

If you've got into this rut, make a list of the main things you do every day. Then sit down with your offspring and go through the list, to see which jobs they could do – and have time for.

Treat it like a 'Job Specification'. The novelty might make them want to do these chores. The following list is taken from a brilliant handbook produced by The Family Caring Trust, which runs programmes for helping families. For more details, contact it at 44 Rathfriland Road, Newry, Co.Down BT34 1LD. Tel 028 3026 4174

Go through this list and tick off anything you do which you think your children might be capable of doing.

- Get them up in the mornings

- Make their beds; tidy their rooms

- Choose and lay out their clothes for the following day

- Dress them; tie their shoes

- Dress the baby

- Choose and buy their clothes

- Make school lunches; prepare breakfast; prepare their meals; cook

- Pick up their clothes; tidy away their toys

- Bath them; wash faces; brush teeth; wash their hair; comb hair

- Supervise their eating

- Iron their clothes; sew; knit

- Lay the table and clear it

- Sweep the kitchen floor; dust the house; vacuum the floor

- Clean and tidy the bathroom

- Clean windows

- Sort out and fold newly washed clothes

- Settle fights and squabbles

- Go to the post office/shop

- Do their homework with them

- Clean the car; change the oil; drive the car

- Paint the inside and outside of house

- Mow the lawn

- Dig the garden; plant flowers and vegetables

- Polish shoes

- Mend bicycle punctures

- Wire an electric plug; change a fuse

- Use saw/hammer; chop firewood

- Make the decisions about their routines, their friends, their lifestyle and their future

The authors Michael and Terri Quinn also suggests asking yourself the following questions:

- What are you doing for your children that they could do for themselves?

- What new responsibilities could you begin to introduce them to, during the next week?

- Be as specific as possible. Who? What? How will you start?

You might like to write down your plans.

The book also has an Encouragement Table to help parents make positive remarks instead of discouraging ones. For example: 'You've got five out of 10. Well done. I notice you're making a greater effort recently.'

This is better than 'You got five wrong out of 10. You'll have to improve on that.'

Other remarks to aim for include:

- 'That's it. Now you're getting the hang of it!'

- 'Now add in the egg and see what happens...'

- 'I see. So it's been very hard for you this week.'

- 'Oh well. We all make mistakes. What can you learn from it all?'

JOBS THAT AREN'T REALLY JOBS BECAUSE THEY SHOULD DO THEM ANYWAY

Wow. This is turning into a 'How to make your kid turn over a new leaf' book. The truth is that when I started, it seemed quite easy to define 'jobs'. But the more I thought about it, the more I realised that what I thought kids should do anyway, my own kids considered a chore. For example, getting up in the morning and cleaning their teeth without being asked etc.

So although these aren't strictly 'jobs', here's some hard earned advice on how to be successful.

Waking them up in the morning

Do this one in stages. Put an alarm clock by their bed. When it goes off, kiss them good morning. Set to snooze button. The next 'good morning' should be slightly louder and more demanding. Give them a drink. Encourage them to sit propped up in bed while daylight dawns. Have their clothes next to the bed. Give them a five minute warning. When they ignore this, tickle their feet. When this doesn't work, strip off the duvet. Then start screaming about how late you're going to be for school.

Getting them to clean their teeth

Of course they should do this anyway but it doesn't work that way. Make it a ritual that they breathe on you after breakfast so you can check. After you've cleaned your own teeth in the morning, put a line of paste on their brushes so you know when they've cleaned their teeth and when they haven't.

Talking nicely to older relatives/friends

The best way to teach them this is to start off by talking nicely to your kids. Ask them about their day. Ask them if they had a good one. If you find it difficult, pretend they're not your own kids at all but visiting children that you have to be nice to.

When your children learn pleasantries like this, it's easier for them to reciprocate. If they say they don't know what to talk about, tell them to ask questions of other people. Explain that older people in particular like talking about themselves. So they could ask them what they did yesterday or if they went to the library recently or how their backs are.

The great thing about this is that these elderly relatives will then be under the misapprehension that you've brought up your kids right.

Writing thank you letters

Give them some nice paper to write on. It might be an encouragement. Even better, slip some personalised notepaper into their Christmas stocking.

Get them to write out a master thank you letter with general information like what they did over Christmas. They can use this for each person with slight variations.

- Check the envelope. My children once sent the wrong thank you letters to the wrong people, each praising the virtue of the other person's present…

- If you're desperate, allow them to type a thank you letter on the computer. It's better than not doing one at all.

- If you're really, really desperate, let them e-mail or even telephone. I personally don't approve but at least it's an acknowledgment.

- As an alternative to a thank you letter, let them take or choose a family photograph taken at Christmas and write a thank you note on the back.

- For younger children, stick on shapes and make a collage card.

Going shopping with you

Yes, they hate it and yes, they drive you mad. So try:

- Giving them a copy of your shopping list and asking them to help you.

- Choosing a shopping time when they're not tired and hungry.

- Having a break with a cup of tea.

- Not taking too long. If necessary, go out another time as well.

- Promise them a small amount of cash that they can spend on themselves if they behave while they're shopping with you.

Washing their hair

If they hate washing their hair – and won't let you do it – see if they'll let an older brother or sister do it for them. Find out why they hate it. Are they worried about getting shampoo in their eyes? If so, you can buy non-sting shampoo. Try out those plastic halo masks. If they're still young, get them to wash a toy in the bath at the same time (as long as it's washable). Compromise. You squirt the shampoo on their hair and they rub it in.

Will you turn that music down?

Forget this one. You're better off doing it yourself. Or else turn your own music up really loudly. This could include the radio. Then tell them that's what it feels like. Alternatively, if you can't beat them, join them. Wait until their friends are round for maximum effect and then suggest they turn their music up even louder. Dance around the room and embarrass them. Hopefully the neighbours will then complain.

Shut the door behind you!

Just keep saying it. A bit like a broken record. Modify it every now and then with different levels of sound. When friends come round, keep going into their rooms and when you exit, leave the door open. When they ask (shout at) you to shut it, say brightly 'Sorry, I can't hear you.'

Turn off the lights when you're not using them

Just go round switching them off yourself (the Queen does this, apparently). Again, when friends visit, turn *on* the lights when they're least expecting it. Tell them you'll stop if they remember to turn them off.

JOBS WHICH, WITH HINDSIGHT, YOU SHOULDN'T HAVE ASKED THEM TO DO IN THE FIRST PLACE

Well, we can all get carried away, can't we? And sometimes we think our kids can do something which in fact they could, but can't be bothered to do properly. Here are some examples. For obvious reasons, the parents who told us about them didn't want to be named.

"'I asked my 16 year old son to wash the dog. He did a great job. But he did it in the middle of our new sitting room carpet. I was sure I had told him to do it outside but my son was worried the dog would get cold. I was out at the time. Another mistake."

"My daughter offered to clean the silver. She didn't read the instructions properly and left the stuff on for too long. It looks worse now than it did before."

"I got my 13 year old to promise to vacuum. He thought he would empty the bag while he was doing it and cracked the case by banging it on the ground."

"I asked my 14 year old son to tidy my study and put all the papers on one side and the files on another. He wasn't listening properly and binned some really important stuff. Luckily I got there before the dustmen but it took me ages to sort it out."

"I thought my daughter was old enough to iron at 16. I showed her how to do it. I only left her for 10 minutes while I did something in another room and she managed to burn three shirts."

"I told my 17 year old son to use distilled water in the iron. I even showed him where the container was. Unfortunately it was next to a juice bottle. And guess which one he used?"

"I asked my son to clean the fridge. He did a great job but then he thought he'd defrost the freezer – while it was still on. He couldn't break the clumps of ice that were forming so he used a knife. He then cut himself and we spent four hours in casualty."

JOBS YOU SHOULD THINK TWICE ABOUT BEFORE LETTING THEM DO THEM

- Light a fire without supervision

- Service the boiler

- Clean sharp knives

- Clean the oven with that caustic stuff that burns hands (unless they're wearing rubber gloves and you're standing nearby)

Feel free to add to this list, drawing on your own experience.

JOBS THEY CAN DO FOR YOU – BECAUSE (LET'S FACE IT) THEY'RE PROBABLY BETTER

There comes a time in every parent's life, when you suddenly realise your kids can do something better than you. This can be very depressing. But it can also be a great help – especially when it comes to jobs round the house. Here are some ideas to boost their ego and save you time.

- Buffing the bathroom taps. Kids have more oomph than many an adult. So twisting a cloth one way and then another is not as much hard work for them as it is for us.

- Setting the video timer. Their brains are wired better than ours when it comes to doing this.

- Transferring your Christmas list onto the computer and printing out labels. If necessary, get them to do this during the summer holidays so you're ready to go.

- Ask them nicely to wrap up Christmas and birthday presents.

- Cleaning windows. They've got more oomph. But don't let them fall out.

- Changing the ringer on your mobile phone. Showing you how all the other bits and pieces work.

- Talking you through your new computer and showing you what else you could do with it, apart from the routine things you already know.

- Setting up an email account for you.

- Working the new camcorder/iPod/anything technical.

- Finding the end of that Sellotape roll (their fingers are niftier than yours).

- Picking you up from the station once they've passed their driving test.

Size really does matter

The Victorians had a point when they sent children up chimneys to sweep them out. Well they were exactly the right size, weren't they? We're not suggesting you do the same but there's no reason why they shouldn't use their small fingers and bodies to do things that we can't. For example, squeezing behind a chair to pick up something. Or putting a key on a key ring.

JOBS THAT SHOULD BE HABITS

How many times have you sat down on the loo for a bit of piece and quiet, only to discover that there's a cardboard roll on what should be the loo roll holder. And what's the betting that the previous occupant (who failed to replace the loo roll) is under 30?

This is when it's time to implement the 'Jobs that should be Habits' solution. It's a bit like the Pavlovian dog theory. If we can get our kids to understand that when A happens, B should follow afterwards, we might just get them to replace the loo roll.

It works like this. Pick five or six crucial habits that you'd like the children to get into. They could include replacing the loo roll/putting their plates in the dishwasher/taking off their muddy shoes when they get into the house/hanging up their clothes when they get undressed.

Now go back a step. What would they be doing just before you want them to do these things? If it's replacing the loo roll, it's using the last square. If it's putting the plates in the dishwasher, it's throwing down – sorry, putting down – their knives and forks. If it's taking off those muddy trainers, it's shutting the front door behind them. If it's hanging up their clothes, it's taking them off.

This is where the tricky bit starts. Every time they reach that penultimate stage, ask them what they're going to do next. Start off with a slightly jaunty tone. 'Aha, so you're home at last even though you're two hours late and dinner was ready ages ago. Shut the front door please. Now what are you going to do? That's right. Take off your muddy shoes.'

And so on. 'Aha, so you're finally going to bed' (try to resist adding 'after I've nagged you for the past five hours'.) 'Great, so you're getting undressed. Now what are you going to do? That's right. Hang up your clothes.'

If the jokey irony doesn't work, you might have to resort to a firmer tone or disciplinary actions such as taking away privileges. (Only half joking here.) The trick is to drum the pattern and habit into their subconscious, so as soon as they do the first bit, they automatically do the second.

Top Tips

- You can also substitute the loo roll for toothpaste. Not literally but every time they get to the end of the tube, they should find the new one.

- Make sure they know where spares are kept. Otherwise, they'll resort to that old excuse that they didn't know where something was, so they couldn't do it.

And other habits to get them into

They've just had a bath? So they rinse it out. They've just been to the loo? So they pull the chain…

DESPERATE MEASURES

This is something I discovered by accident when my then 12 year old son and I were in a strop with each other. I can't quite recall the original reason for our disagreement but suffice it to say that it made us run late for school. I dashed out of the house to the car, laden with books and his sports kit only to find, to my fury, that he failed to hold the gate open for me. This made it very difficult for me to get through with all the paraphernalia which he should, after all, have been carrying. So I politely asked him to come back and hold the gate open for me.

He very impolitely disagreed.

So we had a bit of an argument which resulted in me having a teenage tantrum (even though I'm far too old for this), and declining to take him to school. At this point panic, not to mention reason, set in and my son came back to hold open the gate.

I'm not sure when we both the saw funny side of this but I can assure you that from that time on, he held the gate open for me. Now we are in a house that doesn't have a gate but he still hasn't been let off the hook. Instead, he will (on occasions) get out and hold open the driver's door for me.

I'm not suggesting you have a row with your children in order to get them to do things they hate. But you can make arguments work to your advantage.

FUN JOBS TO MAKE UP FOR THE ROTTEN ONES

Every good boy deserves favour as the piano prompt used to go. And it's true. Encourage them to get into job mode by giving them nice jobs to do.

- Allow them to give you or one of your friends a manicure. Yes, I agree it's dicey but little girls love this. Just make sure that there's plenty of nail polish remover on hand in case they spill it on the carpet.

- Permit them to tidy out your various bags and briefcases. Give them two carrier bags. One for stuff that's obviously rubbish. And a second for things which you will probably want to keep. Go through both afterwards. Their choices may not necessarily be yours.

- Sort out your makeup, tools, train sets, stationery drawer. As a reward, you can give them some cast-offs.

- Thinking of buying something new? Get older kids to price them for you on websites which show you where to buy the cheapest thing. Do the same with holiday offers and get them to find you the best value breaks. Make sure they print out and don't lose the vital information. Suggest they use this as part of their business studies coursework. You never know; you could be cultivating a mini Richard Branson.

- Get them to do a general house sort out and put unwanted rubbish in one room or corner. Once you've checked that no one wants them, allow your kids to sell them either on eBay or in a garage sale or car boot sale. Check the legality of ages and sellers first. You might need to go along. But we bet they won't be able to resist the opportunity of making money.

- Let them ice the Christmas cake even if they get themselves and the kitchen and the cake itself, into a horrible mess.

- Ask them to colour co-ordinate your wardrobe. Put all the blues together and then the browns etc. When they've finished, they could do their own.

Key points

- *Teach them practical jobs* that will come in handy

- *They might be better* at some jobs than you. Accept this gracefully and tell them how brilliant they are at setting the video

- *Write out job specifications*

- *Make jobs into habits*

- *Make a list of jobs you want them to do and they won't* Then use our strategies to get them to agree

Chapter ten

Looking after pets

This is such a big subject that it deserves a chapter of its own. After all, teaching your offspring to look after the resident pets is not only a useful way of sharing chores. It also helps them to learn responsibility. And that's pretty important when a life is at stake. So when the rabbit starts to stagnate, don't give in and clean it out for the kids. *Get them to help* even if it's going to take longer..

"Instead of nagging," says Gaynor Sbuttoni, "try saying something like 'I can hear the dog scratching at the door'. That reminds them that they promised to take him for a walk. We want children to start thinking for themselves and not just do something because we're nagging them."

One of Gaynor's friends has a picture of her daughter's rabbit on the kitchen cupboard door to remind her daughter that the food is inside. "You could also use Post-it stickers as well, saying 'Feed me. I'm starving.'"

FISH

Have fun cleaning out fish by taking them to the pet shop and getting stuff to colour the water. It might encourage them to do the dirtier bit like cleaning out the slime inside the tank. Encourage them to discuss cleaning methods with the pet shop staff.

When it comes to feeding fish, be warned by one of my own experiences which could have had a potentially fatal ending. My then three year old was looking round a nursery (with me in tow) when he decided (uninvited) to feed the class fish. He tipped too much in and the tank had to be instantly cleaned in order to make sure the fish didn't overdose and die. So if you are putting them in charge of feeding duty, make sure they know how much nosh to dish out. And if you've got one of those posh tanks with lighting etc, do check they don't switch the thing off at the mains in their enthusiasm. An entire tank of fish died this way at one of my children's schools. (And no, my kids weren't responsible.)

Teach them responsibility by giving them a fish apiece. They're more likely to take the feeding/cleaning rota seriously if they have a vested interest in something (sorry, someone) that belongs just to them.

CATS

Even smallish children can learn how to feed cats. Keep tins etc. within easy reach and also teach them the importance of washing out food bowls and washing their own hands afterwards.

DOGS

Again, children can and should learn to feed the dog. They can also be taught to groom but do make sure they do it the right way and don't end up annoying the hound. Wiping paws and rubbing canines down after muddy walks is another great way of dishing out chores that you'd rather not do yourself. It's probably a good idea to push the hand washing routine afterwards.

Taking the dog for a walk is something that all kids should do. But it's not always the doddle that it's made out to be. I have a friend whose teenage son was devastated when he accidentally dropped the lead and the dog ran into the road. Sadly the pet was killed. I only tell this salutary tale to enforce the fact that some jobs might not be suitable for some children. You also need to show them through several practice sessions what to do: how to hold the lead; what to do in traffic; how to cross the road safely with a pet and so on.

HAMSTERS, GERBILS, RABBITS AND OTHER SMALL ANIMALS

Clean out regularly; clean out regularly; clean out regularly. This should be written on their bedroom wall or at least on the side of the cage. Don't allow them to get away with it because it's quicker to do it yourself. One of the most important parts of keeping an animal is to learn how to look after it.

PONIES AND BIGGER ANIMALS

If you're going to take on a commitment like this, it goes without saying that the kids have to do their share. Unfortunately, even if it's their animal in theory, there are going to be jobs that they'll need your help with such as mucking out and picking out hooves. So think carefully before you give in to the 'I want a pony' argument even if someone offers to lend you a pony free of charge. When we first moved to the country, a canny farmer offered us his mare for a long term loan and my daughter couldn't believe her luck. Of course, what we soon realised was that looking after a pony was very hard work. And with the best will in the world, kids can't do everything especially when they start getting more homework. So think carefully before you add to everyone's workload including your own.

Key points

- *Only get a pet* for your child if you're prepared to spend time and effort to get them to help.

- *Use the responsibility* factor to get your child to help out. It will teach them the importance of looking after someone else.

Chapter eleven

Paid jobs outside the home

Even though this book is about things that kids don't want to do, we still thought we'd include this. First because there's a lot of confusion about what jobs children can legally do when they are still at school. And secondly, because teenagers often start jobs outside the home and then decide they don't want to carry on.

"Sometimes we need to explain that if we take on a commitment, we need to follow it through," says psychologist Gaynor Sbuttoni. "Obviously, if a child is really unhappy or the employer is not being fair, that's different. But an outside job can be a great way of getting them to swot for their exams. After all, they're going to need to pass them if they're not going to end up doing a boring job for the rest of their lives."

IS IT SAFE AND LEGAL?

When my son was 13, he wanted to do a summer job helping our local milkman deliver in neighbouring villages. I encouraged him, thinking it might instil a sense of responsibility. When he came back, he told me he'd had to cross several main roads and, on one occasion, tripped over a cat's eye and nearly got run over on a notorious blackspot.

I then discovered that according to the law, he should have been 16 before he'd been allowed to do the job.

Paid jobs outside the home can be great. But you need to make sure they are legal. Most children have to be 13-14 before they can do a job – and it's the employer's responsibility to check this. Just as confusing, each local authority has its own by-laws on how old children have to be to do certain jobs. And according to a recent report by the TUC, nine out of 10 local councils get the law wrong on teenage working because the by-laws need updating.

Many local authorities haven't updated old by-laws to adhere with changes at national level. For example, under the 1933 Act, children aged 14-16 can undertake light work, as can 13 year olds in certain circumstances. However, this should only be where the local council by-law specifically sets out the kind of jobs that they may do. Yet the TUC found that over a third of the councils responding (37 per cent) still allow children as young as 10 to work.

Many council by-laws also get the number of permitted hours wrong. Four in 10 (42 per cent) council by-laws contained inaccurate information on working during the holidays, and over two thirds (69 per cent) made a mistake on the hours that children could put in either before or after school. The Children and Young Persons Act says that 14 year olds can only do 12 hours paid employment a week during term time. Yet one London borough and 10 unitary authorities state that 17 hours is the allowed maximum.

According to the Children and Young Person's Act 1933, a 14 yr old (and where local authority by-laws permit it, a 13 year old) may not work for more than five hours on a Saturday nor more than two hours on any other day during term time. Nor may they work for more than 12 hours in total during the week.

During holidays, 14 yr olds (or, where they are allowed, 13 year olds) may not work for more than 25 hours during the week, nor for more than five hours a day. They may not work more than four hours a day without a rest break of one hour. They must also have two consecutive weeks during their holiday without employment.

If they are 15 or 16 (but have not reached the school leaving age) they may work for up to 8 hours on a Saturday during term time, but they can still only work for two hours on any other term time day, and still only a total of 12 hours during a term time week.

During holidays, they may work for up to 8 hours a day and up to a total of 35 hours a week.

If they're under 16, children aren't allowed to work as street traders, according to Section 20 of the Children and Young Persons Act 1933. But if children are at least 14, the local council may have special rules that let kids work for their parents in these jobs. Schoolchildren are not allowed to work in industry, according to the Employment of Women, Young Persons and Children Act 1920.

Complicated, eh? Confused? So are we. The TUC recommends that you ring up the local council to check on the law. You also need to make sure that your child's employer has registered them as an employee and has also covered them for insurance. An employer should also conform to the Health and Safety (Young Persons) Regulations 1997.

HOW MUCH SHOULD THEY GET?

Check they're being paid the right amount of money. Some unscrupulous employers will try to get away with underpaying teenagers. Ask around to see what the going rate is. The national minimum wage of £5.35 an hour only applies to 22 year olds upwards. Sixteen or 17 year olds who are not at school should earn a minimum wage of £3 an hour.

BABYSITTING

Amazingly, there is no law that says a child has to be a minimum age before they babysit for other children. In the absence of legislation, both the Royal Society for the Prevention of Accidents and the

NSPCC recommend that no one under 16 should be left to care for an infant. Parents can be prosecuted and fined if they leave their children in a situation which a court might say is 'neglectful'.

If your teenager does want to babysit, go over 'what if' scenarios and also get them to do a first aid course. It will add to their employability too as parents will be keener on teens who know what to do if a child chokes.

The Royal Society for the Prevention of Accidents has the following useful guidelines. It might be useful to show them to your children and discuss them. They are obviously aimed at potential teenage babysitters but provide some useful food for thought for us parents. Discussing these points will also make your teenager realise that babysitting is a responsible job – and not just an excuse for entertaining the boyfriend or watching TV. It's also crucial that children aren't given responsibility for another child's welfare such as looking after a child in the bath.

Good Practice for Babysitters

Note – these guidelines are addressed to children, which might make it easier for you to show it to them.

Sitting for younger siblings

- Do try and be open with your parent/s about how you feel about babysitting your younger brothers and sisters. If you have any worries or concerns, try to bring them out in the open. Try to talk about it calmly.

- Negotiate. No one can be expected to babysit every night. Agree to sit a few evenings if you, in turn, can have some nights off to do your own thing.

- If you do have to stay in with younger siblings for a whole week, ask if you can have a friend to come and sit with you so that you can share the responsibility of looking after the children.

- Try not to resent or blame your younger brothers and sisters for the situation, it is not their fault. Try to look at the situation from all points of view including that of your parent/s.

- Treat your responsibilities as seriously as you would were you sitting for someone else's children.

- Set up a back-up system. Is there another relative or other adult you can ask for help in an emergency? Would a neighbour help?

- Make sure you know where your parent/s will be and roughly what time they will be back. Give them a little leeway as it can be difficult to return 'on the dot'. Get a contact telephone number, if you can.

- In the unlikely event that something major occurs – illness or accident – would you know what to do? Do you know how to get hold of the family doctor and the Emergency Services? If not, ask a parent to help you find out.

- A knowledge of home safety would be helpful to you. Get to know the hazards and risks in and around your home. Identify the hazards which have potential to cause harm to you and the other children. What are the risks? Do you know how to manage and control those risks?

- If nobody thanks you or praises you for looking after your younger siblings, then give yourself a pat on the back for doing a good job.

Sitting for other people

- Are you aged 16 years or over and able to accept the responsibilities of looking after one or more children?

- Parents are seeking good child care in their absence. You must remember at all times that there is a child in the house in your care. Can you offer such a service?

- Why do you want to babysit? Is it for the love of children or to earn some extra money? Hopefully, it is a combination of both. If it is simply to get away from your own house so that you can do what you like in someone else's, think again.

- Take some basic training in the safe care of young children. Remember that young children are not only prone to illness but also to having mishaps and accidents. It is essential that you can cope with such emergencies. If you can study child development and first aid at school, do so; otherwise, take a first aid course offered by the St John Ambulance or Red Cross.

- A good working knowledge and understanding of safety in the home environment is important so that you can recognise good and bad safety practices. You should be able to identify hazards and risks.

- You ideally need some experience of dealing with and looking after small children and should spend some time with a family where there are small children present. Getting to know the child you will be caring for before you babysit is a good idea.

- Organise a suitable back-up system – such as having a near relative or neighbour available whom you can call upon in an emergency or simply to ask advice about an uncertain situation.

- If you agree to babysit, always be prompt and arrive in good time.

- Try not to let the child's parents leave the home before learning where to contact them. Ask for other numbers, too – e.g. family doctor, other relatives etc. You must feel safe, secure and happy to be left alone with the child or children before the parents depart for the evening.

- Know, in advance, exactly how you will be getting home after the sitting session. You might also like to negotiate terms of payment and whether or not you are allowed to have a friend sit with you.

Make sure you know what you can and cannot do in someone else's home.

COULD AN OUTSIDE JOB INTERFERE WITH SCHOOL WORK?

A recent report claimed that working outside school can reduce a student's chances of getting good GCSE and A level grades.

On the other hand, it can also make them more streetwise – and it gives them something to put on their UCAS form to show they haven't slouched around all their life.

As with many parenting problems, the trick is to find the balance. You don't want your teenager to be so tired after stacking supermarket shelves that they can't write an essay. But a two hour job at the weekend can broaden their personality and also bring in a bit of spare cash.

Holiday jobs are a great way of doing both. Employment agencies often take on teenagers so get them to investigate. Stores like Marks & Spencer tend to recruit several months in advance. The Post Office also has jobs for teenagers and students at Christmas.

Top Tip _____

My then 18 year old son claimed he was too exhausted after A levels to look for a job. So in desperation, I wrote this advert and pinned it on the village noticeboard. Luckily, he saw the funny side.

Lazy, indolent, exhausted (or so he says), post-A level student, reluctantly seeks summer employment at the instigation of his parents. No previous experience. Will consider anything that starts after he gets up (midday at the earliest) and ends in time for 'Neighbours'. Only available for ten days at the end of August due to holiday commitments.

In fact, he got a babysitting job out of it.

Key points

- *Holiday jobs* can be a good way of encouraging your teenager to stick at something/develop initiative/learn that it's nice to earn money.

- *Check with your local council* that the job your child wants to do is legal.

- *Be very careful* not to give your child too much responsibility. An older child may well not know what to do in an emergency. They shouldn't be left in charge of younger children if there isn't an adult on hand or near by. And there are certain situations they should never be allowed in such as supervising younger children in water.

Chapter twelve

Jobs we did as kids – without having to be nagged

"Setting the table and clearing it. Washing up. Boring jobs. There was no choice and no leeway. That's why I like to make jobs fun for my kids."

Sue

"We lived in a large Edwardian six bedroom house and at weekends, the three elder girls had to dust, hoover the sitting room and run an electric polisher over the quarry tiled floor. We often argued about whose turn it was to do which job as some were deemed to be easier than others. I remember once complaining that the sister below me never helped with washing up. My mum said she didn't push it because she couldn't stand her miserable face when she was forced to do it. At weekends, dad and I used to sing while washing up; we usually sang extracts from Trial by Jury because I'd done it at school and he'd done it in the army. One year in my mid-teens, when my mother had had another baby and her home help was ill, I did her job for two mornings a week for the whole summer holiday and was paid what the home help would have received. Apart from that, there were no incentives or bribery. We did them because we were told to."

Jan

"My mother told me to concentrate on homework and that there would be plenty of time for chores later. She was right!"

Sue

"As a child in the fifties, I did all kinds of jobs including helping with the family baking and also the washing which was done in a tube with dolly legs and a manual wringer."

Margaret

"I wasn't paid for doing jobs. It was seen (and this is the view I have as a parent) that doing the chores is a shared responsibility that the family just has to do. There is a responsibility to other members of the family to help each other and not burden any particular person with the responsibility of chores."

Brian

"I used to love drying up while my mother washed up because it gave me time alone with her. We had lovely long chats although I distinctly remember feeling uncomfortable when, at the age of eight, she used the washing up and drying up quality time, to explain the facts of life. Now, as an adult, every time I dry up a wine glass, I am reminded of her going into quite graphic detail about the ins and outs of sex (all puns intended). She was a nurse and believed in being open about most things. I've tried using washing/drying up time to engage my children in meaningful conversation but they usually say 'Oh stop it mum; we knew that kind of things years ago."

Jane

"When I was a child, I was expected to do everything including mowing the lawn and cleaning the car. We certainly didn't get paid. And we wouldn't have thought of asking."

Sara

"I was the eldest of five so I used to help my parents by taking my younger sister out for walks in her pushchair and playing cricket with my brothers. I always went shopping on Saturday for my mother so she didn't have to carry heavy bags. But I remember being told to cut the lawn and giving up because my father only had shears and not a mower. I wasn't very good at washing up either."

Bill

"The key is to start young. It's no good saying 'Now you're 13, you can tidy your room.'"

Paul

"My family owned a pub and we had to help out. We weren't paid but we were allowed to keep loose change which we found on the floor."

Dawn

"I made my bed every day and ran the carpet sweeper over my floor every Saturday. I can't remember how old I was when I started to do it. It was just something I always seemed to do."

John

"I used to clean the car with my dad and two brothers every Sunday. At the end, we were allowed to hose each other down. Mum didn't like this because we'd come in soaking wet. We've continued the tradition with our three girls."

Susie

"I used to make cakes and knead dough with my grandmother because her hands were arthritic. I loved it because she'd tell me stories about her childhood. It taught me what I wanted to do in life."

Sandra (now a professional cook and keen storyteller to her own children)

"I used to chop wood with my dad. One day, I cut my hand and had to have it stitched at hospital when I was about nine. But I don't recall anyone saying I shouldn't have been doing a job like that so young."

Clive

"I'd clear out the firegrate every morning for my mother. We had a real fire right up to the beginning of the sixties. I can still remember how the ash got into everything if you weren't careful. But I wasn't allowed to light the fire until I was about 12 and, even then, my mother used to supervise."

Pat

Chapter thirteen

Homework

This may not be a job, but it's still something they have to do – and we bet they don't always want to do it. So if you're tearing your hair out over a child who's reluctant to open their school bags (and we know the feeling), here are some strategies.

ADVICE FROM THE HORSE'S MOUTH (I.E. A TEACHER)

"Try to get them to do their homework shortly after getting home," advises Amanda Haehner, teacher at a London secondary school and spokesperson for a teaching union. "If they don't, they'll start doing other things and then run out of time. At weekends, when there's more homework, point out that if they do the most difficult bit first, they can get it out of the way."

Amanda also advises the carrot approach. "Ask them what they want to do after their homework and explain that the sooner they do their work now, the sooner they can do what they really want. Also make a copy of their homework timetable and stick it on the fridge door so you know what they're meant to be doing. Combine this with looking in their homework diary. They should have written down what they were told to do."

Organisation is the key word with homework, especially at secondary school. "When your children start doing coursework, they might think they have lots of time to finish it. Parents and teachers need to explain that kids have to get into the habit of working steadily so they don't miss the deadlines. It can help if parents can write down deadline dates next to the timetable on the fridge."

Hopefully you won't have to wipe their bottoms, so to speak, after a few months because by then, they should have learned to organise themselves. But we might have to do a bit of adjusting ourselves, warns Amanda. "Many parents get upset because their kids listen to music or watch television while they do their homework. We need to realise that kids have their own different learning styles. They live in a much busier world than we did and they have learned to fit more in. If they're getting reasonable grades, we shouldn't worry."

And if they're not? "Parents and teachers need to talk to them. Explain to your child that if they don't do their homework, they're going to have to face the consequences. They might fail a unit or an important exam. If you're really worried, talk to the year head and see if you can work out a strategy together."

ARE THEY SITTING COMFORTABLY?

Finding the right place to do the dreaded homework is also vital. "If it's difficult to work because the rest of the family is so noisy, suggest your child goes to the library or even a friend's house," says Amanda.

Even better, switch off these distractions, advises Bob Carstairs, assistant general secretary of the Association of School and College Leaders. "Ideally, there should be an atmosphere of quiet contemplation." (Good thing he hasn't been inside our house.) "There should also be a culture that's conducive to learning such as plenty of books and encouraging parents. If your children are going to do their homework in the bedroom, make sure they don't flick onto MSN when they're pretending to look up something for school on the net. You can buy filters to make sure this doesn't happen. Have a no-mobile-phone policy while they're working. And keep out any distracting brothers and sisters. It's also a good idea to make the occasional foray into your child's bedroom to make sure they're really working."

Funny he should say that. I'm a great believer in quietly checking up myself. But recently, my nearly 15 year old son has told me in no uncertain terms to get out of his territory. And although I don't like to think of myself as a browbeaten mother, it's sometimes easier to do as he says in order to maintain the peace. Mind you, that doesn't stop me from going through his homework diary afterwards to check he's done what he says he has.

GET THEM INTO THE SWING

Bob Carstairs also recommends establishing a homework routine. "Give them a bun and a drink when they come in but then jolly them along so they start their homework. Don't expect them to do two and a half hours all in one batch. They'll be exhausted by the end and won't give it their full attention. Much better to have about three bashes with short breaks in between."

Also show an interest in subjects you can understand. "Trigonometry might not be your specialist area but something like geography is fairly understandable," says Bob. "So you could try to introduce this into conversation."

ALLOW ENOUGH TIME

With younger children, find out what they have to do that night and fit other commitments around it. Don't have too many after-school activities or your child will be too tired.

BREAK IT UP

If your child feels overwhelmed by work, show him or her how to break it up into manageable bits within the time allowed. Sometimes it helps to make out a timetable.

DOESN'T UNDERSTAND?

There are plenty of educational guides for different subjects. There are also various computer programmes which help, although these can encourage children to wander off into cyberspace. Talk to the teacher and see if extra help is needed. My son's school does a maths clinic once a week at lunchtime although I have yet to persuade him to attend.

LEARN TO LET GO

There comes a time in every controlling parent's life when he or she finally realises they have to let go. I found this difficult too. When my older children had tests I would always revise with them and they didn't seem to mind. However my youngest (now 14) deeply resents it and makes a point of not telling me he has a test until after the event. I was hurt at first but have now learned that children have their own learning method. I've pointed out that if he does badly, it means he obviously isn't revising properly or hasn't got the right notes.

Top Tips

- If they hate French, get them to learn 10 new words a week, says Masha Bell, author of *Understanding English Spelling*. "That's what my son did. It helped him understand it better and he was surprised at how much more he learned. A foreign language is all about vocabulary"

- Do the same with English words. Practise one new unusual word every day and promise your child a small reward if he incorporates it into a piece of written work. Also use the odd French word in an otherwise English sentence to reinforce vocab. For example: 'Please make your lit.'

DO NOT DISTURB

If your child is doing homework, don't interrupt.

MOTIVATE THEM

Talk to them about their future, says Jackie Arnold, life coach. Find out what they want to do and discuss what exams and grades they need to achieve that. It gives them a goal to work towards. If necessary, shock them into real thinking by asking if they want to serve burgers all their life. Sometimes this realisation doesn't happen until their grades drop and they have to do something to improve them. Tell them they can only go out if they finish their work.

Get them to write down their goals on notices, advises Heather Summers, language and communication expert. "Then pin these goals on their bedroom wall e.g. 'My goal is to be a doctor. My GCSEs will help me get there.'"

CONSIDER EXTRA TUITION

Ask school if it can help. Or ask friends for word of mouth recommendations.

IS THE COMPUTER GETTING IN THE WAY OF HOMEWORK?

"Promise them 10 minutes on MSN for every 50 minutes of homework," suggests Heather.

NEIGHBOURHOOD WATCH

At the same time, make sure they are not hopping onto My Space or MSN when they are meant to be using the computer for work. This is tricky. Sometimes spot checks are the only things that work although they're not popular with teenagers.

BE AVAILABLE…

If your help is needed, says Masha.

BUT NOT IN HIS OR HER FACE

Try not to interfere if they don't want you to. Sometimes they have to learn by their own mistakes.

LET THEM READ WHATEVER THEY WANT

Well, as long as it's not the kind of magazine you find on the top shelf. Seriously, a comic is better than nothing.

NAGGING

This can work, says Professor Cary Cooper. "But only up to a point. It might encourage them to open a book."

ALLOW THEM TO FAIL SOMETIMES

Professor Cooper says, "Failure is the greatest motivator for children. All but one of our children went to uni but one of them got involved with a boy during her A levels and she didn't do well. Then she did her HNDs instead and went on to take a degree. So if they're not working, say something like 'It seems to me that you're not doing enough work. Well, it's your problem so I'll leave it with you.'"

DRAW UP A HOME TIMETABLE

This is Margaret Morrissey's advice, spokesperson for the National Council of Parents Teachers Association. "For older children I would advocate a discussion which produced a timetable scheduling in homework time. Ensure this time is when you, the parent, will be at home to supervise this happening. Don't let your children go out until you have seen the completed work. Ask school if they can email pupils' homework schedules so you know what is needed when."

Top Tip

Keep spares of pens, glue, calculator, mathematical instruments and so on. Very handy when your child has left an essential item at school.

IT WORKED FOR US! PARENTS' TIPS

"My nine year old son is doing a project on the Second World War at the moment and is learning about evacuees. They were only allowed to take a certain number of things with them so I got my son to show me the things he would take if he was an evacuee. It made the subject come to life."

Laura

"My five year old has one lot of homework once a week but it's quite a lot. So I get her to start early in the week and then break it down into manageable sections. That way, it doesn't seem so scary."

Caroline

"Set time aside when they must do their homework. Help them if necessary and offer something they want as an inducement."

Tim

"It's their fault if they won't do their homework. They need to learn."

Simon

"I try to help by supporting and encouraging my daughter. I make sure she understands what is expected of her. And I get her to recall how the task was achieved in class."

Laura

"I just insist on it. Homework is non-negotiable."

Anon

"If they won't do their homework I cajole, persuade, warn of consequences at school and then give up."

Anon

"I threaten to write to the teacher if he won't do his homework."

Anon

"We get them to do their homework with a lot of encouragement. Threats are counterproductive."

Jane

"I explain how long it will take and then what can be done, once it's completed e.g. going out to play."

Anon

"If your child has been playing on the computer or Playstation and can't seem to concentrate on homework afterwards, let them have half an hour off away from the screen to clear their brain before they get their books out. It seems to work."

Anon

"We have a computer spreadsheet for end of term results to encourage them to do their homework. There's one overall summary to capture the trend over terms and years with additional payments for term on term improvement. The other sheets are for each term."

Suzanne

"If they won't or can't do it, we help them."

Katy

"If there's a lot at the weekend, I usually get him to do it before seeing his friends. Sometimes I allow him to go out for a bit first but we agree a time that he must be home for it. Yes, he does stick to this!"

Anon

"My six year old found reading hard and frustrating to begin with. Forcing the issue only made it worse so I let her try by herself when she wanted to and helped if she needed me. The more confident she became, the more she wanted to do it."

Anon

"Remind them they will have to explain to the teacher why they haven't done the work."

Victoria

"I dish out threats to my 15 and 13 year olds if they don't do their homework."

Beth

"We set tasks to make homework more interesting. Last year, when my son's grades went down in German, we agreed he could have two terms to move the grades back up. If the grade didn't improve, we would pay for him to have extra lessons. However, when he got a new teacher, his grades improved. So it might be worth seeing if it's the teacher that's making him or her worried about home-work."

Anon

"My two are at uni now and managing to fend for themselves, despite having done virtually nil when they were at home. This was my fault and not theirs, an attitude inherited from my mum who thought I should be free to get on with homework. The good news is they both seem to have turned into reasonable individuals who will shop, cook, give lifts etc. and help the place run a bit more smooth-ly when they're home. However, both their bedrooms remain no-go areas…"

Sue

"I 'help' our nine year old by sitting with him while he does it, rather than doing it for him. I also don't allow alternative activities like tel-evision and computer games until it is done."

Alex

"Set a timer. They have the set time allocated by the school. I write a note in the homework diary to say how long they spent on it."

Miranda

"I encourage our children to do homework by talking about what is exciting about the subject they're working on. I ask them questions and see why it interests them. I have always done 'older' activities with them like taking them to galleries and the ballet as tinies. Children can be stretched much more than some people realise and their intelligence is sometimes not respected. This is why they get bored. Homework has to have some purpose and excitement. For example, our five year old daughter loves ballet so we get her reading and writing about ballet."

Sophie

"We arrange time ahead when they will do their homework e.g. after tea, on Tuesday evening. We get homework out and all the equipment needed. And we tidy the table and point out it is ready for them so it's time to start."

Nick

Key points

- *Routine* Get your children into a homework routine. You'll know what suits them e.g. tea, a bit of television and then work. When you find a pattern that works for them, stick to it.

- *Make their environment comfortable* Make sure there's enough light and that no one's going to disturb them.

- *Be there* to guide them if they need you to. But not too much.

- *Motivate them* Talk about what they can achieve if they keep going.

- *Show them how to organise themselves* Wall charts; keeping up to date with homework diaries etc.

Chapter fourteen

What makes us do homework – and what stops us?

Who better to ask than kids themselves?

"I do my prep at school which is good in one way because we have to do it. But we often talk to friends if we can do it without being caught. If you get too much homework, it puts you off. Teachers need to remember that we've been working all day anyway."

Sam, 15

"We have to learn different words once a week. I find it difficult and I don't like it when mum gets upset because I can't remember."

Ellie, six

"My dad helped me with my maths homework but got it all wrong."

Sam, nine

"My room used to be such a mess that I was always losing my homework. Then my mum went mad. She put up a special shelf on my wall to keep my school books and said she didn't care what the rest of my room was like as long as my school books were there and not hidden under clothes. She only did this three weeks ago but it seems to have worked."

Alison, 13

"I do do my homework but my mum doesn't believe me. Then we row about it. She ought to trust me more."

Giles, 14

"I used to hate doing tables but then dad got me a tape with someone singing them. Now we sing them on the way to school and it's much better."

Oliver, eight

"The only thing that gets me to do my homework is when my mum nags me."

Will, 14

"I try to do my homework in my bedroom but my little sister keeps coming in and interrupting me. I've told mum but my sister keeps coming back."

Kieran, nine

"I find it easier to do my homework on the computer because I can look things up on the internet. Sometimes I go on MSN at the same time but it doesn't interfere with my homework. Mum comes in to check on me and then I have to pretend I'm not talking to my friends."

Sophie, 11

"We just get one lot of homework a week. Mum helps me sometimes. We do it as soon as I get it and then we do a bit more later in the week. I've only been late once and that was when I was ill."

Samantha, seven

"I'm tired after school and I just want to chill out. Then it's supper and then there doesn't seem enough time to do it all. Dad's always nagging me to start earlier but I find it difficult."

Kelly, 13

"I made my own personal organiser on the computer and wrote down when my coursework was due in and when my ordinary homework was due in. I stuck it on my wall and it's really helped to see it."

Ann, 15

"Mum never made me do homework. I always just did it. (I am a geek.)"

James, 19

"My parents didn't make me. I did it if and when I had to."

Andrew, 19

"I can only do my homework when I play my music. I'm always arguing with mum over this because she says I can't concentrate. But I do."

Max, 12

"I wish teachers would tell each other how much homework they've each given us. I'm sure they don't realise and then we end up with loads."

Margaret, 14

HOW MUCH HOMEWORK SHOULD YOUR KIDS BE DOING?

This is what the Department for Education and Skills recommends:

Years 1 and 2:   1 hour a week (reading, spelling, other literacy work and number work)

Years 3 and 4:   1.5 hours a week

Years 5 and 6:   30 minutes a day

Years 7 and 8:   45-90 minutes a day

Year 9:   1-2 hours a day

Years 10 and 11:   1.5 – 2.5 hours a day

Chapter fifteen

Pocket money – how to use it to get them to co-operate

Should you pay your kids to do things round the house? There are two ways of looking at this. If we do, they might expect us to pay them for lifting a hand every time we ask them to lay the table/clear the plate. But payment can also act as an incentive and a structure for a weekly family job timetable.

'Earning' money can also make children feel good about themselves, increase self-esteem and learn how to budget. So maybe the answer is to pay them according to the job. Draw up a wage table, writing down the job and how much you'll pay next to it. Some jobs can have the word 'Nothing' next to them because they're the kind of things they should be doing anyway.

One of the parents in our survey sticks a wage chart up on her fridge so her kids know exactly what they can get. 'I pay extra money for tough jobs like cleaning the car and mowing the lawn.'

BUT HOW MUCH POCKET MONEY SHOULD YOU GIVE THEM?

Dr Pat Spungin from **www.raisingkids.co.uk** has some useful advice.

"It all depends on what your kids want to spend their pocket money on. Obviously, your older child will have different needs to your little one but take the time to discuss with them the things that they 'need' rather than 'want' – and the differences between the two. Aside from traditional pocket money gobblers like sweets and

Pokemon cards, are your children (especially your eldest) expected to use the money for Christmas and birthday presents? Do you expect them to save? Has your eldest got a mobile phone, and if so, who pays for that? All of these considerations affect the final sum. Ask around – how much pocket money do friends' children get? How much are your children's classmates given?

"Once you've decided how much, discuss saving and budgeting. Again, this is more relevant for your eldest but even your five year old will be able to grasp the idea of putting away 50p a week towards a new toy. If you haven't already done so, open bank accounts for them."

WHAT'S THE GOING RATE?

Alternatively, you can get your mind boggled with national surveys on pocket money.

According to new research from Halifax, which claims it's the UK's largest savings provider, the average amount of pocket money is £7.82 a week. This amounts to a collective yearly spending power of £70m which goes a long way towards buying a few sweet shops.

Halifax survey covers children aged between seven and 16. The average weekly pocket money according to respondents is:

Seven to 11 year olds   £6.31
12-16 year olds   £9.15

Whatever you do, however, don't move to Scotland or you could find yourself forking out even more. The Halifax survey found out that Scottish children receive the highest amount per week – a staggering £9.23. At the time of writing, there was a big hoo-ha about Scottish children spending pocket money in the local tanning salon so maybe that's where all the money goes.

If you've got boys, you're more likely to be out of pocket. That's because boys in the UK receive 50p more pocket money a week than girls, on average.

If you're a total skinflint and don't believe in giving pocket money, you're in the minority. The survey shows that over two thirds (67 per cent) of seven to 16 year olds get some kind of filthy lucre from their parents.

Key findings of the Halifax research are:

Pocket money in the UK increased at 23 times the rate of inflation between 2003 and 2004. The average UK weekly pocket money is £7.82, an increase from the £5.79 cited the previous year.

- Pocket money has risen by more than double the rate of inflation since the late eighties.

- Most parents seem to give pocket money every week as opposed to every month until children get to 12. About 24 per cent of 12-16 year olds get monthly handouts. Increases in pocket money usually take place on a child's birthday, according to the Halifax, which is another reason for not showing your child this particular chapter.

- The Halifax Pocket Money survey shows that 56 per cent of children get regular pocket money from their parents and 14 per cent get it from grandparents.

- Around 15 per cent of children have to earn their pocket money by doing jobs around the home – Yes! Out of these, 27 per cent clean, 25 per cent do the washing up and 21 per cent do the vacuuming. If they read this book, they'll get some more interesting ideas.

ANOTHER SURVEY

According to another survey by NOP for the Abbey National:

- Children are earning more than £1,000 a year for doing jobs around the house. However, girls receive less than boys for eight out of nine household chores.

- The average child aged under 16 earns £1,200 a year from helping out and 21 per cent of parents with two children say they give away nearly £2,500.

- The most lucrative job is helping to clean the house, for which children earn an average £2.77, followed by loading and unloading the dishwasher, at £2.52. Boys are paid an average of £5.10 for this task, nearly five times more than girls' £1.04.

LEARNING TO BUDGET

If your kids are going to earn money through jobs, they might as well learn to save. Here are some tips on how to encourage them:

- Agree on a fixed amount to put aside every week.

- Shop around for an interesting savings package with building societies or banks. Many offer free gifts/clubs/incentives for young savers.

- Ask them what they really, really want – and then work out a programme on how to save up for it. For example, if they save up half the amount, you might be persuaded to fork out the rest provided they pull their weight round the house.

- When they get birthday or Christmas money, don't encourage them to blow it all at once. Suggest they put some aside for a rainy day.

- Buy young, vulnerable savers a gimmicky savings box to put their money in.

- Set up a swearing/bad behaviour money box in a communal room such as the kitchen. Divide ill gotten gains at the end of the month.

POCKET MONEY GUIDELINES

Fix a definite day for pocket money and stick to it. Use this as a tool if they misbehave. For example, if you don't do x, y and z, you won't get your pocket money on Saturday. It's more effective than threatening not to give them pocket money if they never know when they're going to get it.

Encourage them to keep a pocket money book, listing how much they've got and what they've spent. It will be good practice for the future when they're penniless students.

Give them somewhere to keep their money e.g. piggy bank or wallet (theirs and not yours).

Key points

- *Pocket money* can be a useful tool for getting them to do jobs they hate. But use it wisely. Don't hand out cash for everything. And don't be stingy.

- *Consider* drawing up a list of jobs and corresponding 'payments'.

- *Help them* learn to save.

Chapter sixteen

Facts and figures

To help with the research for this book, we sent out a survey to parents, asking them what kind of jobs their children did and how they encouraged them to do them. Just over 100 parents responded; the ages of the children these replies covered were:

Five and under 20%
Six to ten   30%
Ten to 16   30%
16 to 18   20%

Well, it looks as though some of our kids are a lazy lot. The parents who replied to our survey seemed to be divided sharply between the lucky ones who have children who help, and the unlucky ones whose kids would much rather crash out in front of the TV or send MSN messages to friends.

Below is a copy of the survey, together with the results. Many parents found that merely reading it spurred them on to get their kids to help more. It makes interesting reading …

Do your children help with household chores?

41% of parents said their children helped regularly round the house

54% said it was 'occasional'

And 5% don't lift a finger

Which of the following jobs do your children do regularly?.

Tidying their bedrooms – 15%
Loading dishwasher – 11%
Cooking – 11%
Making own beds – 10%
Washing up/drying up – 6%
Looking after pet – 7%
Gardening – 6%
Helping with younger children – 6%
Vacuuming – 5%
Dusting – 4%
Cleaning car – 0%
Ironing – 0%
Watering houseplants – 0%

How old were your children when they started doing jobs regularly?

Our survey showed the average age to be seven.

It was nice to see that they started young – maybe parents were just desperate for help. Or perhaps it was a good way of keeping them amused.

Which jobs do your kids hate doing most? Our survey revealed the following:

Tidying toys/bedroom – 48%
Washing up – 8%
Washing – 5%
Cleaning – 5%
All of them – 5%
Cleaning the car – 5%
Ironing – 3%
Doing the laundry – 3%
Scraping plates for the dishwasher – 2%
Dusting – 2%

Do you try to persuade them to do these jobs by:

Nagging them – 46%
Paying them – 38%
Positive encouragement/incentive/game – 4%
Agreed to/expected of – 3%
Negotiating – 1%
Feeding them – 1%

If you pay them, do you:

Pay them different amounts depending on the job – 56%
Have a set pay structure – 41%
Forego payment – 3%

If your children don't want to help, do you:

Keep trying to persuade them – 64%
Give up – 36%

If the kids refused to co-operate, many parents also threatened to take something away. But one enterprising respondent played fast music instead. It's slightly unclear as to whether this was to encourage the children or calm parental nerves.

What jobs did you have to do as a child? Our survey showed:

Washing/drying up
Tidying bedroom/making the bed
Cooking
Cleaning
Laying and clearing the table
Vacuuming
Ironing
Cleaning the car
Shopping
Gardening

Were you paid for them or expected to do them for nothing?

Paid – 21%
Expected to do them for nothing – 79%

Do you think children 'get away' with doing fewer jobs nowadays?

Yes – 72%
No – 14%
Don't know – 14%

If so, is this because:

Parents don't have enough time to stick to their guns – 48%
Parents are too weak – 30%
Children are too stubborn – 22%

Are your children reluctant to do their homework?

Always – 9%
Often – 22%
Occasionally – 58%
Never – 11%

Do you encourage them by:

Helping them with it – 65%
Nagging them – 26%
Punishing them if they don't do it – 5%
Offering financial rewards – 5%

Do you help your children with their homework?

A lot – 29%
Occasionally – 65%
Never – 6%

How do you get them to do their homework if they don't want to?

Leave to them/teacher's discipline – 32%

Positive encouragement/reasoning/making it fun – 23%
Set aside time with no alternative activity – 20%
Nag – 8%
Put your foot down – 5%
Short bursts – 2%

These are the top ways that parents use to make their kids knuckle down to maths and so on. Also a couple of rather interesting respondents begged their kids to do it. We couldn't help wondering if they went down on their knees as well. In our day, we would have been caned for not doing it. How times have changed....

What other things do your children hate doing, apart from jobs round the house?

Shopping – 20%
Going to bed – 17%
Early wake up – 8%
Thank you letters – 8%
Walking – 5%
Adult parties/coffee mornings – 5%
Washing – 3%
Dressing smartly for outings – 3%
School – 3%
Music practice – 3%

Contact us

You're welcome to contact White Ladder Press if you have any questions or comments for either us or the author. Please use whichever of the following routes suits you.

Phone 01803 813343 between 9am and 5.30pm

Email enquiries@whiteladderpress.com

Fax 01803 813928

Address White Ladder Press, Great Ambrook, Near Ipplepen, Devon TQ12 5UL

Website www.whiteladderpress.com

What can our website do for you?

If you want more information about any of our books, you'll find it at **www.whiteladderpress.com**. In particular you'll find extracts from each of our books, and reviews of those that are already published. We also run special offers on future titles if you order online before publication. And you can request a copy of our free catalogue.

Many of our books have links pages, useful addresses and so on relevant to the subject of the book. You'll also find out a bit more about us and, if you're a writer yourself, you'll find our submission guidelines for authors. So please check us out and let us know if you have any comments, questions or suggestions.

Fancy another good read?

If you've enjoyed this book, how about reading another of our books for helping busy parents have an easier and more enjoyable time with their children? *The Art of Hiding Vegetables Sneaky ways to feed your children healthy food* does just what it says on the tin.

It's hard enough getting your children to eat two or three portions of fresh fruit and vegetables a day, let alone the recommended five. But have you tried subterfuge? This book is packed with ideas for hiding the fresh food or dressing it up so that even a small child will be seduced into eating it. With tips and suggestions for meals from breakfast to supper, plus snacks, lunchboxes, drinks and parties, this practical and realistic book is designed to help busy parents introduce a healthier diet for their children without spending more money or taking up time they don't have.

Here's a taster of what you'll find in *The Art of Hiding Vegetables*. If you like the look of it and want to order a copy you can use the order form in the back of the book, call us on 01803 813343 or order online at www.whiteladderpress.com.

"As a working mother, this is just the book I need. It's packed with great ideas which are clever, practical and simple to use."

Melinda Messenger

The Art of Hiding Vegetables

Sneaky ways to feed your children healthy food

PARENT-TO-PARENT IDEAS, TIPS AND TRICKS

Almost every parent has at least one way of getting their child to eat fruit and vegetables, from plain old bribery to far more sneaky measures.

Here is a selection of the best ideas, gathered from nutritionists and chefs but mostly from ordinary parents:

DISGUISE WITH CHEESE

If your child likes cheese, and most do, try vegetables in cheese sauce (broccoli, cauliflower, onions, garlic etc) or grated cheese, melted if preferred, over the top.

FONDUE!

Have fun with a savoury sauce like cheese or spicy tomato and either raw or very lightly cooked vegetables. Similarly, a sweet or chocolate sauce can help a whole load of fruit go down without any problem.

USE THE WATER

Always try to save the water in which you cook your green vegetables. Lots of vitamins leak into the water when the vegetables are cooking and rather than throwing this away, use it to make gravy or add to soup and stew.

WAIT UNTIL THEY HAVE VISITORS

The best time to try something new is when your children have friends over for a meal. Whether it is a main course with well hidden vegetables or a pudding consisting mainly of fruit, the friends will not know that this is different from the norm. If other children eat the food without question, yours should too. Don't hover, watch or comment – just serve the food and disappear.

PEEL AND CHOP FRUIT FOR THEM

Children, lovely as they are, can be lazy when it comes to eating. Whether it is peeling an orange or chewing their way through a whole apple (including skin), usually they just can't be bothered. For pudding, snacks or supper, they are much more likely to eat fruit if you do the hard work. Serve it immediately after preparation – brown apples and soggy strawberries are not appetising.

You could include:

- Peeled bananas, chopped into chunks

- A couple of peeled and segmented satsumas

- A few strawberries, washed, dried and without the stalks

- A handful of grapes, washed and dried

- An apple or pear, peeled and chopped

- Some cherries, washed and dried without the stalks (removing the stones is a little extreme, unless your children are young enough to choke on them)

- Sweet oranges, cut into quarters or eighths with the skin on – children love to suck the juice whilst making funny faces with the orange skin over their teeth

- Small, ripe apricots, washed, cut in half with stones removed

- **Kiwi fruit** – peeled and sliced or cut into quarters, or halved so they can be scooped out and eaten with a teaspoon

- **Slices of mango, papaya, and pineapple** add a tropical taste for a refreshing change

START WITH ONE

If your child says that they do not like a certain vegetable, maybe they don't, but maybe they have not even tried it. When serving the vegetable with a family meal, put just one (or one teaspoon) of this vegetable on their plate – yes, even one pea. If they comment, pretend that it slipped onto the plate 'by mistake'. You may need to do this several times before they eat it, but before you know it they may be asking for more.

BARGAINING

Make a meal with three types of vegetable. If they complain or attempt to leave them all, make out you are doing them a favour by letting them leave two if they eat one.

If they protest that they don't want to try vegetables or fruit, agree with them that if they try something 10 times and still don't like it they will not have to eat it again.

GET THEM TO COUNT

Explain to your children about the health benefits of fruit and vegetables – their school should be reinforcing this as part of the curriculum. At the end of the day (just occasionally, not every day) ask them in the evening how many portions of fruit and vegetables they have eaten that day. Praise them or give a small reward (a gold star, 10p) if they have had five or over. The Rainbow Food Activity Chart can help with this.

BRIBE THEM!

Not every parent agrees with bribery, but you may find it works and it can help in the short term to get them used to new foods. Offer them something as a reward for eating up all their vegetables or finishing a plate of fruit, but not every day or every mealtime. The danger is they will expect rewards for eating vegetables, even when they get older. A new bike or a holiday with friends is no fair exchange for your teenager eating their carrots…

SALAD

Start adding a little salad to finger food – sandwiches, chips, pizza or nuggets. Just two or three chunky cucumber slices, a cherry tomato or two and a few little carrot sticks can make quite a difference to the nutritional content of a child's meal or snack. Don't comment if they leave some but give the same amount each time – the amount that they eat should gradually increase.

STIR-FRY

Many children love beansprouts, not least because they look like worms. Stir-fry for just a couple of minutes (not until they go soggy) with finely sliced carrots, peppers and onions and serve with rice or noodles. Speaking of rice, add chopped herbs, finely chopped onions, peas and sweetcorn to your fried rice – delicious!

*f*isheries *and* Uncertainty

A PRECAUTIONARY APPROACH TO RESOURCE MANAGEMENT

EDITORS:
Daniel V. Gordon
Gordon R. Munro

UNIVERSITY OF CALGARY PRESS

Canadian Cataloguing in Publication Data

Main entry under title:
    Fisheries and uncertainty

ISBN 1-895176-68-9

1. Fishery management – Canada. 2. Fishery conservation – Atlantic Coast (Canada). 3. Fishery resources – Atlantic Coast (Canada). I. Gordon, Daniel Vernon, 1953– II. Munro, Gordon R., 1934-
SH225.F574 1996   338.3'727'09715   C96-910125-2

COMMITTED TO THE DEVELOPMENT OF CULTURE AND THE ARTS

Printed and bound in Canada by AGMV.

♾ This book is printed on acid-free paper.

TABLE OF CONTENTS

ACKNOWLEDGEMENTS

The editors gratefully acknowledge the financial support of the Vice-President Research (Publication Subvention Grant), Faculty of Social Sciences and Department of Economics, The University of Calgary toward the publication of this book. We also acknowledge the outstanding editorial contribution by Dr. Steve Mason.

Daniel V. Gordon
Gordon R. Munro

FOREWORD

Gordon R. Munro
Department of Economics
University of British Columbia

The papers in this volume have their origin in a set of panels on fisheries economics, which were staged as a part of the 28th Annual Meeting of the Canadian Economics Association. The Meeting was held in June 1994 at the University of Calgary.

The panel sessions had as their title: *The Atlantic Canada Resource Management Catastrophe and Its Implications for Fisheries Economics*. As the title suggests, the panels were motivated by what was unquestionably a renewable resource management catastrophe off Atlantic Canada. The panelists, who came from across Canada, and who were a mixture of economists and applied mathematicians, from both academia and government, took the view that the catastrophe compelled us to rethink completely our approach to fisheries economics, and to fisheries management in general.

It is perhaps worth emphasizing just how great the catastrophe in fact was. Fisheries have always been important to the economies of Atlantic Canada in general, and to that of Newfoundland in particular. Of the fishery resources off Atlantic Canada, so called groundfish resources (e.g. cod, sole, flounder, turbot) have been dominant. In the years immediately following the implementation by Canada of Extended Fisheries Jurisdiction (EFJ) and the establishment of 200 mile Exclusive Economic Zones (EEZs) in 1977, groundfish accounted for roughly 50 per cent of the Atlantic Canada harvests of fish in value terms (Munro 1980). Of the groundfish stocks, by far the most important historically was a cod stock complex extending from southern Labrador to southeastern Newfoundland, popularly referred to as "Northern Cod". The stock had been the mainstay of the Newfoundland fishing industry, and was important to the fishing industries of other Atlantic Canada provinces as well (e.g., Nova Scotia (Munro and McCorquodale 1981).

Prior to the implementation of EFJ in 1977, Canada's jurisdiction over fishery resources did, by and in the large, not extend beyond 12 miles. Up to the late 1950s, this was not of major concern to Canada, as far as Northern Cod was concerned. The resource had, for centuries, been exploited by Canadians (and Newfoundlanders, before Newfoundland joined Canada) and by fishers from distant water fishing nations. In passing, a distant water fishing nation can be defined as a fishing nation, some of whose fleets operate far from home waters (e.g. Russia and Spain).

In any event, the annual total harvest of Northern Cod was normally in the range of 250-300 thousand tonnes per annum. Marine biologists estimated that the annual Maximum Sustainable Yield (MSY) of the resource was in the order of 550 thousand tonnes. The prevailing resource management criterion of the day was MSY, i.e., stabilizing the resource at a level yielding the MSY. Thus, marine biologists were able to argue that, if anything, the resource was "underexploited."

Since 1949, that part of the Northern Cod resource outside of Canada's narrow jurisdiction was managed by an international body, the International Commission for the Northwest Atlantic Fisheries (ICNAF). Under ICNAF, exploitation of the Northern Cod resource by fleets of distant water fishing nations expanded rapidly in the late 1950s and 1960s. In the late 1960s the total annual harvest of Northern Cod reached a manifestly unsustainable level of almost 800 thousand tonnes. Approximately 85 per cent of the harvest was accounted for by distant water fishing nations (Munro 1980).

In 1973/74, the Atlantic Canada fishing industry, particularly that part of it dependent upon the Northern Cod resource, found itself in deep crisis. The government of Canada became convinced that ICNAF management of the fishery resource off of Canada's Atlantic coast had been ineffective. At that time, the United Nations Third Conference on the Law of the Sea was commencing. The experience with her Atlantic fisheries gave Canada a powerful incentive to join with those in the Conference who were pressing for an extension of coastal state jurisdiction over fishery resources.

The concept of coastal state Extended Fisheries Jurisdiction (EFJ) gained wide support within the Conference. By mid-1975, there was general agreement in the Conference that coastal states should be given the right to extend their jurisdiction over fishery resources out to 200 nautical miles from shore, by establishing so called Exclusive Economic Zones (EEZs). On this basis, Canada established 200 nautical mile EEZs off its coasts on 1 January 1977.

Off Atlantic Canada, large amounts of fishery resource were encompassed by the EEZ and became, to all intents and purposes, Canadian property. Two segments of the famous Grand Bank of Newfoundland were, however, found to lie outside of the Canadian EEZ. These two segments, to be found in the eastern and southern portions of the Grand Bank, and referred to popularly as the Nose and Tail of the Bank respectively, were to be the source of considerable difficulty to Canada in the years to come.

In the case of Northern Cod, however, 95 per cent of the resource was deemed to be within the EEZ, and thus was, to all intents and purposes, a Canadian resource. Northern Cod was the great prize, the great bonanza if you will, for Canada under EFJ.

The resource management plan, which the Canadian authorities developed for Northern Cod, and similar resources, was very straightforward. If the fishery resources had been overexploited when they were international common property under the management of ICNAF, then what was called for was a rebuilding of the stocks, through a program of reduced harvesting. As far as Northern Cod was concerned, the reduction in fishing effort could be achieved at little or no political cost, since the reduction would come at the expense of the distant water fishing nations. As the stocks were rebuilt, the total allowable catches would increase, all to the benefit of the Atlantic Canada fishing industries.

The management criterion of MSY was to be abandoned in favour of criteria leading to the stabilization of the fishery resources at levels exceeding those associated with MSY (Munro 1980). A lower long term sustainable yield would be traded off against lower unit harvesting costs, associated with denser stocks. All of this was consistent with the prevailing fisheries economics.

The scientific advice underlying the management program would be provided by Canadian marine biologists who were acknowledged to be world class in stature. Many of these scientists had had years of experience doing research on the resources through ICNAF scientific committees (ibid.). Thus, the outlook for the resources, and for the industries dependent upon them, was promising.

Returning to Northern Cod specifically, the total allowable catch for 1977/78 was set at a modest 140 thousand tonnes, or about one half of the typical annual harvest in the mid 1950s. It was anticipated that the stock would stabilize at the target level in the late 1980s, and that the resource would support annual total allowable catches (TACs) in the order of 400 thousand tonnes from there on in. To place the TACs in perspective, it was estimated at the time that every 57 thousand tonnes of harvested groundfish would support 1,000 person years worth of employment in the processing sector (ibid.). In addition, of course, there would be added employment in the harvesting sector and in satellite industries.

For a time, all seemed to go according to plan. The authorities did, however, often because of pressure arising from the provinces, permit an overexpansion in both the harvesting and processing sectors. The impetus towards overexpansion was, of course, provided by the promise of a fisheries bonanza.

In any event, with the onset of the worldwide recession, in 1981/82, the overexpansion became starkly apparent, and the Atlantic Canada fishing industry was once again plunged into crisis. The federal government responded by establishing a task force to study the problem, the Task Force on Atlantic Fisheries, chaired by now Senator Michael Kirby (Kirby 1982).

The Task Force brought down its report, referred to hereafter as the Kirby Report, in late 1982 (ibid.). While analyzing the severe economic difficulties created by overexpansion of the fleets and processing sector, the Kirby Report expressed great confidence about the state of the resource. The authors of the Report maintained that:

> The state of the Atlantic fishery in 1982 is not a story of
> unalloyed disaster ... (ibid., 23).

Then noting the increase in total allowable catches off Atlantic Canada had increased by 65 per cent since 1976, the authors of the Report went on to state:

> We face the happy prospect of a 50 per cent increase in the
> groundfish catch between 1981 and 1987 ... almost all of this

increase will consist of cod ... most of the growth will take place off northeast Newfoundland [i.e. Northern Cod] (ibid.).

and further:

Our comments [in the Report] on the resource will be almost perfunctory because we believe its management is quite well in hand (ibid.).

The authors then went on to maintain that the annual TAC for Northern Cod by 1987 could conservatively be estimated to be in the order of 400 thousand tonnes, 95 per cent of which would be taken by Canadian fleets for processing in Canada (ibid., 26).

During the period of time that elapsed between the release of the Kirby Report and the end of the decade something went horribly wrong. The annual TAC for Northern Cod never achieved 270 thousand tonnes, let alone 400 thousand tonnes. From 1989 onwards the Northern Cod TAC was steadily decreased. In mid-1992, a moratorium was declared and the directed Northern Cod fishery was effectively closed. The moratorium, originally set to last for two years, remains in effect at the time of writing, and is expected to remain in effect for the indefinite future. Subsequent to the closing of the Northern Cod fishery, seven other groundfish fisheries were closed off Atlantic Canada. Thousands upon thousands of fishers and processing workers were laid off in Atlantic Canada as a consequence, and the region has been visited by what Canada's leading newspaper, the Globe and Mail, described as a "calamity of Biblical proportions" (Globe and Mail 21 December 1993, B4).

So what in fact did go wrong? The papers of Noel Roy, William Shrank and Eugene Tsoa address this issue. All three authors are from Memorial University of Newfoundland, and thus come from the centre of the disaster.

After reading these papers, we are left with the conclusion that there is no clear single explanation. Schrank focuses on the common property problem of capture fisheries, namely that of excessive exploitation and overcapitalization of the fleet and processing sector. He points out that, at the time of the advent of Extended Fisheries Jurisdiction and the rebuilding of the fish stock, the authorities were presented with a golden opportunity to prevent excess capacity in the Newfoundland fishing industry from re-emerging. The opportunity was, according to Schrank, "thrown away with both hands." Gross excess capacity, in the fleet and processing sector did re-emerge. Implicit in his argument is the view that the chronically undersatisfied fleets and processors may have aggravated a tendency towards excessively liberal total allowable catches and exacerbated the problem of monitoring, control and surveillance.

The paper by Tsoa takes an entirely different tack and emphasizes ecological problems. He focuses on the rapid growth of harp seal stocks, following the successful European campaign to destroy the trade in seal pelts. The seals do not so much predate upon cod, as they do upon capelin. Capelin are, in turn, an important prey for cod.

The paper by Roy provides a survey of all possible causes of the collapse of the stocks. He stresses the fact that no one reason by itself is sufficient to explain the collapse. The reasons put forward run from inadequate controls over harvesting to environmental shocks and surprises. What is made abundantly clear from his paper is that the task of managing even relatively stable fishery resources, such as groundfish, is fraught with a far greater degree of uncertainty than had been realized in the past.

The discussion of these papers by the panel at the CEA sessions led to two conclusions, which were to become the basic themes of the panel. The first was that the degree of "true" uncertainty (situations in which it is not possible to construct objective probability distributions) is far greater in fisheries management generally than we had realized heretofore. Regardless of the economically feasible quantity of scientific research on the resource, and regardless of the quality of such research, there will always remain an irreducible level of uncertainty in fisheries management.

The second basic conclusion of the panel was that it would be folly to suppose that the Atlantic Canada experience is in some sense unique. In fact, subsequent to the panel's deliberations in June 1994, we have witnessed serious difficulties emerging in Canada's Pacific Coast fisheries, with several million salmon disappearing inexplicably. A panel established by the federal government to review the situation in these fisheries has urged the government to adopt a "risk averse" management policy, i.e., a policy which gives clear recognition to uncertainty (Canada 1995).

The stress which the 1994 panel members placed on the role of uncertainty in fisheries management is not a concern confined to

Canada. On the contrary, it is now becoming worldwide. The concern most commonly appears in the form of the *precautionary approach to resource management*. The approach has gained prominence in fisheries through the current United Nations Conference on Straddling Fish Stocks and Highly Migratory Fish Stocks. The precautionary approach to resource management is, according to the FAO (FAO 1995), one which explicitly takes into account the intrinsic inefficiencies in fisheries management, insufficient scientific information and natural variability (ibid., 10).

Two papers in this volume, one by Daniel Lane and Halldor Palsson, the other by Timothy Lauck, address the uncertainty issue directly. The Lane and Palsson paper focuses on Northern Cod, but does not do so in isolation. The authors provide a survey of experiences encountered in other major North Atlantic cod stocks to gain insights into the nature of the uncertainty encountered in the management of Northern Cod. The authors conclude that fluctuations in stock abundance in Northern Cod, and other major cod stocks, are attributable to five factors, these being: recruitment variability, weight at age variability, natural mortality changes, ecosystem and environmental changes, and fishing mortality. Only fishing mortality is subject to management. Of the remaining four, only weight at age variability is directly observable. The others are either partially observable or not observable at all. What is also unknown is the extent to which fishing mortality aggravates the other causes of stock instability. All of this serves to underline the difficulty of making accurate stock abundance estimates and the fact that there exists an irreducible level of uncertainty.

The authors then discuss the moratoria on harvests of Northern Cod and other Atlantic Canada groundfish stocks. They argue that the policy is misguided in the sense that, by refusing to allow a small controlled fishery, the authorities robbed themselves of valuable information and data, which is precisely the last thing one wants to do when confronted by uncertainty.

The authors then end with a plea for radical changes in the way in which stock information is gathered. There must, they argue, be a dynamic ongoing accounting of intra and inter-seasonal stock dynamics through ongoing catch monitoring. This will require:

- a spatial and temporal view of fish stock;
- the development of a "partnership" relationship between the harvesting sector and fisheries managers, and;
- a strategic forward looking view of fisheries decision making.

The paper by Lauck discusses one possible means of addressing uncertainty in fisheries management. This involves establishing large fishery reserves, and in a sense follows on from the Lane/Palsson insistence that fish stocks must be viewed on a spatial and temporal basis.

Lauck notes that in other fields of economic activity where true uncertainty is encountered, risk averse participants will follow so called "bet hedging" strategies. In the management of financial assets, for example, risk averse wealth holders will adopt the rule of diversifying their assets, and will further protect themselves against disaster by holding low yielding, but safe, liquid assets in their portfolios. In fisheries management reserves play a role analogous to "safe" assets in a financial wealth holder's portfolio.

In his paper, Lauck demonstrates that even a conservative harvesting strategy can bring with it the risk of stock collapse if the entire resource is being exploited. He then goes on to demonstrate that the use of fishery reserves, so long as they are substantial, can sharply reduce the risk of a stock collapse.

Along with considering the direct role of uncertainty in fisheries management, the members of the panel directed their attention to two specific fisheries management policy issues, which are both of immediate relevance to the Atlantic Canada catastrophe, and are of interest and concern in the management of fishery resources in many different parts of the world. The first is the management of transboundary fishery resources, particularly in the form of so called "straddling" stocks. The second concerns the attempts to address the problem of overcapitalization of fishing fleets, which arises as a consequence of the common property nature of the resources. Programs of limited entry to the fishery are contrasted with schemes involving the use of individual harvest quotas.

The paper by Gordon Munro addresses the first of the two issues. One factor which greatly aggravated the fishery resource management problems off of Atlantic Canada was the fact, mentioned at an earlier point in the foreword, that the 200 mile boundary of the EEZ slices off two portions of the Grand Bank of Newfoundland. As a consequence, important groundfish stocks are found to "straddle" the boundary of the EEZ and the adjacent high seas. Since 1979, the management of the high seas portions of these so called straddling stocks has been under the direction of an international body, the Northwest Atlantic Fisheries Organization (NAFO), which has as members Canada and relevant distant water fishing nations. While the NAFO management regime had proven to be reasonably effective up to 1985, it has proven to be decidedly ineffective since that time.

The Munro paper points out that an important reason why straddling stocks have proven to be so difficult to manage is to be found within the Law of the Sea Convention, now international treaty law, which emerged from the UN Third Conference on the Law of the Sea. That section of the Convention pertaining to high seas fisheries management (Articles 116-120) is seriously inadequate. One consequence is that the rights, duties and obligations of coastal states, as opposed to those of distant water fishing nations, with respect to the high seas portions of the straddling stocks are exceedingly unclear. This is exemplified by the Canada-Spain turbot dispute, which burst on the scene in February-March 1995.

Turbot (or Greenland halibut) straddles the Canadian EEZ boundary with the Nose of the Bank. One school of thought argues that coastal states, like Canada, have rights superior to those of distant water fishing nations in the high seas adjacent to the EEZ. The Canadian authorities, obviously sympathetic to this school of thought, took action against the vessels of Spain, a distant water fishing nation, which Canada deems to have been engaging in "illegal" fishing activity destructive to the turbot resource. Spain has responded by denouncing the Canadian action as an unequivocal violation of international law, and as being tantamount to piracy.

Munro's paper also argues that the economic analysis of the management of straddling fish stocks makes it absolutely clear that, if cooperation in the management of a straddling fish stock breaks down, the relevant parties, or "players," will be driven to adopt strategies which all recognize as destructive to the resource. Once again, the Canada-Spain turbot "war" demonstrates the validity of the analysis in stark terms.

With regards to the second fisheries management issue, that of dealing with the chronic problem of fleet overcapitalization, which plagues Canadian fisheries off both Atlantic and Pacific coasts, the seemingly obvious way of addressing the problem is to set up barriers to prevent an excessive number of vessels from entering the fleet. This is the basic purpose of limited entry or license limitation programs, which first made their appearance in Canada in the Pacific salmon fishery in 1969. The paper by Diane Dupont examines the Canadian experience with limited entry programs.

The basic point made in the Dupont paper is that fishing effort, or fishing power, does not consist of a single input such as a "vessel." Rather it consists of a bundle of inputs. It has not proven possible for the authorities (i.e., the government) to restrict, to control all inputs constituting fishing power. Since the incentives which individual fishers have to compete for shares of the valuable harvest remain, the issue then becomes to what extent can fishers substitute uncontrolled inputs for controlled ones. The answer appears to be that the degree of substitution, particularly over the long run, is high indeed.

As a consequence, the experience which Canada (and other countries) have had with limited entry programs has been disappointing. There is no question, for example, that there is still severe overcapitalization in the British Columbia salmon fleet, even though a program of limited entry has been in effect in this fishery for over twenty-five years.

The limited entry programs in Canada vary in terms of the disappointment they have caused the resource managers. Most disappointing of all have been the programs introduced into the Atlantic groundfish fisheries.

Finally, the Dupont paper draws to our attention the consequences for resource conservation of overcapitalization that is not effectively addressed. First, an excessively large fleet exacerbates the monitoring and surveillance problem of the authorities, making the achievement of total allowable catch goals much more difficult. Secondly, a chronically unsatisfied fleet will push the authorities towards adopting excessively liberal total allowable catches. Given the uncertainty within which the authorities must formulate harvest policies, the aforementioned pressure could have particularly unwelcome consequences.

In making these points, the Dupont paper buttresses and supports similar points made in the Schrank paper on the causes of the collapse of the Northern Cod stock.

The disappointment with limited entry programs has led Canadian resource management authorities to consider other management approaches, approaches which attempt to alter the incentives influencing the fishers. One such approach, which has aroused considerable interest and controversy in Canada, is the use of individual transferable quotas (ITQs). Individual fishers (or companies) are issued shares of the total allowable harvest. Such individual quotas can come to acquire the attributes of property rights to shares of the harvest.

The issue is discussed in two papers, one by R. Quentin Grafton, an academic, and one by Paul Macgillivray, an official with the Department of Fisheries and Oceans. The Grafton paper is an investigation into the question of the consequences of extending the use of ITQs in Atlantic Canada. In so doing, he surveys the use of such quotas in Canada and other countries (e.g., Australia, New Zealand, and Iceland). The Macgillivray paper examines the use of ITQ schemes, from a practitioner's point of view, in both Atlantic Canada and British Columbia.

In theory, ITQs should lead to enhanced economic efficiency in resource management, by eliminating (or at least sharply reducing) the incentive for fishers to compete for shares of the total harvest. The fishers would, moreover, then have an incentive to use the most efficient methods possible in taking their particular harvest shares.

The experience in Canada, and elsewhere, indicates clearly that, while there have been some very encouraging examples of the use of ITQs, there is no guarantee of success. Grafton emphasizes the fact that the harvest quotas must be transferable, i.e., salable, if excess capital is to be eliminated from the fishery and maximum economic efficiency is to be achieved. He does agree, however, that care must be taken to ensure that transferability does not lead to excess concentration.

The question of the term of ITQs is a key issue. Short term quotas may give the fishers little incentive to conserve the resource. Long term quotas, on the other hand, may do just that. The Macgillivray paper's discussion on the individual harvest quota scheme in the British Columbia halibut fishery is particularly instructive on this issue.

The importance of giving fishers an incentive to take "the long term view" of the resource, and hence an incentive to conserve the resource, cannot be overemphasized when uncertainty in resource management is inescapable.

The importance of this incentive should, among other things, lead fishers and resource managers to move from the traditional adversarial relationship to one of partnership. The panel was in full agreement that the existence of an adversarial relationship between fishers and resource managers, when attempting to manage a resource under irreducible uncertainty, is an invitation to disaster.

Both Grafton and Macgillivray agree that effective monitoring of the quota scheme is critical. Ineffective monitoring can lead readily to quota "busting," i.e., outright cheating, or to a discard problem in which less valuable fish are simply thrown overboard (high grading). As well as constituting manifest waste, discarding makes the measurement of true fishing mortality much more difficult. In any event, as Canadian experience shows, ineffective monitoring can lead to the rapid disintegration of the individual harvest quota scheme.

Both authors appear to agree that ITQ schemes, while not being universally applicable, are worthy of very serious consideration in resource management programs off both of Canada's Atlantic and Pacific coasts.

To summarize overall, the papers in this volume were written in response to an upheaval in renewable resource management, which has forced us to rethink the way in which we approach fisheries economics. The purpose of the papers is, not to provide definitive answers, but is rather to provide direction for the urgently required research, as we confront the aforementioned upheaval.

REFERENCES

Canada. 1995. *Report*. Ottawa: Fraser River Sockeye Public Review Board.

Food and Agriculture Organization of the United Nations. 1995. *The State of World Fisheries and Aquaculture*, Rome: FAO.

Kirby, M. J. L. 1982. *Navigating Troubled Waters: A New Policy for Atlantic Fisheries*. Report of the Task Force on Atlantic Fisheries. Ottawa: Supply and Services Canada.

Munro, Gordon R. 1980. *A Promise of Abundance: Extended Fisheries Jurisdiction and the Newfoundland Economy*. Ottawa: The Economic Council of Canada .

Munro, Gordon R. and Susan McCorquodale. 1981. *The Northern Cod Fishery of Newfoundland*. The Public Regulation of Commercial Fisheries in Canada, Technical Report No. 18. Ottawa: The Economic Council of Canada.

1

WHAT WENT WRONG AND WHAT CAN WE LEARN FROM IT?

Noel Roy
Department of Economics
Memorial University of Newfoundland

INTRODUCTION

The recent closure of the Northwest Atlantic Cod and other groundfish stocks off the east coast of Canada has prompted calls from several quarters for a reconsideration of our understanding of fisheries stock dynamics. It is disturbing to acknowledge that in 1979, immediately after Canada had declared Extended Fisheries Jurisdiction (EFJ) off its shores, the Total Allowable Catch (TAC) of Northern Cod (2J3KL Cod) had been expected to rise to 402 thousand tonnes by 1985 (Department of Fisheries and Oceans 1981). This outcome was expected to result from the rebuilding of the stock from the depleted state to which it had been reduced as a result of the actions of distant-water fleets over the previous two decades.

In fact, the TAC for this stock never rose above 266 thousand tonnes, and beginning in 1989 the TAC was progressively reduced until the directed fishery was effectively closed in mid-1992. Subsequently, seven other cod stocks, and several flatfish and redfish stocks in the Northwest Atlantic have also been closed. This outcome would have had no credibility, even as a worst-case scenario, a few years ago. Indeed, the East Coast fishery was the subject of numerous studies in this period immediately after the establishment of EFJ (see, for example, Government of Newfoundland and Labrador 1978; Economic Council of Canada 1980; and Task Force on Atlantic

15

Fisheries 1982). None of these studies anticipated a problem resulting from a shortage of fish.

While stock assessment methods have been the focus of considerable attention as a result of the collapse of the groundfish stocks (see, for example, Northern Cod Review Panel 1990), the enormity of the catastrophe suggests that some aspects of fisheries bioeconomics theory deserve reconsideration as well.

My intent in this paper is to discuss the origins of the recent fisheries catastrophe in Atlantic Canada, and draw out some lessons for fisheries economics and for the future management of fisheries.

WHAT WENT WRONG?

We cannot be sure about what went wrong. There are about half a dozen (at least) explanations that are credible, in the sense that they are broadly consistent both with the evidence, and with our understanding of how fisheries work. These explanations include the following:

1. Water which is unusually cold and/or of low salinity, possibly because global warming has resulted in greater melting of the polar ice cap. These changes are hypothesized to cause a substantial increase in the natural mortality of the spawning and/or juvenile stocks, or low egg survival.
2. Food-chain changes: either an increase in the number of non-human predators (e.g., seals) or a reduction in the number of prey (e.g., capelin). Of course, the latter change could well be induced by the former.
3. Changes in the spatial distribution of the stocks: either there has been a long-range migration of the Northwest Atlantic stocks elsewhere, or the stocks are concentrating somewhere else in the Northwest in a location that has yet to be discovered. These changes are sometimes ascribed to the environmental changes delineated in (1) above.
4. Overfishing by distant water fleets.
5. Overfishing generally.

In my view, none of these explanations is entirely consistent with the facts; that is to say, each of these explanations, left to stand by

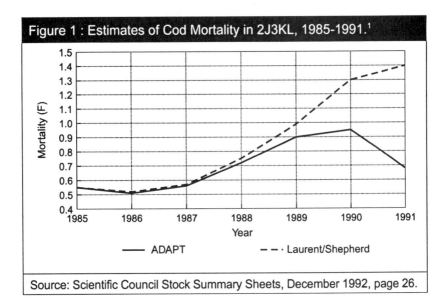

Figure 1 : Estimates of Cod Mortality in 2J3KL, 1985-1991.[1]

Source: Scientific Council Stock Summary Sheets, December 1992, page 26.

itself, is an unsatisfactory one. However, some of these explanations have more credibility than others.

The simplest and most parsimonious explanation is that the disaster is the result of overfishing. It is evident that massive overfishing took place in the Northwest Atlantic in the 1980s. For example, the $F_{0.1}$ policy goal adopted by the Department of Fisheries and Oceans (DFO) in the late 1970s (see Munro 1980) was generally interpreted as implying an annual rate of fishing mortality (generally denoted by F) equal to 0.2 for Northern Cod.[2]

It is now clear that actual fishing mortality far exceeded this target in the 1980s. The December 1992 stock summary sheets issued by the

---

[1] Figure 1 presents estimates of fishing mortality based on two methodologies for estimating population biomass, one generated by the ADAPT model and the other using the Laurent/Shepherd method. Given the uncertainties inherent in the stock assessment process, the two methods can be said to yield essentially similar estimates up to the final two or three years.

[2] F is theoretically defined as the *instantaneous* rate at which biomass is removed through fishing per unit time interval. Thus, an F of 0.2 implies that fish are being caught at the rate of 20% of the biomass per annum. Values of F in excess of unity are possible because, as the stock is depleted, the amount caught (for a given value of F) declines proportionally, so that, in fact, some fish remain even if such a value of F were sustained for an entire year. Within this theoretical framework, only an infinite value of F can catch the entire stock.

Scientific Council of the Northwest Atlantic Fisheries Organization (NAFO), parts of which are represented in Figure 1, estimate fishing mortality for the spawning stock (ages 7-9) of Northern Cod in excess of 0.5 in 1985-87; in excess of 0.7 in 1988; in excess of 0.9 in 1989; and, by one measure, 1.3 in 1990 and 1.4 in 1991. Similar stories could be told for other groundfish stocks. Whether fishing cod at such high rates is sustainable is apparently open to some debate. While such rates seem outrageously high to the non-biologist layman, some cod stocks in Iceland and Norway have sustained similar rates of exploitation without catastrophic collapse. However, I want to raise a more fundamental point. Clearly, fishing mortality exceeded the target set by the regulator to such an extent as to represent a *fundamental policy failure* with respect to the management of virtually all groundfish stocks in the Northwest Atlantic. This failure was clearly systemic rather than accidental. The causes of this policy failure must be explained if we are to avoid repetitions in other fisheries.

Part of the blame must be assigned to what, in retrospect, we now know were poor policy choices. For example, in 1990 the scientific advice provided to the manager for Northern Cod was for a TAC of 125 thousand tonnes. Such a catch would have all but closed down the Newfoundland offshore cod fishery and so, on "socioeconomic" grounds, the regulators chose to set a TAC at 199 thousand tonnes, nearly sixty percent greater. With the benefit of hindsight, we now know that even the scientific advice proved to be well in excess of the target F of 0.2.

A more fundamental failure was an unwillingness to face the fundamental uncertainties associated with the stock assessment exercise. These uncertainties were basically treated as random error which, since we cannot explain them, we must therefore ignore. Those responsible for stock assessment only claim accuracy within ±30%, and, given the uncertainties involved, this is reasonable enough. By the late 1980s, however, it had become clear (see, for example, the Report of the Task Group on Newfoundland Inshore Fisheries 1987) that this error had consistently been on the plus side. One would expect rational planners, confronted with evidence of consistent upward bias in their predictions, to incorporate some allowance for this consistent prediction error in subsequent predictions. This did not happen.

One lesson that we can derive from the disaster, then, is that fisheries policy should explicitly incorporate within its formulation the existence of uncertainty and error. Policy should be based on the knowledge that the data on which we are formulating that policy are probably wrong. What we need here is not so much better theory, as better consistently applied practice. I will have more concrete suggestions later.

The finger points strongly toward overfishing as the main culprit underlying the disaster. However, overfishing cannot explain everything that we observe. For example, we would expect that in a conservative ecological system, overharvesting of particular target species would result in a decline in the biomass of these target species and a concomitant expansion in the biomass of less desirable species, as the latter occupy the ecological niches vacated by the former (cf. Wilson et al. 1991). This is broadly what has happened, at least until very recently, on the Georges Bank off Nova Scotia and New England, as heavily harvested cod, flounder, and haddock has been displaced by species such as sand lance and dogfish. Overfishing, then, has an impact less on the total biomass in the system than on the distribution of biomass across species.

This is not what has happened in North Atlantic waters. The devastation has hit noncommercial as well as commercial species. Division 2J, off the Labrador coast, has become a marine desert. Similar, although less devastating changes have occurred in Division 3K, off the northeast coast of Newfoundland. The more southerly divisions off Newfoundland do have some (limited) fish of commercial size. This evidence strongly suggests that there are factors besides overfishing which are affecting the resource.

Some elements (although by no means all) within the Department of Fisheries and Oceans suggest the occurrence of an environmental disaster of unprecedented magnitude and unknown cause, but possibly related to cold water and changes in salinity. This explanation could be interpreted as somewhat self-serving, in that it tends to absolve the managers of any responsibility for the disaster. Nonetheless, the hypothesis must be taken seriously, since it is compatible with the evidence.

Supporting the hypothesis of an environmental cause is the fact that the Research Vessel (RV) surveys report that Northern Cod stocks have continued to decline throughout the so-called moratorium. However, the RV survey is a small sample of the stock, and is generally regarded as subject to high standard error of estimate (anywhere from one-third to three times the value of the assessment, depending on the stock). Therefore, the "finding" that the Northern Cod stock has continued to decline must be treated as highly tentative.

Moreover, the moratorium has not been a total one. There was a so-called "recreational" catch that has fed a thriving black market (this fishery was closed in 1994 except for a brief period); a substantial by-catch both inside and outside Canadian waters; a directed European Union fishery in international waters (now suspended) and fishing by non-NAFO countries in international waters (which is the subject of recent disputed Canadian legislation). Much of this fishing is undocumented but has probably been in the range of 10-40 thousand tonnes per year.

Inshore fishing interests have an alternative explanation. They cite the unselective harvesting methods of offshore trawlers, and damage to habitat allegedly caused by continuously dragging the ocean bottom, to explain the widespread devastation. This explanation is arguably as suspect as that of a manager blaming cold water. But it cannot be casually rejected either. If valid, this hypothesis has major implications for harvesting policy in a rejuvenated cod fishery.

The counter-argument to the "blame the trawlers" explanation is that cod stocks are also depressed in the Gulf of St. Lawrence, which has been off limits to trawlers since the 1960s. However, inshore draggers work these waters, and these craft are not very selective either. ITQs may also have played a role here, as I will mention in a minute.

Other villains are cited as well. While there is little direct evidence that seals eat a lot of cod, we have to recognize that the seal (along with humanity) is a major predator at the top of the food chain in the North Atlantic. It is hard to imagine that an increase in the seal population would not have had a major impact on the ecosystem. At the same time, the extent (or even the existence) of any increase in the seal population is subject to considerable controversy. My colleague, Dr. Eugene Tsoa, has more to say about this possibility in his contribution to this volume.

Foreigners are also often blamed, although it seems clear to me that at least until the time of the moratorium, distant water nations played a minor role in the overfishing that took place after Canada declared Extended Fisheries Jurisdiction (EFJ). This is not to say that what foreigners do, or are allowed to do, will not have a major influence on the rebuilding of the resource. We should be concerned that since the international fishery is effectively an open-access fishery, any stock recovery may simply induce additional foreign effort in the international zone, thereby aborting the recovery.

WHAT LESSONS CAN WE LEARN?

One fundamental truth we have relearned is the fragility and unpredictability of the resource, which contradicts the illusion of control on which most of our models are founded. Management has been based on the premise that our knowledge of the resource is "good enough", and our control over the harvesting process is good enough. Neither has been true for Northwest Atlantic groundfish.

Fisheries management should be based on the premise that the consequences of our actions are inherently uncertain. While the existence of uncertainty creates modeling difficulties, some of the implications for management are straightforward. A bias to conservative management seems appropriate, particularly when the consequences can be irreversible. More generally, actions with consequences that are reversible should be favoured over those with consequences that are not. We should seek advice in terms of confidence intervals rather than point estimates, and base policy on estimates towards the lower end of the range of scientific advice rather than the top end. If this seems to be an obvious point, recall that so far we have been doing the exact opposite. (It has been stated that stock assessors have been reluctant to provide a confidence interval rather than a point estimate to fisheries managers, because of an alleged tendency on the part of the latter to go to the end that benefited the industry.) Ludwig, Hilborn and Walters (1993) have further suggestions along these lines that bear careful consideration.

We should perhaps be looking at alternatives to quota management; for example, we should consider additional biological controls to ensure greater selectivity in harvesting. It is apparent to me that quota management has failed in the North Atlantic groundfishery. It is not apparent that there is a superior alternative, but we surely have to look for one. We may have overreached ourselves in attempting to control more than our ability or information will permit . Tim Lauck's modeling exercises (presented in this volume) imply that diversification is likely to be an optimal response to uncertainty in resource management just as it is in portfolio management. This hypothesis has several provocative implications, one of which is the need for diversification in management techniques. We have been putting most of our management eggs in quota techniques, to our detriment.

THE ROLE OF ITQs

It has been suggested that Individual Transferable Quotas (ITQs) may have made some contribution to the disaster. I would like to make a few brief comments on this issue.

For several years, ITQs have been in place in the offshore ground-fishery and in the Gulf of St. Lawrence otter trawl cod fishery. All these fisheries (except for some redfish stocks) are now closed. At the very least, then, the presence of ITQs in these fisheries did not prevent the disaster.

In my opinion, it would be unreasonable to have expected ITQs to have done so. ITQs are designed to achieve economic goals, not biological ones. They are designed to maximize the economic rent obtained from a given level of harvesting. For this to be successful, we have to get the global quota right. If we get this global quota wrong (as we have done), then all that ITQs will do (at best) is ensure that we will overexploit the resource in an economically efficient manner. ITQs, then, are not directed to the problem that is the subject matter of this paper. However, it has sometimes been claimed that the presence of ITQs, by adding an element of proprietorship to the resource stock, would reduce the incentive for harvesters to place political pressure on fisheries managers to set the quota higher than it should be. Our recent experience in Atlantic Canada does not provide much support for this hypothesis.

Could ITQs have positively contributed to the disaster? ITQs are believed to encourage discards and high grading (Copes 1986), and in the early 1980s there was apparently a considerable amount of this activity in the offshore groundfishery. But the general view has been, at least until recently, that the introduction of onboard observers in the mid-1980s, accompanied by gear design changes at about the same time, have reduced the incidence of this behaviour. This view is currently being reassessed in the light of the retrospective analysis referred to above, which has revealed a consistent downward bias in fishing mortality estimates for Northern Cod. One good candidate process for this bias is misreporting and dumping.

The Gulf cod stocks are another matter. There is considerable anecdotal evidence (and some physical evidence) in the Gulf of substantial high grading of cod. The otter trawl fishery is characterized by dockside monitoring only. ITQs could well have contributed to the collapse of the Gulf cod stocks.

CONCLUSION

Whether overfishing actually caused the collapse of the Northwest Atlantic groundfish stocks is open to some debate. There are aspects of this collapse that cannot be explained by overfishing alone or by overfishing per se.

Nevertheless, it is incontrovertible that massive overfishing did take place in the 1980s, in the sense that actual fishing mortality far exceeded the target set by the managers. There is some suggestion, and some limited hard evidence, that this overfishing was accompanied by substantial unreported by-catch and discarding, particularly of juvenile fish. Given the enormous fecundity of most groundfish species, it is hard to see how the population declines which we are presently experiencing could have occurred without substantial mortality in juvenile, pre-spawning age-classes.

This overfishing either induced the collapse of the stocks, or seriously aggravated a population decline induced by other, unknown causes. Either way, the implications for fisheries management are serious. If overfishing is the cause of the collapse, then the implication is that quota management as presently constituted alone cannot control fishing mortality. If the collapse is due to other causes (perhaps environmental fluctuations), then the implication is that we are unable to respond to these fluctuations sufficiently promptly to adjust our fishing effort to prevent the huge variations in fishing mortality which we have been experiencing recently. Whichever is true, major changes in the way in which we have been managing our ground fisheries is called for.

While it would be premature to recommend a specific management regime, it would seem prudent to move in the direction of greater selectivity, both with respect to species and with respect to age-class. Moreover, the existence of significant environmental uncertainties would commend techniques which either maintain fishing mortality (or at least fishing effort) at a particular (safe) level or automatically induce compensating (protective) changes in response to biomass changes. Quota management is not the technique of choice in dealing with an uncertain and rapidly changing environment. A diversified set of strategies, properly designed, will reduce risk, although it might increase costs as well. Finally, we must confront uncertainty in a fundamental sense.

REFERENCES

Coady, L..W. 1993. The Groundfish Resource Crisis: Ecological and Other Perspectives on the Newfoundland Fishery. Pages 56-77 in *The Newfoundland Groundfish Fisheries: Defining the Reality*, edited by K. Storey. Institute of Social and Economic Research, Memorial University.

Copes, P. 1986. A critical review of the individual quota as a device in fisheries management. *Land Economics* 62(3):278-91.

Department of Fisheries and Oceans. 1981. *Resource Prospects for Canada's Atlantic Fisheries 1981-1987*. Ottawa: Supply and Services Canada.

Economic Council of Canada. 1980. *Newfoundland: From Dependency to Self-Reliance*. Ottawa: Supply and Services Canada.

Government of Newfoundland and Labrador. 1978. *Setting a Course: A Regional Strategy for Development of the Newfoundland Fishing Industry to 1985*. St. John's: Government of Newfoundland and Labrador.

Ludwig, D., R. Hilborn, and C. Walters. 1993. Uncertainty, Resource Exploitation, and Conservation: Lessons from History. *Science* 260:17.

Munro, Gordon R. 1980. *A Promise of Abundance: Extended Fisheries Jurisdiction and the Newfoundland Economy*. Ottawa: Supply and Services Canada.

Northern Cod Review Panel. 1990. *Independent Review of the State of the Northern Cod Stock*. Ottawa: Supply and Services Canada.

Task Force on Atlantic Fisheries. 1982. *Navigating Troubled Waters: A New Policy for the Atlantic Fisheries*. Ottawa: Supply and Services Canada.

Task Group on Newfoundland Inshore Fisheries. 1987. *A Study of Trends of Cod Stocks off Newfoundland and Factors Influencing their Abundance and Availability to the Inshore Fishery*. A report to the Honourable Tom Sidden, Minister of Fisheries, Canada .

Wilson, J. A., J. French, P. Kleban, S. MacKay, and R. Townsend. 1991. Chaotic Dynamics in a Multiple Species Fishery: a Model of Community Predation. *Ecological Modelling* 58:303.

2

ORIGINS OF ATLANTIC CANADA'S FISHERIES CRISIS

William E. Schrank
Department of Economics
Memorial University of Newfoundland

INTRODUCTION

This paper argues that the current crisis in the Canadian east coast fisheries is rooted in the management practices of the late seventies and early eighties. In 1977, Canada declared Extended Fisheries Jurisdiction (EFJ) with the hope and expectation of achieving an economically viable fishing industry. I argue that critical errors in management of the Canadian east coast fisheries were made during the period 1977-1981. These errors created circumstances that led to the fisheries crisis of the 1990s.

At the start of the period, the number of fishers of eastern Canada was declining, the result of poor harvests. As I will show, there was a clear understanding by government at that time that the population of fishermen and fish plant workers was too large, that too many families were dependent on the fishery, that the fishery was inefficient, and that unless the fishery was cut in size it would never be economically viable. The hopes that came with Extended Fisheries Jurisdiction set the stage for a relatively painless transformation of the fishery into an economically viable industry. Given the increased harvests expected, and the overcapacity in the industry's harvesting and processing sectors, the size of the industry could be kept at its then-current level, or even further reduced, and much greater output and income generated. A commercially viable industry could result.

27

But this is not what happened. Instead of further decreasing the size of the fishery, or holding it constant, or even increasing it slowly as harvests increased, there was a mad rush to expand the industry. The implications for overfishing are obvious, I think, and I will say nothing about them. A very expensive and economically unviable behemoth was created and we are still living with the consequences. Why did this happen if the government was well aware of the problem? That is what my paper is about.

I do not mean this to be a history lesson for its own sake. With the fishery currently in perhaps its greatest crisis ever, there is an obvious opportunity to "downsize", in the current jargon. We hear a lot about downsizing. As I show, we have been there before. Unless we under-stand the reasons why the fisheries were permitted to grow in 1977-1981, we are in serious danger of repeating the mistakes; the indus-trial, social, economic, and political pressures that existed nearly twenty years ago are still with us.

THE FEDERAL GOVERNMENT AND ATLANTIC CANADA'S FISHING POPULATION

There is nothing new in the recent observation of the Cashin Task Force (Cashin 1993) that the fishery is too large, that it is trying to employ too many people.[1] What is particularly interesting is that, despite the fact that the fundamental problem has not changed, the fisheries department of the Federal Government fully understood the situation twenty-five years ago.

At the end of 1969, the minister responsible for fisheries[2] stated in a major speech to the House of Commons that "we are beginning to manage our living resources in an intelligent manner. We are assessing

---

[1] See, for instance, p. 14 where among the fundamental problems of the fishery is listed the fact that there is "over dependence on the fishery ... there are more people and capacity than the fishery can sustain." More than a quarter of a century ago, the Pushie Commission in Newfoundland (Pushie 1967, 185) noted that "the number of people dependent on the inshore fishery should be reduced...". In a 1986 paper, Schrank and his colleagues estimated that a commercially viable Newfoundland fishery would not employ more than 6,000 fishermen, and this estimate was based on an inflated projected annual sustained Northern Cod catch of 450 thousand tonnes (Schrank, Roy, and Tsoa 1986, 253).

[2] The Honourable Jack Davis, Minister of Fisheries and Forestry.

fish populations and estimating maximum sustainable yields. *We are trimming our fishing fleets down to size and increasing the income of the average Canadian fisherman*" [my emphasis]. In 1964, Canada had shifted from a three mile control zone to twelve miles and the minister now announced that a headland to headland baseline system was being adopted which would close certain bays and coves to foreigners. According to the minister, because of foreign overfishing, Newfoundland inshore fishermen were catching only half the fish they caught in the 1950s and, while earning more per pound, were still earning lower real incomes than before (Commons 1969, 411-417).

In a memorandum prepared for cabinet at about this time (Canada undated) the department noted that while "the fishing industry is an important source of employment and income in ... the Maritime Provinces and Newfoundland ... [the] commercial fishery is ineffi- cient ... [and] could produce its present output with a smaller amount of capital and less than half its present labour force." The memoran- dum recommended that action be taken to double the fishing income of the average Canadian fisherman by 1980 by cutting the number of fishermen overall from 71 thousand in 1968 to 42 thousand in 1980 (Newfoundland figures were 19,800 and 10,000) and concomitantly cutting the number of plant workers from 18,300 to 12,700 (4,400 to 3,000 in Newfoundland).

A variant of this policy recommendation went to cabinet in June 1970. While the cabinet decision of October 1970 recognized that the "basic objective was to rationalize the fishing industry with a view to creating a viable self-sustaining industry" it also recognized that "the pursuit of this objective would raise important social and other questions ... " and did not give the fisheries department the regulatory authority it had requested (Cabinet 1970, 33-34).

No major fishery policy changes emanated from cabinet during the next few years. By 1974, fish stocks were in serious decline and markets were devastated by world recession. "The crisis of the present, the chronic problems of the past, the expectations of national jurisdiction over offshore fishery resources in the future, the evidence of a potential for the development of a viable fishing industry and the deepening financial involvement of government" (Canada 1976, 49-50) led the fisheries service to undertake a new review of policy. The review led to the adoption of a new fisheries policy by govern- ment in 1975 and the publication of the policy and its justification in a

100-page document in 1976. This document makes it clear that the federal fisheries service understood the problems of the Canadian fisheries and the actions that were required (Gough 1993).

Embedded in the policy statement is a perceptive summary of a general problem of industry which affects the fisheries and goes beyond that of common property. The focus is on the great uncertainty that characterizes both the market demand for fish products and the supply of fish in the sea. The fact of uncertainty on both the demand and supply sides of the market provokes a reaction in the private sector that results in increasing overcapacity and recurring crises:

> Resource-based fluctuations of this magnitude [changes in catch of up to 90% in a year] from time to time may be superimposed on the movement in costs and prices stemming from ... other sources. The results can be a steep, and usually unforeseen, fall or rise in earnings and profits. Industry reaction to this form of uncertainty frequently has been to install sufficient catching and processing capacity to handle the peaks in supply, thereby inflating industrial overheads and reinforcing the inherent tendency toward over-expansion in the commercial fisheries (Canada 1976, 44-45).

Recognizing overcapacity as a basic problem, and understanding the underlying cause, as it did, the policy statement called for a "fundamental restructuring of the fishing industry", referring to changing the fleet mix and reducing overcapacity. The restructuring was seen as being "inevitable", coming "about either in an orderly fashion under government auspices or through the operation of inexorable economic and social forces" (ibid., 53). There was a third option, which was not mentioned but which was in effect implemented. That is, in the words of Michael Kirby (1982a), to adopt the "pothole theory of government", i.e., to leave the existing system intact and fill the potholes with money.[3]

Of great interest, considering the sequel, is the comment that "The prospect of Canada achieving extended offshore jurisdiction does nothing to lessen the urgency of the matter" (Canada 1976, 56). Yet despite this comment, the caveat of 1970 was elaborated upon:

---

[3] Handwritten note on draft of a speech, February 22, 1982. National Archives of Canada (NAC) Kirby files, RG 23, Volume 2018, File 9000-9 (Pt. 1).

... fisheries development is synonymous, in this context, with a restructuring of the industry itself for its very survival. Where adverse social side-effects such as reduced employment opportunities can be kept within acceptable limits, restructuring should proceed. Where damage to the community would outweigh advantages in the short run the changes must be postponed. In the inshore fisheries generally, especially those of the Atlantic region, the labour force far exceeds the industry's capacity for employment at an adequate level of income" (ibid., 56).

Then comes the element that plays such a large role in Newfoundland, "to be sure, many residents of these [small inshore communities with underdeveloped basic services] may have a satisfying life notwithstanding" (ibid., 57). We shall later take a look at the cost of maintaining a satisfying life in this way.

The report estimated that there were 9 thousand inshore fishermen on the eastern coast of Newfoundland and on the Labrador coast, and that they earned an average of $1,500 from fishing, continuing with the speculation that with modern technology and with feasible inshore catches of 200 thousand tonnes per year, average income could rise to $5,000. Of course, even at 1976 prices, $5,000 was a derisory level of income. Therefore, even under optimal conditions the number of fishermen would have to be reduced (ibid., 58).

However, with the vision of EFJ before them, the authors of the report backtracked and emphasized that "fewer people [need] be employed in relation to output ... This does not mean drastic dislocation of the people now dependent on the fishing industry. It does mean that where it is feasible to expand, this expansion should be accomplished without increasing employment in the fishery itself" (ibid., 58). A drastic reduction of the fisheries labor force was not seen as necessary. But the discussion of incomes earlier on the same page implies that even with a substantial increase in catch the number of fishermen would have to be reduced.

Nonetheless, the authors concluded that "the 200-mile limit as a simple answer for the problems of Canada's fisheries has been greatly exaggerated" (ibid., 62). The critical factor was that the Department was not prepared to insist on either a sharp reduction in the number of fishermen, or even on a planned, phased, reduction. Rather, it was prepared to await events. The report ends with a list of 25 strategies for improving the fishery, including provision for "the withdrawal of excessive catching capacity in congested fleet segments" (ibid., 64). Without details telling how this was to be done, it was unlikely that action would be taken, and it was not. The only really hopeful sign was that the number of fishermen in Newfoundland had already fallen about halfway to the goal the department had tried to set in 1970.

EXTENDED FISHERIES JURISDICTION

The policy statement was published in 1976. On June 4, 1976, the Canadian Minister of External Affairs announced in the House of Commons that by 1 January 1977, Canada would unilaterally adopt a 200-mile fishing control limit. The Minister was quoted in the New York Times (1976) as saying that "catch quotas are expected to be set back sharply ... to allow overfished stocks to recover" and in the Toronto Globe and Mail (1976) as saying that "the state of our fishery resource and the situation of our fisheries, fishing industry and of our coastal communities make this action imperative." The Globe went on to say that "Walter Carter [Newfoundland's Minister of Fisheries] was jubilant ... he said he believes the stocks can be built up and, 'if the quotas have to be reduced, Newfoundland fishermen are prepared to cooperate'." If there was ever to be an opportune time for a cooperative effort to limit the fishery, this was it.

A Fisheries and Marine Service summary written later in the year (Molson 1976) noted that "the problem now is with the Canadian industry which is highly fragmented, suffers from substantial over-capacity and in which many plants and communities may not be viable in the long term" and went on to indicate that harvesting policy under EFJ would see:

> ... foreign fishing ... reduced and Canadian effort ... remain the same except in the Gulf of St. Lawrence where it will be dramatically reduced. We will have spent, by April 1977, $140 million compensating for displacement in the various sectors of the Canadian industry, just to keep it in existence, not to change anything.

It was perhaps an evil portent that at precisely the moment when EFJ was being declared, the Newfoundland fishery was booming. Cod and total sea fish landings were at their highest level in half a decade and cod prices were rising.[4] The current state of the fishery encouraged the general inclination to do nothing about the structure of the fishery, to wait and see.

But "nothing" was not done. The then current structure, with its overcapacity, was not frozen in size; instead the industry was permitted to grow helter-skelter out of control until it was too late. We are still paying the price because of the resultant overfishing and because government now has to support, at great expense, a large number of fishing families.

Table 1 shows the growth of the Newfoundland fishery from 1976 to 1980, just before the fishing economy collapsed again in the wake of economic recession in the United States. Instead of care being taken to adjust the size of the fishing industry to achieve an economically viable fishery, there was a tremendous expansion. It is apparent from the table that the number of registered fishermen and inshore vessels, the value of the inshore and offshore fleets, the number of fish processing plants and their freezing capacity, Unemployment Insurance benefit payments, loans from the Fisheries Loan Board, and expenditures by both the provincial and federal governments increased enormously. The total of $125 million in federal and provincial expenditures for 1980/81 were nearly equal to the value of the entire landed catch (Schrank et al. 1987).

1980/81 was not the end of the story. The events of the preceding few years tied both levels of government to supporting an increasingly bloated fishery. Accordingly, their expenditures continued to rise. Including loans as well as expenditures, transfers and subsidies, federal and provincial financial outlays on the Newfoundland fishery[5] nearly doubled from $211,300,000 in 1981/82 to $408,700,000 in 1990/91, shortly before the Northern Cod moratorium came into force. For the five provinces participating in the Atlantic fishery, the total financial outlays grew from $505,300,000 in 1981/82 to more than $1 billion in 1990/91 ($1,038,600,000), a figure that exceeded the $918,700,000 value of the landed catch. Over the same decade, the total financial outlay on the Atlantic fishery is conservatively

---

[4] Historical Statistics of Newfoundland and Labrador. 1990. Volume 2(6), Tables K-1 and K-2.

[5] Excluding portions of Newfoundland included in DFO's Gulf Region to which they were attached in 1981.

Table 1 : Newfoundland's Fishing Industry : 1976-1980.			
	1976	1978	1980
Registered Inshore Fishers[a]	13,736 (1975)	25,060	33,640
Registered Inshore Vessels[b]	9,517	16,656	19,594
Value of Inshore Vessels[b]	$42,420,000	$79,214,000	$129,921,000
Registered Offshore Vessels[b]	84	89	90
Value of Offshore Vessels[b]	$73,470,000	$113,546,000	$131,880,000
Federally Registered Fish Processing Establishments[c]	147 (1977)	174	225 (1981)
Freezing Capacity (tons)[d]	180,550 (1974)	308,804	466,543
Net UI Benefits Paid to Inshore Fishers[e]	$9,774,000 (1976/77)	$22,252,000 (1978/79)	$36,534,000 (1980/81)
Outstanding Loans of the Fisheries Loan Board[e]	$12,488,000 (1976/77)	$21,587,000 (1978/79)	$43,796,000 (1980/81)
Total Provincial Expenditures[e]	$13,377,000 (1976/77)	$20,148,000 (1978/79)	$19,320,000 (1980/81)
Total Federal Expenditures[e]	$60,086,000 (1976/77)	$97,270,000 (1978/79)	$105,712,000 (1980/81)

Sources:
a. Canada 1982, Table 2.
b. Canada 1982, Table 7.
c. Canada 1982, Table 4C-1.
d. Canada 1982, Table 4C-2.
e. Schrank et al. 1987, 550,571,573. Government "expenditures" include expenditures, transfer payments, and subsidies.

estimated as $8 billion, equal in value to the landed catch and somewhat less than half the $19 billion value of production of the fish products industry in the five provinces (Schrank 1994). Somewhat less than half of the $8 billion was paid as Unemployment Insurance benefits.

POLITICAL PRESSURES AND THE EFFECTIVENESS OF FISHERIES POLICIES

Perhaps the fundamental source of the problem is that DFO has suffered from a policy schizophrenia, never being able to determine whether its chief goal is to set and implement policy for the fishery as a viable industry or whether it is to maximize employment and save nonviable rural communities.

Perhaps a convenient way to elucidate the schizophrenia argument is to review some early internal documents of the Kirby Task Force which started working early in 1982, following the collapse of the fishing industry after its enormous expansion of the late 1970s.

In a document dated 12 February 1982, Peter Nicholson, a member of the Task Force, prepared a draft statement on the goals of the future east coast fishery. The first goal was that it be profitable, the second that it be organized as a business, and another, that the resource base be stabilized. Nicholson comments that of all the goals listed only the goal of a stable resource base "seems well within reach" (Nicholson 1987). Shortly thereafter, in a draft speech of 22 February 1982, Kirby (1982a) was to state his belief that:

> ... we can ensure we never again have disasters such as the collapse of the Northern Cod stocks in 1973/74, where offshore fishing at a level of some 800,000 tonnes decimated the inshore catch to about 40,000 tonnes.

Kirby's faith, unfortunately, was not sustainable. As the draft speech approaches its end, Kirby notes that:

> I've highlighted a number of the factors that affect the viability of the East Coast fishery. But overlaid on the whole economic picture has to be the issue of the social responsibility of the fishery. It's of no small consequence.

> Today we have neither a fully economical fishery, nor a social welfare fishery. We're somewhere in the middle with the government footing the bill. Withdrawal of federal financial support would likely result in very few fishermen, operating in a highly capital intensive industry.

> Let's be realistic. If there is a problem of too much harvesting capacity, then it must be reduced. Or, it must be subsidized.

It comes down to a basic decision on the part of government. Either we're going to have to exercise some discipline over all sectors of the industry, or we're going to have to subsidize it massively.

While Kirby was sounding the alarm only in 1982, after the expansion of the post-EFJ period had occurred, his comments, as he implicitly recognized, related to a fishery that had not changed fundamentally in many years. His comments would have been equally appropriate twenty years before, or now.

A month later, Kirby followed up his [draft] speech with a memorandum to the members of the Task Force in which he forcefully indicated that it must clearly enunciate the objective of fisheries policy, "By clearly articulating the objective of Atlantic fishery policy, the government will be able to have a reasonably objective measure against which it can assess the value of various policies." But now, only six weeks after Peter Nicholson had proposed profitability as the goal of the fishery, Kirby suggested that, "The proposed objective of federal Atlantic fishery policy is: to maximize employment subject to two constraints," (Kirby 1982b) where the constraints referred to the income of the fishermen, not directly to the profitability of the enterprise. Once again, fully cognizant of the fundamental problems of the fishery, and in this case being particularly cognizant of the need for a clear policy, the focus became employment maximization, not economic viability.

Perhaps the clearest statement of the problem appeared in a memorandum from another member of the Task Force, Dr. A.W. May, to Kirby in response to his document of 29 March (May 1982). May commented that he believed:

> ... the employment objective has always been implicit in Atlantic Fisheries policy. Thus it is about time that we made it explicit and dealt with it on the table. Incidentally, the employment objective has been much stronger provincially than federally. Since the declaration of the 200-mile limit, it has been the provinces which pushed the development theme and the federal government which has preached restraint.

May thus introduced the possibility of conflict among the players in the industry as a factor in policy implementation. He further suggested that the inshore and offshore fisheries be divided, "so that the maximum employment model applies inshore and the maximum economic rent offshore." May concluded by stating both that he was unsure that such a bifurcated system could work and that the government must decide on "whether or not there shall be a population on the northern part of the east coast of Canada".

A few days later yet another member of the Task Force proposed as the primary objective the maximization of employment in the industry where "employment is taken to mean the number of fishing and processing jobs yielding at least sufficient incomes, which, taken with other income opportunities available, generate decent annual cash household incomes..."(Roberts 1982). Employment maximization was to be subject to the constraints that fishing and processing enterprises generate normal economic returns and that the concern to rural survival be on a "small area basis", not necessarily on an individual community basis.

When finally published, the Kirby report (Kirby 1982c) stated that its first two objectives were:

1. The Atlantic fishing industry should be economically viable on an ongoing basis, where to be viable implies an ability to survive downturns with only a normal business failure rate and without government assistance.
2. Employment in the Atlantic fishing industry be maximized subject to the constraint that those employed receive a reasonable income as a result of fishery-related activities, *including fishery-related income transfer payments* [my emphasis].

It is now clear that neither the recommendations of the Kirby report, nor the financial restructuring of the industry which followed, were the salvation of the Atlantic fishery. Despite the early hopes of the members of the Task Force, their final report so hedged its basic premise that in retrospect it is clear that what was needed for a viable fishery was not even mentioned. Answers to the questions of how many fishermen there were to be, and how any downsizing was to be accomplished, were totally lacking. In going from Peter Nicholson's comments on profitability in February to the final report's comments on employment maximization in December, the game had been given away — as it always had been in the past.

Whether or not it has ever been explicit, it is clear that the social goal of the fishery has consistently taken precedence over the goal of economic viability.

FEDERAL/PROVINCIAL RELATIONS

As a member of the Kirby Task Force, May referred to pressure on DFO from the provinces. He specifically referred to provincial emphasis on "development" during the post-EFJ expansion period, but the pressure has been consistent. To illustrate the nature of provincial pressure I cite a single example from an earlier period: the example for 1973-74 of the Fishing Vessel Assistance Program (FVAP), where a federal initiative to reduce subsidies was effectively squelched by the provinces.

FVAP was a federal subsidy program for fishing vessel construction or refitting.[6] The program originated in the 1940s and was first applied in Newfoundland in 1953/54 when FVAP subsidies of $7 thousand were granted. By 1967/68, payouts in Newfoundland reached more than $1 million, fell to $400 thousand in 1969/70 and rose again to nearly $4 million in 1973/74, 1973 having been the most profitable year for fish processors in living memory and which just preceded the disastrous year of 1974, when oil prices increased dramatically.[7] The basic shortsightedness of policy is implicit in these figures, which show fleet expansion in the face of short-term profitability which, presumably, is assumed falsely to last forever. In this case, profits turned to losses in one year, but the vessels had been built and continued to be part of the fixed capital of the fishery. In the expansion of the fishery that followed the declaration of EFJ, FVAP payments (for the entire country) grew from $4 million in 1977 to $11 million in the following year, continuing at more than $6 million per year until it fell

---

[6] For details of the history of the FVAP program, see Crowley, McEachern and Jasperse (1993).

[7] Data from NAC, RG 23, Acc 82-83/151, Box 110, File 1439-U6-7 (Pt. 4). The 1973 "boom" resulted from rapidly increased market prices, despite rapidly dropping catches. The boom ended abruptly when world recession combined with reduced catches to devastate the industry which was only saved by the institution of the Temporary Assistance Program which almost immediately attracted countervail attention from the United States. Catch and price statistics are from Canada (1976), Tables 10 and 11.

in 1982 (again a year of bankruptcies), rising to nearly $8 million in 1983,[8] immediately following the publication of the Kirby and Pearse reports (Kirby 1982c; Pearse 1982).

FVAP payments in Newfoundland which were more than $2 million in 1981/82, fell dramatically in 1982/83 and rose to more than $1 million for each of the next two years (Schrank 1994).

FVAP was therefore a vehicle for the expansion — nay overexpansion — of the fishery through the building in of over capacity during short periods of high profitability and optimism.

The Canadian government was aware quite early on that the FVAP program was likely to get out of financial control. Late in 1973 Treasury Board decided that future funding under FVAP would be contingent on a new subsidy policy which accounted for budgetary constraints. At its meeting of 1 November 1973, the Federal/Provincial Atlantic Fishery Committee (FPAFC: consisting of senior representatives of DFO and the provinces) established a task force "to develop a new subsidy policy". The guidelines for establishing the policy, as set out in the minutes of the FPAFC, stated that:

> ... a completely new approach should be taken to the subsidy problem with the major aim being to develop an innovative and imaginative policy ... the basic premise [of which] should be that any financial assistance would be selective and be an incentive performance grant directly related to productivity of the vessel and exploitation of the types of species we are trying to encourage rather than a universal subsidy.

The task force met three times, issuing its final report after its meeting of 22 January 1974. Having been established with the aim of reforming subsidy policy, the task force came forth with the meagre recommendation:

> BE IT THEREFORE RESOLVED THAT, for a period of two years, and in respect to fishing vessels from 35 feet to 75 feet in length, subsidy assistance at the rate of 35% be continued, with such incentives as may be found necessary and useful in the development of under-exploited species or areas.

---

[8] See Crowley, McEachern and Jasperse (1993, 351).

No policy change was suggested and the task force essentially voted itself out of existence, having accomplished nothing.

The task force was aware of its anemic performance and in the letter transmitting its recommendation noted that the solutions were complicated by a number of factors including the lack of a precise data base, the fragility of the Atlantic economy, uncertainties regarding federal licensing policy, the potential effects of the pending Law of the Sea Convention, and the long history of the FVAP program. It was further noted that "the attitude of Task Force members ... is somewhat conditioned by the social ["socio-political" was deleted at the last minute], as well as economic concerns, of the respective Provinces" ["Provincial Governments" was also deleted]. Finally, passing the buck in grand style, they recommended "that the two-year period ... should see productive effort in development of ...", among other things, "thrusts for developing possible phase-out, or redirection, of subsidy assistance". Even this final comment was watered down in the final document, "phase-out" being replaced with "selective levels".

Thus, an attempt to seriously review a growing subsidy was almost immediately aborted amongst excuses and dreams for future work (which, needless to say, was not undertaken). Reading between the lines, one might see this as an effort instigated by the federal government and sidetracked by the provinces. This pattern of a grand start followed by a rather meagre result characterizes nearly all efforts to reform Canada's fisheries policies.[9] The FVAP program was finally phased out a dozen years later.

It is difficult enough for a government to maintain a long term policy — such as one which would limit the size of a fishery over an extended period. Governments lose office and policies change. It is particularly difficult in the Canadian federal system where jurisdiction is divided, the federal government having jurisdiction over fish

---

[9] The minutes and drafts discussed here can be found in the NAC, RG 23, Acc 86-87/149, Box 29, File 1475-87/F6 (Pt. 1). It is characteristic of Canada's fisheries policy that there is recognition that the industry is over-expanded and that adjustments need be made, but economic, social and political forces act to slow the adjustment until a major crisis occurs. It then becomes urgent to shift labor out of the fishery, but the lack of employment alternatives elsewhere creates a situation where the government increases its subsidization of the industry until the crisis passes when a new and ineffective "go slow" policy is adopted and the cycle starts again. For a historical survey of some of these topics see Schrank et al. (1992).

harvesting and the provinces controlling the fish processing sector. One result is that even when DFO takes a firm stand to stop the expansion of the fishery, and does not yield as it did in the FVAP case, it may not have the power to implement its policies. Again we cite a single example.

THE PRIVATE SECTOR

Most of the expansion of the fishery followed immediately after the declaration of EFJ. By early 1979, DFO started applying the brakes on the fishery. It was possible, however, for the provincial governments, in league with the private sector, to render the federal effort ineffective.

A particularly well documented example is that of the Jackson's Arm Seafoods Ltd. This company, a subsidiary of H.B. Nickerson and Sons, applied in April 1979 to the Department of Regional Economic Expansion (DREE) for financial aid under the Regional Development Initiatives Act (RDIA) to build a new plant in Jackson's Arm. DFO recommended against the application on the grounds that P. Janes & Sons already had a plant in that community (which was being expanded with DREE funding) and that the fish resource in White Bay was insufficient to warrant additional processing capacity. DREE accepted the DFO recommendation and rejected the application (Follett 1982). That was not the end of the story.

During a 1978 campaign to increase its presence in Newfoundland, the Royal Bank had agreed to finance a new plant in Jackson's Arm so the plant was built despite the refusal of DREE to help.[10] The Jackson's Arm plant was only utilized at 12% and 28% of capacity in 1980 and 1981 before being closed in October of 1981 (ibid.). The Jackson's Arm plant made no economic sense, as was recognized by the federal government. It is clear that DFO was outflanked by the Royal Bank with the help of the Province of Newfoundland which licensed the new plant. In microcosm, this example illustrates the interaction of economics, politics, entrepreneurial greed, and the complex of federal/provincial relationships in the management of the Canadian fishery.

---

[10]Memo from Dave Patterson to Michael Kirby, February 17, 1982. NAC Kirby files, RG 23, Volume 2031, File 9090-1 (Pt. 2).

Regardless of the source of pressure, DFO's record is one of inconsistency, at best. While provincial governments could license fish plants and banks could finance them, despite attempts by DFO to control processing overcapacity, DFO provided the licenses ("registrations") for the vessels and the fishermen without which the expansion of the harvesting sector could not have occurred. DFO must at least share in the responsibility for the great and fateful expansion of the industry.

CONCLUSIONS

In the absence of a strong and unequivocal policy by government on goals of the fishery, the easiest approach at any time is to allow the fishery to grow if someone, somewhere thinks there is money to be made. When the situation turns sour, the pressure will be inexorable for the government to pay the bill. This has happened repeatedly, for instance, with the Temporary Assistance Program (TAP) in the mid-1970s, the financial restructuring of the fishing industry in the mid-1980s, and the Northern Cod Adjustment and Recovery Program (NCARP) now. Perhaps given the federal structure of government, the permanently depressed state of the Newfoundland economy, and the political and economic climate that envelopes all of these factors, the apparent wishy-washiness, and the great expense, are necessary.

My fear is that a government will some day decide to stop "filling the potholes", causing incredible hardship. But it has never proven possible to systematically downsize the fishery. This was tried in the early seventies; we know with what effect.

I cannot believe that the fish will not be back. The issue is whether there will still be a bloated, economically unviable, fishery when it does — with the usual cycle of repeated crises — or a much smaller economically self-sufficient industry. I fear that as soon as a profitable fishery reappears, the over expansion will be repeated. If there is a lesson from the past, it is that the necessary policies must be in place before the "boom" reappears or we will be back in a few years where we are now.

REFERENCES

Canada. Minister of Fisheries and Forestry. undated. *Memorandum to the Cabinet.* National Archives of Canada (NAC) RG 23, Acc 86-87/150, Box 10, File 1410-3 (Pt. 1).

Canada. House of Commons. 1969. *Debates,* 3 November.

Canada. Cabinet. 1970. *Minutes of the Cabinet of the Government of Canada.* 27 October. Ottawa.

Canada. Department of the Environment, Fisheries and Marine Service. 1976. *Policy for Canada's Commercial Fisheries.* Ottawa.

Canada. Department of Fisheries and Oceans. 1982. *Atlantic Fisheries Review* 2 (10 May). NAC Kirby files RG 23, Volume 2014, File 9000-0 (Supp. A).

Cashin, R., chairman. 1993. *Charting a New Course: Towards the Fishery of the Future.* Report of the Task Force on Income and Adjustment in the Atlantic Fishery. Ottawa: Fisheries and Oceans Canada.

Crowley, R. W., B. McEachern, and J. Jasperse. 1993. A Review of Federal Assistance to the Canadian Fishing Industry, 1945-1990. Pages 339-367 in *Perspectives on Canadian Marine Fisheries Management,* edited by L. S. Parsons and W.H. Lear. Ottawa: National Research Council of Canada.

Follett, Wayne. 1982. *Report on Jackson's Arm Seafoods Ltd.* Ottawa: Department of Fisheries and Oceans. NAC Kirby files, RG 23, Volume 2032, File 9100-2 (Pt. 1).

Gough, J. (1993). A Historical Sketch of Fisheries Management in Canada. Pages 5-53 in *Perspectives on Canadian Marine Fisheries Management,* edited by L. S. Parsons and W. H. Lear. Ottawa: National Research Council of Canada.

Kirby, M. J. L. 1982a. Draft speech dated 22 February. NAC Kirby files, RG 23, Volume 2018, File 9000-9 (Pt. 1).

———. 1982b. *The Objective of Federal Government Atlantic Fisheries Policy.* 29 March 29. NAC Kirby Files, RG 23, Volume 2014, File 9000-0 (Pt. 2).

———, chairman. 1982c. *Navigating Troubled Waters: A New Policy for the Atlantic Fisheries.* Report of the Task Force on Atlantic Fisheries. Ottawa: Supply and Services Canada.

May, A. W. 1982. Memorandum to Michael J. L. Kirby, 5 April. NAC Kirby Files, RG 23, Volume 2014, File 9000-0 (Pt. 2).

Molson, C. R. 1976. *Notes on a meeting held Tuesday, October 5 between Messrs. Love, Daniels, McGee (DREE) and Messrs. Lucas, McEachran, MacKenzie and Molson (DOE).* NAC RG23, Acc. 82-83/151, Box 95, File 1438-R1 (Pt. 1).

New York Times. 1976. 5 July, page 5.

Nicholson, Peter J. 1982. *A Future for the East Coast Fishery - 1987.* 12 February. NAC Kirby Files, RG 23, Volume 2018, File 9000-9 (Pt. 1).

Pearse, P. H. 1982. *Turning the Tide: A New Policy for Canada's Pacific Fisheries.* Final Report of the Commission on Pacific Fisheries Policy.

Pushie, G. F., chairman. 1967. *Report of the Royal Commission on the Economic Prospects of Newfoundland and Labrador.* St. John's: Office of the Queen's Printer.

Roberts, R. 1982. *Objectives of Atlantic Fisheries Policy.* Memorandum to P.J. Nicholson , 8 April. NAC Kirby files, RG 23, Volume 2014, File 9000-0 (Pt. 2).

Schrank, William E. 1994. *Government Financial Outlays on the Atlantic Canadian Fishery, 1981/82 to 1990/91.* Discussion Paper #94-01 of the Department of Economics, Memorial University of Newfoundland, Table 2, p. 21.

Schrank, W.E., Noel Roy, R. Ommer, and Blanca Skoda. 1992. An Inshore Fishery: A Commercially Viable Industry or an Employer of Last Resort? *Ocean Development and International Law* XXIII:335-367.

Schrank, William. E., Noel Roy and E. Tsoa. 1986. Employment Prospects in a Commercially Viable Newfoundland Fishery: An Application of An Econometric Model of the Newfoundland Groundfishery. *Marine Resource Economics* III.

Schrank, William E., Blanca Skoda, Noel Roy, and Eugene Tsoa. 1987. Canadian Government Financial Intervention in a Marine Fishery: The Case of Newfoundland, 1972/73-1980/81. *Ocean Development and International Law* XVIII:533-584.

Toronto Globe and Mail. 1976. 5 July, page 1.

3

THE COLLAPSE OF THE NORTHERN COD FISHERY : PREDATOR-PREY AND OTHER CONSIDERATIONS

Eugene Tsoa
Department of Economics
Memorial University of Newfoundland

INTRODUCTION

It is well known that Northern Cod fishery constitutes the most important fishery of the Canadian Atlantic coast. For centuries, the fishery was the raison d'être for the existence of a community in Newfoundland. The collapse of the Northern Cod stock is a serious blow to the Newfoundland economy which until recently relied heavily on the fishery for employment of a large proportion of its rural population, albeit at a subsistence level with considerable amount of government financial support.[1] For its importance, the Northern Cod fishery has also been one of the most studied fisheries. In addition to the work of scientists and other staff members in the Newfoundland region of Department of Fisheries and Oceans, there have been reports after reports from numerous task groups commissioned by the government. Since the 1980s, we have seen major studies chaired by Kirby (1982), Alverson et al. (1987), Harris et al. (1990), and Cashin et al. (1993). One would lament the collapse and closure of a fishery with such magnitude of research attention. Many important factors contributing to the failure of the Northern Cod fishery have been identified. For example, the Report of the Task Force on Income and Adjustment in

---

[1] See Schrank et al. (1992) for a discussion of how the Newfoundland inshore fishery was heavily subsidized historically for the sake of providing employment.

the Atlantic Fishery chaired by Richard Cashin (Cashin 1993) gives half a dozen reasons for the collapse of the Northern Cod stock. They are:

1. high TAC levels due to overoptimistic scientific projections, inadequate understanding of the stock dynamics and inaccurate data on commercial fishing activity;
2. underreporting of catches and misleading data for management;
3. destructive fishing practices such as high grading, discarding and dumping;
4. foreign overfishing on the Nose and Tail of the Grand Banks;
5. failure to control expansion of fishing effort due to the demands of a processing sector with excess capacity and failure to minimize the adverse impact of various fishing gear technologies, and;
6. unforeseen ecological changes, including cooling water temperature since the mid-1980s, changes in water salinity, and shifting predator-prey relationships, particularly among seals, capelin and cod.

While the above list of factors leading to the collapse of the Northern Cod fishery appears to be fairly exhaustive, it is not my intention in this paper to put together every piece of the puzzle. Instead, I shall concentrate on a couple of factors that I consider strikingly notable after some preliminary investigation. I shall begin with a brief account of the statistics involving a major fleet of Canadian offshore vessels fishing Northern Cod during the last decade and then consider the predator-prey relationship in light of these and other recent statistics.

OFFSHORE CATCH OF NORTHERN COD

The Northern Cod fishery had provided a livelihood to thousands of Newfoundland fishermen for centuries. The growth of a Newfoundland offshore sector in this fishery did not occur until recently. Data on actual catch and Total Allowable Catch (TAC) of Northern Cod from 1960 to 1991 presented in Table 1 show that the stock was heavily fished by foreign vessels in the 1960s and the first part of 1970s. TACs first introduced in 1973 by ICNAF were set too high to be a binding constraint. As a result, Newfoundland inshore catch in 1973-1975 was reduced to less than 50 thousand tonnes annually, the lowest level in recent history. In 1977, for the plight of inshore fishermen and other reasons, the Government of Canada declared Extended Fishery

Table 1 : Historical vs. Total Allowable Catches of Northern Cod.					
	Actual Catches			TAC	
Year	Inshore	Canada	Total	Canada	Total
1960	157	164	459		
1961	119	124	498		
1962	139	143	503		
1963	145	149	509		
1964	131	141	603		
1965	111	118	545		
1966	111	119	525		
1967	102	116	612		
1968	101	122	810		
1969	97	115	754		
1970	77	82	520		
1971	63	67	440		
1972	62	66	458		
1973	42	44	355	-	660
1974	35	36	373	-	657
1975	41	42	288	-	554
1976	60	63	214	-	300
1977	73	80	173	-	160
1978	81	102	139	100	135
1979	86	131	167	130	180
1980	97	147	176	155	180
1981	80	133	171	185	200
1982	113	211	230	215	237
1983	106	214	232	240	260
1984	97	208	232	246	266
1985	80	193	231	250	266
1986	72	207	267	250	266
1987	79	209	240	247	256
1988	101	245	269	266	266
1989	103	215	254	235	235
1990	113	188	219	197	199
1991	60	133	161	188	190
Source: Department of Fisheries and Oceans.					

Jurisdiction (EFJ) unilaterally. In the first few years following EFJ, the Canadian offshore sector was allowed to expand dramatically by increased allocation of the TAC, while foreign fishing effort had disappeared from this fishery. Figures in Table 1 show that as Canadian TACs increased during this period, offshore catches rose much more dramatically than did inshore catches. In 1978, Canadian offshore catch of Northern Cod was only slightly over 20 thousand tonnes, about one quarter of the inshore catch. However, by 1982, it had increased almost five times and stayed over 100 thousand tonnes until 1990.

While the inshore sector had experienced intermittently several bad years in which the actual catch rate fell short of its allowance during the 1980s, the offshore fleets had little difficulty in filling their quotas. Unlike those fishing inshore, offshore vessels need not wait for fish to migrate and they are able to fish all year round. In addition, they have the mobility to travel to more distant waters.

The expansion of Canadian offshore sector fishing Northern Cod has been striking. For almost the entire decade of 1980s, the Canadian offshore catch surpassed the inshore catch. The actual recorded level of catch would have been substantially higher if considerations were given to the notorious practices of underreporting and dumping starting from the early 1980s when the system of enterprise quota was first introduced. According to a document issued by Canadian Atlantic Fishery Scientific Advisory Committee (CAFSAC),[2] the discard rate by number of fish was estimated to be 7.2% in 1981, rising to a high of 24.4% in 1986, and by weight of fish, it was 1.5% in 1981, rising to high of 10.7%. There is little doubt that the younger fish dumped would have deleterious effects on the health of the future stock.

Due to its rapid growth, Canadian offshore fishing activities have been singled out as one of the obvious factors leading to the collapse of Northern Cod stock. Despite the continued high level of offshore catch, statistical evidence did not seem to suggest any sign of an imminent crisis. Productivity of the offshore sector remained high. To demonstrate this, I have calculated the catch per unit effort for a fleet of Newfoundland trawlers in the tonnage class of 500-1,000 tons equipped with bottom otter trawls fishing cod as the main species in area 2J3KL. The results are presented in Table 2. Before we look at the figures, it is important to note that the majority of the offshore catch of Northern Cod was landed by this fleet of Newfoundland trawlers. Data on fishing effort in terms of hours and days fished for the recorded catch of these vessels are available in the NAFO Statistical Bulletin. Data are aggregated to obtain annual time series of catch per hour and catch per day for the entire area of 2J3KL as reported in

---

[2] See *Advice on the Status and Management of the Cod Stock in NAFO Division 2J, 3K and 3L*. CAFSAC Advisory Document 86/25, page 5.

Year	Cod Catch	Total Catch	Hours Fished	Days Fished	Catch/hour Cod	Catch/hour Total	Catch/day Cod	Catch/day Total
Table 2 : Catch and Effort of Newfoundland Vessels between 500-1000 Tons Using Bottom Otter Trawl Fishing Northern Cod.								
1980	34,348	40,672	25,899	1,846	1.33	1.57	18.6	22.0
1981	46,295	51,828	23,586	1,940	1.96	2.20	23.9	26.7
1982	63,381	70,947	37,053	3,137	1.71	1.92	20.2	22.6
1983	71,242	82,560	41,411	3,195	1.72	1.99	22.3	25.8
1984	63,328	73,497	36,803	2,881	1.72	2.00	22.0	25.5
1985	61,701	70,254	35,418	3,041	1.74	1.98	20.3	23.1
1986	79,332	87,799	46,798	4,181	1.70	1.88	19.0	21.0
1987	76,983	85,262	47,311	4,229	1.63	1.80	18.2	20.2
1988	88,245	95,845	50,542	4,608	1.75	1.90	19.2	20.8
1989	64,139	71,396	41,903	3,470	1.53	1.70	18.5	20.6
1990	49,520	55,658	37,611	3,077	1.32	1.48	16.1	18.1

Note:
1. Catch is measured in tonnes.
2. Data includes only effort directed to fishing cod as main species as reported in NAFO Statistical Bulletin. Thus, the difference between cod and total catch constitutes the by-catch of other species.
source: NAFO Statistical Bulletins

Table 2. It shows that both catch per hour and catch per day, regardless of whether only cod catch or the total catch (i.e., with by-catch included) is used for the numerator, rose sharply in 1981 but declined in the following year. However, they stayed relatively stable for the remaining years until 1989. In comparison with the figure in 1980, the catch per hour or catch per day for these vessels in 1990 does not seem to have dropped significantly to signal that a crisis was looming.

It is true that catch per hour or per day may not be an ideal index of stock abundance as the fishing technology (involving either the vessel or the gear used) advances. It is also true that underreporting and discard may render catch per unit effort an inaccurate index of stock abundance. However, it is unlikely that there would be very significant improvement in technology for this particular fishing fleet during the decade under investigation. Likewise, at the time the discard rate was said to rise during the first part of 1980s, one would expect the reported catch per unit effort to fall. This however was not the case. Catch per hour or day in this period was fairly stable. To the extent that errors due to discards and underreporting are systematic, catch per

Eugene Tsoa

Year	Cod Catch	Total Catch	Hours Fished	Days Fished	Catch/hour Cod	Total	Catch/day Cod	Total
				Area 2J				
1980	9,435	9,849	4,657	339	2.03	2.12	27.8	29.1
1981	15,855	16,070	2,806	327	5.65	5.73	48.5	49.1
1982	38,745	39,634	10,226	1,151	3.79	3.88	33.7	34.4
1983	22,915	23,299	3,886	532	5.90	6.00	43.1	43.8
1984	4,390	4,461	1,035	126	4.24	4.31	34.8	35.4
1985	1,106	1,201	663	65	1.67	1.81	17.0	18.5
1986	2,608	2,627	672	115	3.88	3.91	22.7	22.8
1987	26,470	26,879	8,529	1,052	3.10	3.15	25.2	25.6
1988	27,046	27,207	8,916	1,042	3.03	3.05	26.0	26.1
1989	22,279	23,977	9,374	937	2.38	2.56	23.8	25.6
1990	13,920	14,916	11,871	998	1.17	1.26	13.9	14.9
				Area 3K				
1980	16,138	19,692	12,520	893	1.29	1.57	18.1	22.1
1981	15,255	16,669	4,949	496	3.08	3.37	30.8	33.6
1982	7,267	9,095	4,855	433	1.50	1.87	16.8	21.0
1983	22,114	24,910	11,481	882	1.93	2.17	25.1	28.2
1984	25,388	27,952	8,376	865	3.03	3.34	29.4	32.3
1985	36,704	38,755	9,633	1,152	3.81	4.02	31.9	33.6
1986	40,477	43,155	15,348	1,598	2.64	2.81	25.3	27.0
1987	24,806	25,330	6,265	854	4.00	4.04	29.0	29.7
1988	26,618	27,143	5,458	873	4.88	4.97	30.5	31.1
1989	20,601	21,046	5,848	685	3.52	3.60	30.1	30.7
1990	18,173	18,663	3,280	553	5.54	5.69	32.9	33.7
				Area 3L				
1980	8,775	11,131	8,722	614	1.01	1.28	14.3	18.1
1981	15,185	19,089	15,831	1,117	0.96	1.21	13.6	17.1
1982	17,369	22,218	21,972	1,553	0.79	1.01	11.2	14.3
1983	26,213	34,351	26,044	1,781	1.01	1.32	14.7	19.3
1984	33,550	41,084	27,392	1,890	1.23	1.50	17.8	21.7
1985	23,891	30,298	25,122	1,824	0.95	1.21	13.1	16.6
1986	36,247	42,017	30,778	2,468	1.18	1.37	14.7	17.0
1987	25,707	33,053	32,517	2,323	0.79	1.02	11.1	14.2
1988	34,581	41,495	36,168	2,693	0.96	1.15	12.8	15.4
1989	21,259	26,373	26,681	1,848	0.80	0.99	11.5	14.3
1990	17,427	22,079	22,460	1,526	0.78	0.98	11.4	14.5

Table 3 : Catch and Effort of Newfoundland Vessels between 500-1000 Tons Using Bottom Otter Trawl Fishing Northern Cod by Area.

For notes and source, see Table 2.

unit effort remains an useful index of stock abundance. Finally, it has been pointed out that as the stock becomes smaller, effort may fall with catch, mitigating the decline in catch per unit effort. It follows that one may cast doubt on the validity of using the variations in catch per unit effort to interpret changes in stock size. However, there is no evidence that fishing effort had dropped more in the later part of the decade than it had risen in the earlier part of the decade. The total number of hours or days fished in 1989/90 period was much higher than that in period of 1980/81. Fishing effort may have been reduced in the latter years, but it remained at a high level. Granted the possible weaknesses discussed above, catch per unit effort may remain a useful index of abundance.[3]

It has been well known that in the area of 2J3KL there may be several distinct substocks.[4] Unless the stock of fish and fishing effort are uniformly distributed over the area, the aggregated catch per unit effort may be misleading. For this reason, we also present the catch per hour and catch per day by subdivision in Table 3. The figures in Table 3 show large differentials in productivity over various subdivisions. The difference in catch per unit effort may simply reflect the relative abundance of an individual substock vis-a-vis another substock in the area. One would however expect that catch per unit effort should decline over time in each subdivision to harbinger the current disaster. However, the results show that there are conflicting patterns of movement over time in the three subdivisions. Subdivision 2J is the only subdivision showing both a falling trend and a sharp decline in catch per unit effort in the last few years. The decline in catch per unit effort in 3L is not as discernible as in 2J. In 3K, on the contrary, catch per unit effort had been rising over the entire period. Correlation coefficients for catch per hour and catch per day between any two of the three subdivisions in the sample period are also

---

[3] Catch per unit effort data from the offshore fleet and research vessels are used by the DFO scientists in tuning the Virtual Population Analysis for the purpose of stock assessment. One of the main conclusions of Harris report (1990) is that this is inadequate. It is suggested that other indices of abundance, including those based on catch per unit effort data from inshore fleet and acoustical surveys, should be developed.

[4] These substocks may intermingle in the summer but remain separated in the winter when offshore fishing activities are more intense. For a discussion of tagging and other scientific studies to determine various substocks of Northern Cod, see Alverson et al. (1987, 24-29).

52   *Eugene Tsoa*

Table 4 : Correlation Coefficient Matrices Relating Catch Rates between Areas.			
Catch per Hour between Areas			
	2J	3K	3L
2J	1.0000		
3K	-0.4557	1.0000	
3L	0.4017	-0.3150	1.0000
Catch per Day between Areas			
	2J	3K	3L
2J	1.0000		
3K	-0.2597	1.0000	
3L	0.3852	-0.0398	1.0000

computed and reported in Table 4. The low and in some cases negative correlation coefficients further confirm the disparate nature of the individual stock in the each subdivision and lack of systematic movements in catch per unit effort across various subdivisions.[5]

The implications of the above discussion are quite obvious. First, the disparity in catch per unit effort as well as its conflicting patterns of movement over time in various subdivisions suggest that each subdivision should be treated separately for the purpose of setting TACs and its allocation. Further, to the extent that they are accurate, the data examined above could not have foreshadowed the ensuing collapse of the fishery, except perhaps in 2J. It is difficult to determine how the growth of offshore sector is responsible for the collapse of the fishery. During the fifteen years before declaration of EFJ, total Northern Cod catch as shown in Table 1 was close to 8 million tonnes. In comparison, it had diminished to a mere three million tonnes in the fifteen years during the post-EFJ and pre-moratorium period. Why can't the stock sustain such a low level of catch?

---

[5] To verify the representativeness of the statistics reported in Table 3 and 4, it would be ideal if similar types of statistics can be obtained for each class of Canadian vessels fishing Northern Cod. Unfortunately, the only other Canadian offshore vessels which had harvested significant amount of Northern Cod during this period are those of a fleet of smaller vessels in the tonnage class of 150-500 tons equipped also with bottom otter trawls fishing primarily in 3L and 3K. Since similar results are obtained for this fleet of vessels, they are not reported separately. It is therefore not unreasonable to believe that the results shown in Table 3 and 4 are fairly typical of all vessels fishing in the area.

It may be possible that the catch data are inaccurate. It is also likely that the Northern Cod stock had been more severely depleted than it was thought to be in the late 1970s. In hindsight, if the fish stock had indeed been depleted due to overfishing, it would have been more appropriate and beneficial to impose a brief moratorium at the time. However, it was not suspected that the stock could not sustain any further fishing effort then.   On the contrary, there existed a prevailing sense of optimism that the fishery would soon take off as foreign fishing activities were eventually phased out and measures to rebuild the fishery implemented. The optimism might not have been unfounded when the stock seemed to recover following a few years of conservation. In 1978, TAC was set at 135 thousand tonnes, a very low level relative to the level of past catches, and raised to a level of 260 thousand tonnes over a period of five years. Since 1983, TAC had stayed around that level. It was generally believed that the stock was stabilized in this latter period and a TAC of 260 thousand tonnes, based on the $F_{0.1}$ rule,[6] could be sustained. Unfortunately, inshore catch fell well below the allowance in 1984-1987, although the offshore sector was able to increase its catch continuously in the same period. The overall TAC was not reduced until 1989.

SEALS, COD AND CAPELIN

There is little doubt that the size of Northern Cod stock had grown substantially for the first five years following EFJ due to conservation measures. One significant factor that may have been contributing to the growth of the Northern Cod stock may be the size of seal herds at the time. Harp seals in the Northwest Atlantic areas had been hunted for centuries. Annual catch of harp seals for the period of 1952-1990 are shown in Table 5. Statistics indicate that the harp seal catch rate was high during the 1950s and 1960s. An annual harvest of more than 300 thousand harp seals was fairly common. This had led to a continuous downsizing of the harp seal population. In a study by Lett, Mohn and Gray (1979), the harp seal population in the Northwest Atlantic Area was estimated for the period of 1952-1977. The population estimates by Lett, Mohn and Gray (ibid.) are reproduced in Table 5 for

---

[6] See footnote 2, Chapter 1, for an explanation of F.

Eugene Tsoa

| Year | Harp Seal | | Capelin Catch in SA2 and SA3 |
| | Catch | Population | |
	x 1000		x 1000 Tonnes
Table 5 : Historical Harp Seal Catches, Population estimates[a] and Capelin Catches in Northwest Atlantic Areas.			
1953	291	2380	
1954	285	2286	
1955	350	2144	
1956	402	2020	
1957	260	1975	
1958	316	1873	
1959	331	1709	
1960	295	1654	
1961	202	1610	
1962	330	1636	
1963	354	1503	
1964	353	1463	
1965	245	1395	
1966	332	1316	
1967	340	1198	
1968	202	1097	
1969	297	1160	
1970	265	1083	
1971	238	1036	3
1972	137	1026	71
1973	135	1147	269
1974	156	1215	288
1975	182	1260	366
1976	175	1310	361
1977	167	1339	227
1978	176	1379	85
1979	174	1408	23
1980	181	1443	24
1981	211	1473	37
1982	184	1481	41
1983	77	1512	40
1984	49	1626	59
1985	38	1757	50
1986	26	1892	79
1987	43	2037	61
1988	44	2162	108
1989	65	2277	114
1990	70	2358	166

Source: NAFO Statistical Bulletins

[a]Estimates taken from Lett, Mohn, and Gray (1979) for the period of 1953-1977 and using the algorithm listed in the Appendix for the period of 1978-1990.

reference.[7] According to their estimates, the harp seal population was around one million in the early 1970s, down from a higher level about 2.5 million in 1952. Environmental groups began mounting their attacks on seal hunt in the 1960s. However, a substantial reduction in the catch rate did not take place until 1972.

While biologists cannot determine for certain that the harp seal is a direct predator of cod, it is certain that harp seals and cod both feed on capelin. Reduced harp seal populations in the 1960s and early 1970s would have allowed the stock of its prey and hence that of its competing species to grow. One would expect that natural mortality rate would be lower for capelin as well as cod in the period. However, capelin stocks were heavily fished in the early 1970s, primarily by Russian vessels. Data for the annual capelin catch in NAFO subarea 2 and 3 between 1971 and 1990 are also presented in Table 5. Prior to 1971, capelin catch was negligibly small. The abrupt expansion of Russian fishing effort exerted on capelin during 1972-1977 may not have been detrimental to the ecological balance as the harp seal herds and cod stock were both depleted at this time. The declaration of EFJ afforded the Government of Canada the power to control and reduce capelin catch. Although the capelin catch was cut substantially following EFJ, the harp seal population has been steadily rising since the mid-1970s following several years of reduced catch.

The harp seal population was estimated by Lett, Mohn and Gray (ibid.) for the period of 1952-1977. While I could not find any estimates of a consistent time series of more recent harp seal population, I have conducted a simulation exercise to extend the series of harp seal population estimated by Lett, Mohn and Gray (ibid.) beyond 1977. My simulation is based on a simple model proposed by Conrad and Bjorndal (1991).[8] Using the harp seal catch data obtained from NAFO Statistical Bulletin, the parameters estimated by Conrad and Bjorndal and initial populations for 1976 and 1977 estimated by Lett et al., I have calculated an annual series of harp seal population estimates from 1978 to 1991. Details of all calculations can be found from the BASIC program provided in the Appendix of this paper. The

---

[7] See Lett, Mohn and Gray (1979), Table 3.
[8] The model used for simulation consists of equations (1) and (2) in Conrad and Bjorndal (1991). It is a more simplified multicohort model than that of Lett, Mohn and Gray (1979).

result of the simulation suggests that harp seal population increased only marginally during the first five years following EFJ. The total increase from 1978 to 1982 was merely about one hundred thousand. Thus, with the seal herds remaining relatively small and capelin catch being slashed, from the perspective of predator-prey relationship, the task of rebuilding of cod stock was certainly made easier. This would certainly be consistent with the general belief that cod stock had recovered in the early 1980s discussed above.

However, when the environmental group Greenpeace successfully lobbied the European Community to ban the import of seal products in 1982, it had the effect of forcing a moratorium on the Newfoundland seal hunt. Subsequently, the harp seal catch rate declined to a historical low level as shown in Table 5. The reduced number of harp seals taken allowed the population to grow rapidly. My simulation shows an increase of almost one million harp seals by 1991 over 1982. An adult harp seal weighs roughly 400 pounds and is said to consume daily a diet equal to 6% of its body weight.[9] It would not be difficult to imagine the impact of one million more harp seals on the stock of its prey, including capelin and possibly young cod as well. Unfortunately, the capelin catch was allowed to increase substantially at the same time as the seal population was growing. This had arisen from an increased demand for capelin from Japan. During the period 1979-1983, annual capelin catch had been kept below 50 thousand tonnes. However, in 1988, it increased drastically to more than 100 thousand tonnes and by 1990, it was further raised to 166 thousand tonnes. While the capelin catch rates may still be lower than those in the early 1970s when the Russian vessels were present, the harp seal population was considerably larger in the late 1980s.

The increased harvest of capelin and the continuously rising harp seal population are, in my opinion, two crucial factors leading to the subsequent collapse of Northern Cod stock. On the basis of catch history for half a century prior to the excessive foreign fishing in the 1960s and 1970s, the Northern Cod stock was believed able to sustain a yield much higher than the annual TAC of 260 thousand tonnes set for the 1983-1988 period.[10] Why didn't the stock, which had been

---

[9] See Harris et al. (1990,87).

[10] See Munro (1980, 26) for a discussion of projected biomass and TACs made in the late 1970s. For an estimation of the biomass of Northern Cod stock and its productivity

subjected to an average annual harvest of over 500 thousand tonnes for over a decade in 1960s, collapse in the mid-1970s the way it did in the early 1990s? Why did it fail after fifteen years of reduced catch under government management? The answer may be found in the context of a broader predator-prey relationship involving seal, cod and capelin highlighted in our earlier discussion.[11] The capelin catch had been negligibly small, while the harp seal catch high before 1970s. In the 1970s, the Northern Cod stock did not fail perhaps because of the ecological balance in predators and prey. Its breakdown in the 1990s can certainly be linked to the large seal herds after more than a decade of ban on seal hunt as well as to the high capelin catch rate in recent years. To some extent, the events surrounding the populations and catches of seal, cod and capelin discussed above are inopportune in timing. They may also have been overlooked. After more than two years of the moratorium, there is still no sign of recovery for the stock. This could be further evidence that ecological factors cannot be overemphasized as the major explanation for the current failure of the fishery.

---

using the 1953-1979 data, see also Tsoa, Schrank and Roy (1985). These estimates were obtained without any predator-prey and other ecological considerations.

[11] Some may argue that Northern Cod could be considered overexploited on the basis of the recorded catch figures and high discard rates in the 1980s. While I am not suggesting that overfishing is not a factor, I believe that the word overfishing is meaningful only with reference to predator-prey and other ecological considerations.

REFERENCES

Alverson, D. L., F. W. H. Beamish, J. Gulland, P. Larkin, and J. Pope. 1987. *A Study of Trends of Cod Stocks off Newfoundland and Factors Influencing Their Abundance and Availability to the Inshore Fishery*. Ottawa: Fisheries and Oceans Canada.

Bowen, W. D. 1982. Age Structure of Northwest Atlantic Harp Seal Catches, 1952-80. *NAFO Scientific Council Studies* 3:53-65.

Cashin, R., chairman. 1993. *Charting a New Course: Towards the Fishery of the Future*. Report of the Task Force on Income and Adjustment in the Atlantic Fishery. Ottawa: Fisheries and Oceans Canada.

Conrad, J. and T. Bjorndal. 1991. A Bioeconomic Model of the Harp Seal in the Northwest Atlantic. *Land Economics* 67(2):158-71.

Harris, L., chairman. 1990. *Independent Review of the State of Northern Cod Stock: Final Report*. Ottawa: Fisheries and Oceans Canada.

Kirby, M. J. L., chairman. 1982. *Navigating Troubled Waters: A New Policy for the Atlantic Fisheries*. Report of the Task Force on Atlantic Fisheries. Ottawa: Supply and Services Canada.

Lett, P. F., R. K. Mohn, and D. F. Gray. 1979. *Density-Dependent Processes and Management Strategy for the Northwest Atlantic Harp Seal Population*. International Commission for the Northwest Atlantic Fisheries, Selected Paper 5: 61-80.

Munro, Gordon R. 1980. *A Promise of Abundance: Extended Fisheries Jurisdiction and the Newfoundland Economy*. Ottawa: Economic Council of Canada.

Schrank, W. E. , N. Roy, R. Ommer, and B. Skoda. 1992. An Inshore Fishery: A Commercial Viable Industry or an Employer of Last Resort? *Ocean Development and International Law* 23 (2): 335-67.

Tsoa, E., W. E. Schrank, and N. Roy. 1985. Generalizing Fisheries Models: An Extension of the Schaefer Analysis. *Canadian Journal of Fisheries and Aquatic Sciences* 42 (2):44-50.

APPENDIX

```
10 REM This program estimates harp seal population for 1978-91
20 REM using the model in Conrad and Bjorndal (1991)
30 R=.4
40 K=4040000
50 DIM X(16),H(14),Y(14)
60 REM X(0) & X(1) are pop. estimates for 1976 & 1977 in Lett et al
   (1979)
70 X(0)=1310197
80 X(1)=1339052
90 REM Data for 1976-80 from Bowen (1980) and 1981-90 from NAFO
   Stat. Bul.
100 DATA 134892,121750,137315,136417,178394,145274,50058
110 DATA 23827,13334,21888,32156,33275,54724,33728
120 FOR T=1 TO 14
130 READ H(T)
140 NEXT T
150 DATA 31973,54257,37272,44724,33033,38709,26570
160 DATA 24749,24345,4046,10418,10340,19341,36529
170 FOR T=1 TO 14
180 READ Y(T)
190 NEXT T
200 FOR T=1 TO 14
210 X(T+1)=.775*(R*X(T-1)*(1-X(T-1)/K)-H(T))+.925*(X(T)-Y(T))
220 NEXT T
230 PRINT " YEAR     Population "
240 PRINT "........................."
250 FOR T=1 TO 15
260 PRINT T+1976,X(T)
270 NEXT T
280 PRINT "........................."
300 END
```

4

STOCK REBUILDING STRATEGIES UNDER UNCERTAINTY : THE CASE FOR SENTINEL FISHERIES

Daniel E. Lane
Faculty of Administration
University of Ottawa

Halldor P. Palsson
Bureau of Competition Policy
Industry and Science Canada

INTRODUCTION

On July 2, 1992 then Fisheries Minister John Crosbie announced to a stormy session of the Atlantic Groundfish Advisory Committee (AGAC) that there would be a two-year moratorium on fishing the 2J3KL Northern Cod stock.[1] The 1992 moratorium on the Northern Cod stock broke new ground in fisheries management decision making by setting commercial catch quotas at zero for a stock previously exploited annually on the order of 200 thousand tonnes. The primary reason for this decision was to rebuild the very low levels of estimated spawning stock biomass. The initial two-year moratorium eliminated tens of thousands of jobs in harvesting and processing and necessitated massive aid to Atlantic Canada, Newfoundland in particular. In 1993, the moratorium was extended indefinitely on the advice of the Fisheries Resource Conservation Council (FRCC) and a follow-up financial

---

[1] Department of Fisheries and Oceans (DFO) Press Release, NR-HQ-92-58E, 2 July 1992.

aid package was put into place by the new Liberal administration. Indications are that the stock will not recover "before the year 2000 at the earliest" (FRCC 1993).

To deal with this latest crisis in the Atlantic fishery, politicians and administrators have stated their commitment to ensuring the livelihood of the people directly and indirectly affected by the groundfish moratoria. As yet, no policy directives for the post-moratorium future of the Atlantic fishery, its potential new structure, size, or conditions for resumption of fishing have been issued. The moratorium precludes data required for the annual stock assessment process and erodes the usual sources of information about stock status.

In previous stock crises, government fisheries agencies typically lowered catch quotas to smaller but nontrivial exploitation levels. The evidence presented here from other major cod stocks fished commercially in the North Atlantic show that despite apparent stock collapses, commercial fishing at reduced levels throughout periods of stock decline have not precipitated commercial extinction. Moreover, by continuing to monitor reduced fishing activity, control was enhanced and information sources remained in place.

Advice provided originally to the Minister preceding July 1992 by the Canadian Atlantic Fisheries Scientific Advisory Commission (CAFSAC) was that catches should not exceed 25 thousand tonnes for the remainder of the year.[2] This was consistent with the findings of the requested special assessment by NAFO for this stock (NAFO 1992). The decision to proceed with a complete moratorium was apparently taken after realization of the difficulties of suballocating such a small Total Allowable Catch (TAC) among inshore and offshore interests in the summer and fall fisheries. However, these same decisions must eventually be taken in order to define the fishery of the future.[3] The inability to control fishing is not seen as a valid reason to close a fishery that may sustain lower, but not unappreciable, harvesting levels. In the face of expected levels of misreporting of actual catches, it is unlikely that proclaiming a moratorium will result in catches of zero, in any case. It is also argued that the danger of moratoria is

---

[2] DFO Press Release, NR-HQ-92-58E, 2 July 1992.

[3] The Task Force on Incomes and Adjustment in Atlantic Canada recommend Industry Renewal Boards be established for this precise purpose.

precisely that valuable information about catches are ignored or otherwise lost, thus eliminating and complicating forward-looking evidence about when fishing may again be acceptable after the stock has regrown.

This paper evaluates the impact on the fishery system — including stock dynamics and commercial sector socioeconomics — of closing the Northern Cod fishery versus a strategy of controlled but reduced fishing. Specifically, we challenge the wisdom of the accepted policy to close the fishery versus controlled operation of the fishery at reduced levels. To evaluate these options of alternative stock rebuilding strategies, a bioeconomic model of the Northern Cod stock is presented. The modeling exercise is necessary because policy evaluation is at best a look at "tradeoffs" between harvesting levels and expected stock size. The feasibility of investing forgone catches in an effort to rebuild the cod stock is evaluated in an environment of dynamic uncertainty.

In order to obtain a perspective view on the 2J3KL Northern Cod situation, comparisons are made to its stock collapse relative to other cod stocks around the world. A range of evidence supports the view that high fishing mortalities combined with recruitment failure are responsible for serious stock declines. The key note of importance with respect to all cod stocks is the series of recruitment failures that has preceded major stock declines. In a forward-looking view of fisheries stock management, it will be incumbent upon decision makers to examine stock recruitment projections directly.

Next, the bioeconomic impact of the closure of the 2J3KL Northern Cod fishery is examined by analyzing its impact on future stock status and the commercial fishery compared to a policy of controlled fishing.

MAJOR NORTH ATLANTIC COD STOCKS

This section presents brief histories from four major cod stocks in the North Atlantic area. These include:

- the North-East Arctic (also referred to as Arcto-Norwegian) Cod stock;
- the Icelandic Cod stock;
- the West Greenland Cod stock, and;
- the 2J3KL Northern Cod stock.

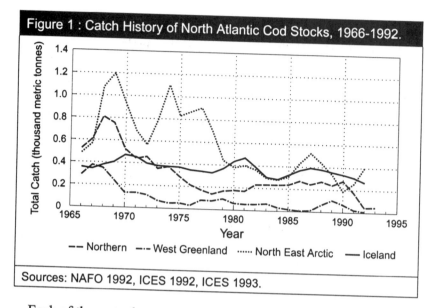

Figure 1 : Catch History of North Atlantic Cod Stocks, 1966-1992.

Sources: NAFO 1992, ICES 1992, ICES 1993.

Each of these stocks are examined with respect to their recent catch histories and biomass trends. Figure 1 presents the catch histories of these four cod stocks from 1966 to 1992 for comparative purposes. All four stocks exhibit declining catch trends over the period: North-East Arctic Cod catches since the 1980s are roughly half the catches for the 1960s and 1970s; West Greenland Cod catches fell off in the late 1960s and have not returned to those levels to date; Icelandic Cod catches have remained relatively flat over the period but have declined relative to catch levels of the 1950s; Northern Cod catches have declined over the period from 1968 to 1977 when they stabilized until 1989 after which time a second decline has occurred.

With regard to the cod stocks, the dynamics are highly stochastic. Average weights by age from catch data among these cod stocks may fluctuate by as much as 30% from year to year. Stock recruitment, as measured by the size of year classes entering the fishery, are so highly variable that they obscure any potential relationship that may exist between the size of the current parent stock and the size of future year classes. Natural mortality may vary considerably depending on environmental conditions and pressure from predators. As Jakobsen reports,

There is little direct evidence to support the exact figure [for natural mortality, 20%], but most assessment biologists would probably agree that 0.1-0.3 is a likely range (Jakobsen 1992, 157).

Cod grow rapidly and growth by weight from year to year is high. The average weight at age from catch data for the four stocks under consideration is comparable. The Icelandic stock is a faster growing stock than the others and is more directly comparable to the North-East Arctic stock. The West Greenland stock and the 2J3KL Northern cod stock are more closely related in their annual growth rates.

As is noted in the following stock-by-stock analysis, the assessed status of the stocks have fluctuated markedly over time. Norway and the Community of Independent States (CIS) are rehabilitating the North-East Arctic Cod stock after the brief "collapse" in 1989. Iceland may be facing a substantial decline in its cod stock because of recruitment failure combined with fishing pressure. The West Greenland stock was a significant stock that collapsed in the late 1960s and has not recovered. Finally, the collapse of Northern Cod is examined in light of the evidence from these comparable cod stocks.

North East Arctic Cod Stock

Catches from this stock peaked at about 1.2 million tonnes in the late 1960s and early 1970s (Figure 1). The stock declined drastically between 1986 and 1990. This is thought to have occurred because the Barents Sea capelin stock declined severely from 1983 to 1986 (Tjelmeland and Bogstad 1993, 120). The mean weight of 4-year-old cod was reduced by 61.5% from 1984 to 1988 (Jorgensen 1992, 269; Jakobsen 1992). As time passes it is clear that the extent of the stock decline starting in 1986 was overestimated. To see this, a comparison of the population estimates in the 1989 assessment are made with those in 1992 in Table 1 for the years 1984 to 1991.

The current biomass assessment of the stock is provided in Figure 2a. The stock

... has improved much quicker than expected after the current severe management strategy was introduced in 1989. This rapid development is due mainly to good growth (ICES 1992, 4).

The "severe management strategy" put into place at the end of 1989 slashed quotas and closed northern areas of the fishery after a poor

Table 1 : Comparison of 1989 and 1992 Stock Assessments for the North-East Arctic Cod Stock.

Year	1989 Assessment		1992 Assessment	
	Total	Spawning	Total	Spawning
	------------------------ metric tonnes ------------------------			
1984	912,227	280,846	908,418	269,476
1985	1,244,177	287,891	1,008,247	199,402
1986	1,440,832	239,583	1,296,222	171,243
1987	1,080,733	256,816	1,129,213	149,112
1988	686,079	188,978	833,000	156,188
1989	673,166	135,298	933,645	169,660
1990	-	-	1,083,613	346,521
1991	-	-	1,418,815	680,283
Source: ICES 1992.				

start to the season. The management measures lowered overall F^4 (5-10 year olds) from 1.02 in 1987 and 0.91 in 1988 to 0.63 in 1989 and 0.24 in 1990 (ICES 1992, table 3.30). The International Council for the Exploration of the Sea (ICES) working group recommended that the main management objective should be to maintain the spawning stock biomass at a high level to avoid further long periods of very poor recruitment. Recruitment had been poor since the early 1970s (Figure 2b).

The North-East Arctic Cod stock recovered quickly because weight at age increased rapidly and maturity at age increased substantially after 1989. By 1991 quotas were increased with the finding of large populations of cod along the coast of Norway. As Jentoft notes,

> We got lucky. It turned out that the fisheries crisis did not last as long as many had feared, after all. By the fall of 1992 it appeared that we had ridden out the storm. Reports by the oceanographers on fish populations in the Barents Sea in 1992 were as surprising as they had been in September 1989. But this time the message was encouraging: The fry production has never been so good since measurements were begun in 1965 ... (Jentoft 1993, 135).

In 1993, the quota was set at more than twice the 1990 level (248 versus 113 thousand tonnes).

---

[4] F is the continuous rate of stock depletion due to fishing; see footnote 2, chapter 1.

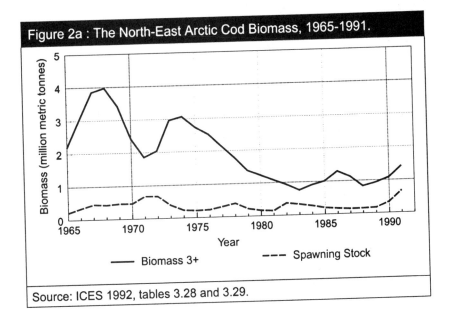

Figure 2a : The North-East Arctic Cod Biomass, 1965-1991.

Source: ICES 1992, tables 3.28 and 3.29.

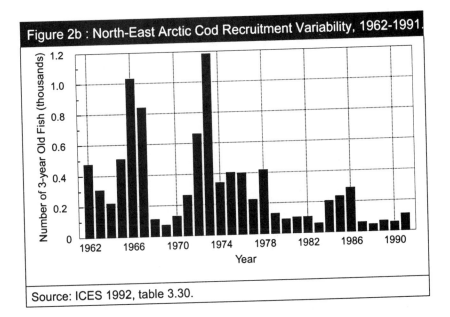

Figure 2b : North-East Arctic Cod Recruitment Variability, 1962-1991.

Source: ICES 1992, table 3.30.

The Icelandic Cod Stock

The average catch for this stock in the period 1905-1992 is 318 thousand tonnes. The peaks in catches at Iceland in the early 1930s and 1950s coincide with large in-migration of cod from Greenland to Iceland (Cushing 1982, 31). Cushing estimates that a 30% reduction in recruitment to the stock if Greenland migrants have ceased to join the Icelandic spawning stock.[5] A downward trend in catches and biomass from the early 1950s is evident (Figure 3a). The Icelandic Cod stock has declined as a result of five small successive year classes recruited to the stock (Figure 3b). The biomass estimates from the 1993 assessment are in Figure 3a. The stock is at a low level. Recruitment in 1994-1996 is expected to be low and the stock will likely be fished at 165 thousand tonnes for the next 2 to 3 years.

The prognosis for a quick recovery of the Icelandic stock is poor because most of the gains in weight at age and maturity have already been realized.[6] The F (5-10 years olds) for 1986-1992 has been in the range 0.77-1.00 (F_{1991}=0.91, F_{1992}=0.88).[7] When fishing this hard the fishery is recruitment driven because it is carried principally by two or three year classes. Iceland is going through the downside of this fishing strategy and the stock is expected to recover if and when a good recruiting year class enters the fishery (Baldursson, Danielsson, and Stephansson 1993, 33).

---

[5] ICES (1993, 12) notes that the 1984 year class hatched at Iceland migrated to Iceland in 1990 and 1991. The concern is migrations from Greenland to Iceland are smaller and less frequent than in the 1930-1970. Only the 1973 and 1984 hatches have migrated back to Iceland in any numbers in the last 25 years.

[6] Ibid. p. 13, "Great care needs to be taken with the maturity at age in the prediction. Firstly, the maturity at age is at record high levels in 1992 and 1993, and it is not felt reasonable to let this drop to the long-term average in 1994 nor is it reasonable to assume these record-high levels far into the future".

[7] Ibid. Table 3.3.12.

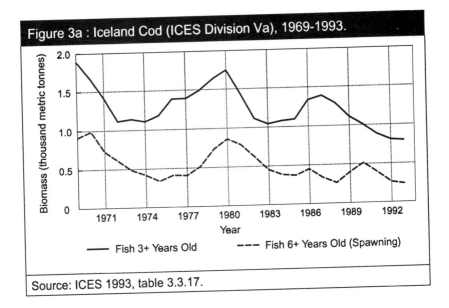

Figure 3a : Iceland Cod (ICES Division Va), 1969-1993.

Source: ICES 1993, table 3.3.17.

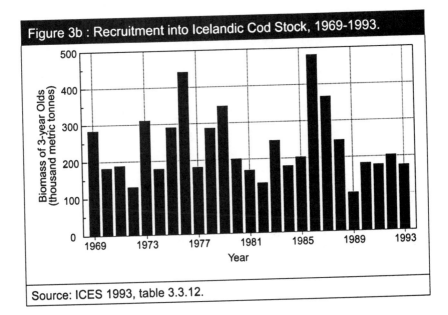

Figure 3b : Recruitment into Icelandic Cod Stock, 1969-1993.

Source: ICES 1993, table 3.3.12.

West Greenland

The landings of West Greenland Cod averaged about 350 thousand tonnes between 1960 and 1969 (Figure 1 and Garrod 1988, 202). The stock has yielded an average of about 50 thousand tonnes per year ever since with little or no stock rebuilding. The cod fishery of West Greenland collapsed in the late 1960s following a series of poor recruiting year-classes. Recruitment estimates are unavailable for this stock. The most recent assessment by ICES concludes that: "The offshore stock may, therefore be considered to be almost non-existent at the present time" (ICES 1993, 20). There continues to be a small inshore fishery in this stock. According to Garrod (1988, 202):

> The collapse is widely regarded as the effect of persistent low water temperatures on year class strength. But the cumulative fishing mortality has been close to 2.0 throughout the 1970s and this is probably high enough to prevent recovery, even if environmental circumstances [had] been more conducive to successful survival of juvenile cod.

The West Greenland Cod stock illustrates the downside associated with fishing a collapsed cod stock at continually high levels. However, the decline in weight at age for cod at West Greenland in recent years (Figure 4) makes it difficult to argue that the stock may be rebuilt at all.

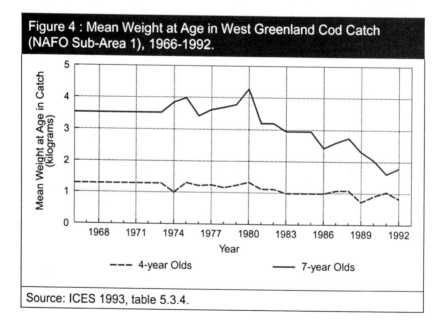

Figure 4 : Mean Weight at Age in West Greenland Cod Catch (NAFO Sub-Area 1), 1966-1992.

Source: ICES 1993, table 5.3.4.

Northern Cod (NAFO 2J3KL)

The peak in catches of Northern Cod in 1968 at 810 thousand tonnes occurred under the management of the International Commission for the Northwest Atlantic Fisheries (ICNAF) by mesh size restrictions. Under Canadian management (CAFSAC) since 1977, catches have been kept under 300 thousand tonnes. It is well known from Alverson et al. (1987), Rivard and Foy (1987), Rice and Evans (1988) and Restrepo et al. (1990) that the Northern Cod stock complex is difficult to assess. Additional information has occasioned large revisions in stock status as can be seen from comparisons of pre-crash assessments estimates (Figure 5a). We are unable to provide a comparative post-crash virtual population analysis (VPA) because DFO scientists do not have sufficient information to partition total mortality into fishing and natural components for 1991 and 1992.

The 1992 stock assessment estimated that the drop in 3+ biomass was from 1.1 million tonnes to 780 thousand tonnes in 1992[8] (Figure 5b). More seriously, the 7+ biomass plunged from 270 thousand tonnes to 130 thousand tonnes. On this basis a reduced TAC of 120 thousand tonnes was set for 1992.

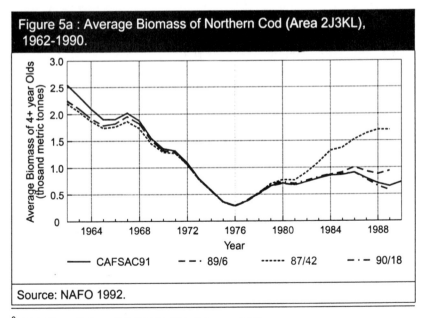

Figure 5a : Average Biomass of Northern Cod (Area 2J3KL), 1962-1990.

Source: NAFO 1992.

---

[8] DFO News Release NR-NF-92-12E, February 1992.

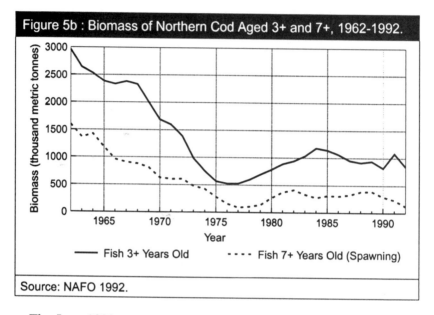

Figure 5b : Biomass of Northern Cod Aged 3+ and 7+, 1962-1992.

Source: NAFO 1992.

The June 1992 NAFO assessment (NAFO 1992) concluded that the age 3+ biomass was about 520-640 thousand tonnes and that the age 7+ biomass was 72-110 thousand tonnes. Fishing mortality (F) for 1989 in the assessment was revised higher, from about 0.5 to 0.7-1.0.

The NAFO (1992) assessment notes that temperatures in 75-175 metre deep water continued on a declining trend that began in the 1980s. The area coverage of the cold intermediate layer of the Labrador Current (water under zero degrees Celsius) are at or near its long term maximum. The NAFO assessment finds a negative relationship between the area extent of the cold intermediate layer and recruitment to 2J3KL cod. The cause of the sudden decline in 7+ cod could not be determined with the available information. The NAFO assessment concludes:

> Under the most optimistic option, to achieve a fishing mortality rate of 0.25 ($F_{0.1}$) in 1992 the total catch should not exceed 91,000 tonnes. Given the uncertainties in the assessment and the obvious requirement for caution, it would be wise to consider the $F_{0.1}$ catch to be at the lower value of 50,000 tonnes (NAFO 1992, 32).

The moratorium on fishing for 2J3KL cod in Canadian waters for 2 years was announced on 2 July 1992. Fishing continued on the nose

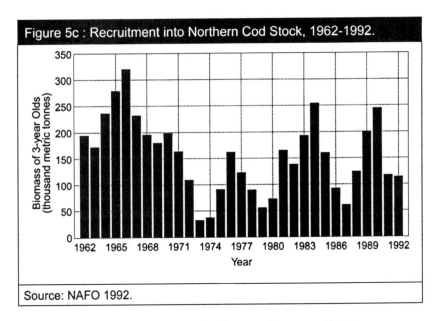

Figure 5c : Recruitment into Northern Cod Stock, 1962-1992.

Source: NAFO 1992.

and tail of the Grand Bank by foreigners plus a small inshore recreational food fishery. Recent statements about the stock note that it has continued to decline despite the moratorium. Average weight at age 7 in the commercial catch in 1992 was the second lowest since 1977 (Sinclair 1993).

The 1993 stock report concludes that based on the 1992 survey, the total biomass could be as low as 100-150 thousand tonnes. Two competing hypothesis are offered for the decline in 2J3KL cod:

1. Decline in stock biomass was abrupt and occurred between January and June 1992.
2. Gradual decline that began in the north in 2J in 1990 and propagated southward (deYoung and Rose 1993).[9]

There is no explicit conclusion on which hypothesis is more appropriate, but (1) seems to be the working assumption in the 1993 DFO stock report. The prognosis for Northern Cod is grim:

---

[9] The authors offer an elaboration of the West Greenland story. They claim that northerly spawning and warm ocean conditions are prerequisites for strong recruitment. The current stock decline is therefore driven by cold water.

The population appears to have continued to decline in 1992,
even in areas in which no fishing occurred ... Any recovery will
depend on the appearance of and survival of strong year-classes.
... The 1988-1991 year-classes are all expected to be below
average in abundance. Recovery of the spawning stock biomass
is unlikely for several years (Sinclair 1993, 58).

The decline of the Northern Cod stock in 1992 remains a puzzle.
The stock was exploited at the lower end of fishing mortality for cod
stocks in comparison with the other major stock referred to above.
Larger year classes (1986 and 1987) were poised on entering the
harvestable stock, especially when compared to recruitment in the
early 1970s (Figure 5c). Recovery may yet be aided by gains in
weight at age, early maturity, and more favourable environmental
conditions. Recruitment of large year classes remains critical for the
recovery of the stock.

COD STOCK COMPARISONS

On the basis of the review of major North Atlantic cod stocks, fluctuations in stock status are largely attributed to:

1. recruitment variability (observable only after a lagged time
   period);
2. weight at age variability (observable on an ongoing basis while
   data is being collected);
3. natural mortality changes (unobservable);
4. ecosystem and environmental conditions (partially observable but
   not on a concurrent basis), and;
5. fishing mortality (not observable directly, but estimated from
   population analyses).

It would appear that among these general causes, management
controls may be initiated only with respect to fishing. However, the
extent to which these other independent major causes are aggravated
by fishing mortality is not known. In other words, major fluctuations
in stock status may occur whether or not there has been some fishing
induced mortality. Fishing doubtless becomes a major cause of stock
change at high levels of mortality. We seek to define a level of fishing
that may not be considered a significant cause of stock change
independent of other major and uncontrollable factors. Moreover,

substantive efforts to control fishing for the primary purpose of gathering information about the stock is a responsible approach to stock management.

From the evidence of the four major cod stocks presented above, similarities, summarized below, are found between explanations for declines across the stocks, and in particular, in reference to the 2J3KL Northern Cod stock.

Recruitment failure

In all observed cases, stock declines were precipitated by a series of annual recruitment failures. This has, in turn, led to a dominance of a reduced number of year classes of harvestable ages in the stock, decreasing weight at age, increasing maturity at age, and higher relative fishing mortalities. While the recovery of a depleted stock depends on improved future recruitment, it is not clear that controlled exploitation, at any level, can ensure reproduction. The available evidence on stock-recruitment in cod is that modest changes in the size of the parent stock may not measurably affect the size of year classes that will be produced.

Fishing mortality

Retrospective analyses on the 2J3KL stock now indicate high rates of fishing mortality in recent years on the order of F=1.0 for fully recruited ages (7 to 9 years). These high Fs approximate the levels of fishing mortalities regularly attained by the other major stocks at or during stock declines. For Northern Cod, at the time, Fs were thought to be more on the order of F_{max} or approximately F=0.5. The argument then being, based on the evidence from other cod stocks (e.g., Norway, Iceland) being fished regularly at F greater than 0.7, was that F=0.5, or in this neighbourhood, was "sustainable". However, when combined with recruitment failure, higher Fs on fully recruited ages (7 to 9) shrink the dependency of harvest on these few year classes. When the low recruits reach these ages (in 1992) the results are predictable.

Ecosystem factors

In the case of North-East Arctic Cod, a decline in the Barents Sea capelin stocks was credited with the subsequent stock declines in cod. This is analogous to the 2J3KL situation where the abundance of capelin had an effect on the condition and survival of cod. The return of the capelin in the North-East Arctic Cod case, was similarly noted as reasons for the rapid recovery in the cod stocks. Recent evidence off Newfoundland for the recovery of capelin stocks[10] may indicate a similar pattern, as well. Analogous to the West Greenland stock declines, low water temperatures in 2J3KL are increasingly credited with the recent cod stock declines.

Survey variability

Difficulties in estimating the abundance of cod stocks is often noted. Rivard and Foy (1987, 977) in their study of errors in catch projections state that,

> ...the error of 30-47% for 2J3KL cod in 1980 and 1982 corresponds to a difference of about 70,000 t between the $F_{0.1}$ catch and the initial projection. This difference is small with respect to the catches that could result from the application of excessive fishing mortalities.

Wide swings occur in VPA assessed stock estimates. For example, the case of the 1989 to 1992 estimates for North-East Arctic Cod (Table 1), and the successive assessments by NAFO of the 2J3KL stock (June 1992 and June 1993) show a halving of the spawning stock biomass estimate and a threefold increase in estimated F for 1991. The reliance on indexed vessel surveys for determining estimates is not consistent with dynamically shifting and migrating stocks. As Sinclair (1993) notes, in the case of 2J3KL cod:

> The only significant concentrations were located outside the normal survey area in waters 930m deep where the foreign fleet was fishing (Sinclair 1993, 55).

The indication here is that stock estimates may not account for such occurrences and lead to potential bias in results. If stock status estimates are to rely primarily on survey results (as is the overwhelming case in Atlantic Canada[11]), variability and their sources

---

[10]Report on the Status of Pelagic Fishes. May 1994. p.5.

[11]The case of 2J3KL Northern Cod stock assessments document this point. The assessment estimates are calibrated against survey results. Commercial catch and effort data have been excluded as an index of abundance on the basis of model fit

need to be systematically diagnosed and incorporated into the estimation process.

Information needs

It is evident that more reliable information would be helpful in improving our understanding of stock status. This important consideration is noted as policy in the recent ICES assessment of the Faroe Bank cod stock:

> Since the groundfish surveys do not seem to describe the state of the stock accurately enough, the Working Group recommends that a strictly controlled fishery be set up in order to obtain the required indices of abundance. This must be based on the same vessels every year using comparable gear." (ICES 1993, 4).

With respect to Icelandic Cod, the recommendation of Baldursson, Danielsson and Stefansson (1993) is similar:

> ...the most difficult part of the problem is to determine how to build up a stock that has shrunk to a very precarious economical and biological level.... Thus, it seems likely that the right approach is to catch some cod each year while making sure there is an overwhelming probability of the stock size increasing.

Communality of these cod stocks with the Northern Cod stock suggest that such a policy of "controlled exploitation" could be applicable in that case as well. There is evidence that cod stocks have never completely disappeared even after decades of extensive fishing. The following sections describes and analyses a controlled exploitation strategy for 2J3KL Northern Cod.

NORTHERN COD: MORATORIUM VERSUS CONTROLLED EXPLOITATION

The bioeconomic impact of the closure of the 2J3KL Northern Cod fishery is examined by projecting its impact relative to a policy of controlled fishing at a reduced level. The performance of the alternative strategies are evaluated using the biological (stock) and economic (commercial fishery) model described in Lane and Kaufmann (1993).

---

performance. This issue is discussed further in Schnute and Hilborn (1993).

The strategies for 2J3KL cod are based on historical data for the period 1989 to 1992. The post 1992 period under the moratorium scenario is assumed to have fishing mortalities related to by-catch in the order of 20 thousand tonnes annually. Under the controlled exploitation strategy, post 1992 catches are twice this amount, or 40 thousand tonnes annually. Assuming the annual deterministic projection of stock biomass attains levels approaching the Dunne targets (Dunne 1990)[12], annual exploitation will be assigned at levels of $F_{0.1}=0.25$ to the end of the planning horizon at year 2001.

The deterministic age-structured population model is constructed using data from most recent stock assessment information for the 2J3KL cod stock. Model dynamics are based on well-defined relationships that have been used elsewhere (Rosenburg and Brault 1990, Schnute 1985, and Walters 1986) in modeling single stock population dynamics subject to exploitation. The model uses initial year stock data including numbers at age, average weight at age, partial recruitment, natural mortality and fishing mortality data (from the corresponding TAC schedule) to determine year-over-year stock at age distributions for

- numbers of fish,
- stock biomass, and
- catch (weight and numbers).

Table 2 presents a summary of model inputs and outputs for the test period, 1989 to 1992.

The deterministic commercial fishery model is subdivided into three sectors that represent the major activities in groundfish production in Atlantic Canada. These sectors include:

1. an inshore harvesting sector of fixed and mobile gear including traps, longliners, and small trawlers;
2. an offshore (domestic and foreign) harvesting sector comprised primarily of large mobile otter trawlers, and;
3. the processing sector comprised of plants that produce processed fish products.

---

[12]Northern Cod targets were 1.3 million tonnes of age 3+ cod and 650 thousand tonnes of age 7+ cod. The long term objective was to reach these targets by year 2000 after which fishing mortality levels of $F_{0.1}=0.25$ were to be enforced.

Table 2 : Initial Years Stock Age Distribution Values.

Global Parameters

Parameter	Value	Description
N	1600	Initial Stock Size (millions of cod), all ages at start of period 1989
M	0.2	Continuous rate of natural mortality (for all years and all ages of cod)

Age Input Parameters

Ages	1	2	3	4	5	6	7	8	9	10	11	12	13	14	15	16
Initial (%)	14.6	35.7	20.7	10.4	5.95	4.49	4.55	2.2	0.73	0.32	0.17	0.06	0.04	0.03	0.03	0.03
PR	0	0	0	0.14	0.4	0.7	1	1	1	1	1	1	0.5	0.5	0.5	0.5
Ave Wt (kg)	0.1	0.24	0.42	0.68	1.02	1.45	1.88	2.19	2.57	3.07	3.78	5.02	6.41	8.45	10.47	10.97

Start of Year Numbers (millions of fish)

Ages	3	4	5	6	7	8	9	10	11	12	13	14	15	16
Years						---- millions of fish ----								
1989	250	166	95	72	73	35	12	5	2.7	1	0.6	0.5	0.5	0.5
1990	275	201	119	53	30	23	11	4	1.6	0.9	0.3	0.3	0.2	0.2
1991	157	220	137	58	17	7	5	2	0.8	0.4	0.2	0.1	0.1	0.1
1992	120	71	158	66	16	5	3	2	0.8	0.2	0.1	0.1	0.05	0.05
1993	100	97	56	116	45	3	3	1.6	1.1	0.5	0.1	0.1	0.07	0.04

Initial Years Values

Year	F	Catch (,000 tonnes)
1989	0.968	253
1990	1.300	219
1991	1.280	171
1992	0.274	45

The economic status of the primary (harvesting) and secondary (processing) sectors in the fishery depend on the annual exploitation levels. Annual economic measures of comparison are calculated for each defined sector of the fishery and include:

- Net Operating Income (the difference between operating revenues and costs including labour),
- Cash (the Net Operating Income less fixed costs, debt expense, and income tax payable), and
- Value Added (the Net Operating Income plus labour less fixed costs).

Input data for the three sectors of the cod fishery are taken from Lane and Kaufmann (1993). All values estimate real 1991 prices and costs. The data are applied to each year of the planning period, 1991-2001.

Comparative Results - Deterministic Analysis

The results of the deterministic model analyses for the two scenarios for Northern Cod are presented in tables 3-6. The biological (tables 3 and 4) and economic (tables 5 and 6) implications of the two strategies are discussed below.

Population Dynamics. For both scenarios, the reduced fishing mortality levels after 1992 contribute to expected growth in the stock even at lower than historical average recruitment levels (200 million versus 300 million age 3 cod annually). Under the moratorium, stock biomass indicators roughly attain the Dunne (1990) target levels by 1999 (table 3). For the controlled exploitation scenario, the same target levels for 3+ and 7+ biomass are met one year later in 2000 (table 4). The return to fishing at $F_{0.1}$ levels result in TACs of approximately 170 thousand tonnes. Under the existing assumptions, this represents an equilibrium catch level for the stock. Biomass levels at the end of the planning period are stable and nearly identical for both scenarios at levels over 1.1 million tonnes of 3+, and approximately 650 thousand tonnes of 7+.

Fishing mortalities for the controlled exploitation scenario are approximately twice those of the moratorium over the control period. However, consistent with the inter annual growth, exploitation of 20 or 40 thousand tonnes annually results in Fs well below 0.2 and falling to below 0.1 in the moratorium and control periods.

Table 3 : Deterministic Model Stock Summary Report: Moratorium Scenario.							
Year	Catches (,000 tonnes)				Fishing Mortality	Biomass (,000 tonnes)		Ave Wt (kg)
	Inshore	Offshore	Foreign	Total	F	Age 3+	Ages 7+	Ages 5+
1989	103	114	36	253	0.968	609	265	1.46
1990	113	79	27	219	1.300	518	150	1.31
1991	60	62	49	171	1.280	431	70	1.13
1992	20	15	10	45	0.275	350	55	1.08
1993	18	2	0	20	0.082	393	116	1.31
1994	17	3	0	20	0.062	479	255	1.45
1995	17	3	0	20	0.054	578	294	1.59
1996	17	3	0	20	0.045	685	355	1.59
1997	17	3	0	20	0.037	810	404	1.59
1998	17	4	0	21	0.031	952	510	1.68
1999	130	48	0	178	0.025	1104	651	1.77
2000	123	45	0	168	0.025	1101	646	1.81
2001	122	45	0	167	0.025	1106	648	1.84

Note:
1. Inshore, offshore and foreign catches are based on an 80%, 20%, 0% split of total catch.
2. Average weights (Ages 5+) are for the estimated start of year cod population numbers.

Table 4 : Deterministic Model Stock Summary Report: Controlled Exploitation Scenario.							
Year	Catches (,000 tonnes)				Fishing Mortality	Biomass (,000 tonnes)		Ave Wt (kg)
	Inshore	Offshore	Foreign	Total	F	Age 3+	Ages 7+	Ages 5+
1989	103	114	36	253	0.968	609	265	1.46
1990	113	79	27	219	1.300	518	150	1.31
1991	60	62	49	171	1.280	431	70	1.13
1992	20	15	10	45	0.274	350	55	1.08
1993	30	10	0	40	0.170	393	116	1.31
1994	29	11	0	40	0.136	459	237	1.44
1995	29	11	0	40	0.122	538	257	1.56
1996	29	11	0	40	0.105	625	298	1.53
1997	29	12	0	40	0.088	731	329	1.52
1998	29	11	0	40	0.072	851	415	1.59
1999	29	11	0	40	0.061	981	532	1.66
2000	127	46	0	173	0.250	1114	646	1.74
2001	126	46	0	172	0.250	1113	653	1.80

see table 3 notes.

Daniel E. Lane and Halldor P. Palsson

Table 5 : Deterministic Model Economics Summary Report: Moratorium Scenario.

Year	Inshore Catch (,000 t)	Gross Revenue ($,000)	Year End Cash ($,000)	Value Added ($,000)	Harvest Employ (PYs)	Inshore Catch (,000 t)	Gross Revenue ($,000)	Year End Cash ($,000)	Value Added ($,000)	Harvest Employ (PYs)
1989	103	69,554	13,537	49,592	2,369	114	78,172	5,631	55,551	685
1990	113	75,411	15,373	53,768	2,599	79	53,393	2,018	37,761	474
1991	60	39,503	6,705	28,165	1,380	62	41,299	43	28,960	374
1992	20	13,449	251	9,589	460	15	10,511	-3,760	7,446	93
1993	18	11,874	-222	8,466	404	2	1,693	-5,258	1,209	15
1994	17	11,812	-318	8,422	397	3	1,929	-5,455	1,379	17
1995	17	12,060	-329	8,599	401	3	1,985	-5,587	1,431	17
1996	17	11,680	-491	8,328	389	3	2,255	-5,687	1,625	19
1997	17	11,464	-608	8,173	381	3	2,431	-5,783	1,756	20
1998	17	11,692	-610	8,336	389	4	2,583	-5,879	1,864	22
1999	130	90,031	19,040	64,192	2,997	48	33,902	-1,358	24,429	287
2000	123	85,083	18,241	60,664	2,831	45	31,563	-1,519	22,738	267
2001	122	84,574	18,482	60,301	2,816	45	31,796	-1,522	22,913	269

Note:
1. Gross Revenues are total sector Northern Cod landed values.
2. Year End Cash position is based on assumed depreciation and calculated income tax payable.
3. Value Added figures are calculated as Gross Revenue less Operating Costs plus Labour Costs.
4. Employment figures are based on 23 person years (PYs) per 1000 tonnes of Northern Cod for the inshore and 6 person years per 1000 tonnes for the offshore.

Economic Impacts. The inshore and offshore sector summary reports of tables 5 and 6 for the two scenarios detail the commercial sector impacts. The major advantage of the controlled exploitation strategy (table 6) is noted as a consequence of the doubling of employment in harvesting and processing in the post 1992 period relative to the moratorium case (table 5). Economic benefits from low level exploitation result in an income earning inshore sector and a profitable processing operation from cod. The limited degree of the controlled exploitation effectively means that perhaps as many as two or three offshore vessels, and as many processing plants can continue to operate viably dedicated to cod.

Comparative Results - Stochastic Analysis

Analysis of uncertainty typically involves describing the key sources of random fluctuations in model inputs and quantification of the impact these fluctuations make on model outputs. This is carried out in a stochastic simulation analysis of the population dynamics and economic impacts models for cod. Randomness in cod population dynamics are applied to the following model inputs:

1. *Natural mortality*. The continuous rate of natural mortality, M is assumed to vary uniformly between 0.15 and 0.25 in each year.

2. *Stock-recruitment*. Annual numbers of age 3 "recruits" are determined as a "flat" Beverton-Holt function of the size of the spawning stock (cod ages 7+) biomass that approximates 200 million age 3 fish annually for the post 1994 period. The randomized stock-recruitment relationship is assumed to have log normally distributed errors with a normally distributed single parameter, having mean zero and standard deviation of 0.25.

3. *Initial population distribution*. In this analysis, the total number of cod across all age classes (ages 1 to 16 years) in 1989 is assumed to be normally distributed with mean equal to 1600 million fish and standard deviation of 300 million fish.

4. *Weight at Age*. Randomized weight at age data were calculated to correspond to the range of values imputed from annual data. Annual realizations were made based on a uniform distribution of weight at age between the "low" and "high" values.

5. *Cod Prices and Costs*. All unit prices and cost at age data for the harvesting and processing sectors are subject to random annual

Daniel E. Lane and Halldor P. Palsson

Table 6 : Deterministic Model Economics Summary Report: Exploitation Scenario.

Year	Inshore Catch (,000 t)	Gross Revenue ($,000)	Year End Cash ($,000)	Value Added ($,000)	Harvest Employ (PYs)	Inshore Catch (,000 t)	Gross Revenue ($,000)	Year End Cash ($,000)	Value Added ($,000)	Harvest Employ (PYs)
1989	103	69,554	13,537	49,592	2,369	114	78,172	5,631	55,551	685
1990	113	75,411	15,373	53,768	2,599	79	53,393	2,018	37,761	474
1991	60	39,503	6,705	28,165	1,380	62	41,299	43	28,960	374
1992	20	13,449	251	9,589	460	15	10,408	-3,774	7,373	92
1993	30	20,316	1,901	14,485	693	10	6,908	-4,549	4,917	60
1994	29	20,020	1,800	14,274	676	11	7,481	-4,638	5,340	65
1995	29	20,263	1,834	14,448	678	11	7,431	-4,731	5,347	63
1996	29	19,623	1,648	13,991	658	11	8,023	-4,777	5,770	68
1997	29	19,656	1,630	14,015	659	12	8,145	-4,864	5,867	69
1998	29	19,964	1,682	14,235	669	11	7,904	-5,015	5,688	67
1999	29	20,029	1,677	14,281	669	11	7,809	-5,131	5,621	66
2000	127	87,977	18,746	62,727	2,929	46	32,273	-1,623	23,238	274
2001	126	87,347	18,997	62,279	2,907	46	32,394	-1,449	23,339	274

see table 5 notes.

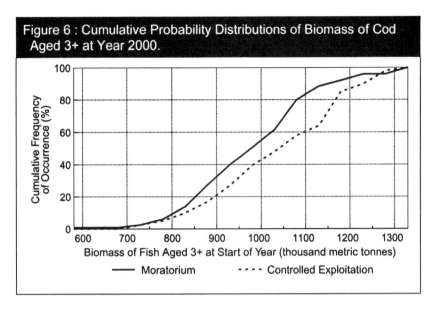

Figure 6 : Cumulative Probability Distributions of Biomass of Cod Aged 3+ at Year 2000.

fluctuations. Annual random realizations affect each age of cod similarly (where applicable). Cod prices and costs are assumed to vary from year to year uniformly at an amount plus or minus 20% of the deterministic value.

Each trial of the simulation model is initialized at the start of year 1989. The dynamics of the first four initial years, 1989 to 1992, are generated for annual random selections of M, and age 4 recruitment. The 1989 to 1992 TACs are fixed at actual values of 253 thousand tonnes, 219 thousand tonnes,171 thousand tonnes,and 45 thousand tonnes, respectively. These results provide the initialization of the stock by age distribution for 1993 when the scenario definitions apply. Thereafter, the generation of random natural mortality and recruitment combined with the selected total catch schedule for 1994-2001 determine the yearly distributions of stock at age.

Population Dynamics. Summary biological results of each simulation include annual descriptive statistics for 3+ and 7+ biomass values at year 2000. Summary results for the cases are presented in Figures 6 and 7. Figure 6 shows the relative frequency distribution for 100 trials of ages 3+ cod biomass at year 2000 for the moratorium and controlled exploitation, respectively. Similarly, Figure 7 shows the relative frequency distribution for 100 trials of ages 7+ cod (spawning stock) biomass at year 2000.

Expected biomass levels do not exceed the specified targets levels at 1994 and 2000 for either scenario. From Figure 6 and Table 7, it can be noted that of the 100 trials in the simulation of both TAC strategies, only about 10 out of the 100 trials were observed to be at or above the 3+ biomass target in year 2000 (1.3 million tonnes). Similarly comparable measures of riskiness were found for the year 2000 ages 7+ spawning stock biomass (10% of observations at or above the 650 thousand tonne target). A summary of statistical measures for ages 3+ and 7+ biomass measures of the population dynamics are found in Table 7.

Economic Impacts. The economic results of the stochastic analysis for the two scenarios measure total discounted operating incomes. These aggregate measures are nearly identical for both cases with very little differences in any one discount indicator. Effectively, the inter annual differences are "washed out" in the aggregate: the moratorium scenario benefits from an additional year of fishing at $F_{0.1}$; whereas the controlled exploitation strategy earns ongoing benefits throughout the post 1992 control period. This being said, there are no costs imputed

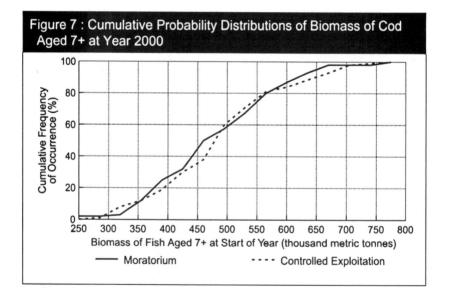

Figure 7 : Cumulative Probability Distributions of Biomass of Cod Aged 7+ at Year 2000

Item	Mean	Std Dev	95% CI on Mean	Range min	max	t-test on Mean	% Above Target
Table 7 : Summary of Simulation Results for Moratorium and Controlled Exploitation.							
Moratorium							
Ages 3+ Biomass, Start of Year 2000	963,000 tonnes	139	935-991	530	1303	-24.24 H$_0$:μ=1300	10%
Ages 7+ Biomass, Start of Year 2000	485,000 tonnes	108	463-506	216	790	-15.37 H$_0$:μ=650	10%
Total Discounted NOI - Inshore	$176,400,000	15.6	173-180	133	216	-	-
Total Discounted NOI - Offshore	$37,600,000	9.6	35.6-39.5	18	59	-	-
Total Discounted NOI - Processing	$376,200,000	51.3	366-386	264	516	-	-
Controlled Exploitation							
Ages 3+ Biomass, Start of Year 2000	965,000 tonnes	130	939-991	685	1294	-25.76 H$_0$:μ=1300	5%
Ages 7+ Biomass, Start of Year 2000	476,000 tonnes	105	455-497	267	746	-16.57 H$_0$:μ=650	10%
Total Discounted NOI - Inshore	$164,900,000	11.6	163-167	132	193	-	-
Total Discounted NOI - Offshore	$32,500,000	8.2	30.9-34.1	15	54	-	-
Total Discounted NOI - Processing	$343,200,000	40.9	335-351	253	479	-	-

for subsidies under the moratorium period that could otherwise be relieved in the controlled exploitation strategy.

CONCLUSIONS

We challenge the policy to close the fishery versus controlled operation of the fishery at lower levels. To evaluate these options of alternative stock rebuilding strategies, a bioeconomic model of the Northern Cod stock is presented that examines the "tradeoffs" between harvesting and moratorium. We conclude that a strictly controlled exploitation strategy would not be detrimental to the resource, *ceteris paribus*, and would provide valuable socioeconomic and stock information benefits. A coordinated program of exploitation specifically designed and allocated to the harvesting sectors as partners in research on the spatial and temporal tendencies of the stock would provide the extension of much needed longitudinal information on stock dynamics. This comanagement aspect provides for continued information to be collected to increase knowledge of the fishery system dynamics, scientific testing and analysis of specific hypotheses, and a forward looking (versus retrospective) view toward system controllability. The moratorium effectively severs the flow of stock observations and results in a substantial information loss that has "value" relative to the management capability.

This paper suggests that radical changes take place in the way stock information is gathered (Lane and Stephenson 1995). These include moving from the current independent research vessel survey information system with its aggregated and static stock assessment procedure, toward a dynamic ongoing accounting of the intra seasonal and inter seasonal stock dynamics through ongoing catch monitoring. This requires:

- a spatial and temporal view of fish stocks;
- development of a "partnership" (as opposed to an adversarial) relationship between the harvesting sector and fisheries managers, and;
- a strategic forward-looking view of fisheries decision making that includes the need to develop ongoing operational hypotheses and target-setting on unknown stock abundance.

REFERENCES

Alverson, L., D. Beamish, J. Gulland, P. Larkin, and J. Pope. 1987. *A study of trends of cod stocks off Newfoundland and factors influencing their abundance and availability.* A report to the Honourable Tom Siddon, Minister of Fisheries by the Task Group on Newfoundland Inshore Fisheries. Ottawa: Department of Fisheries and Oceans.

Baldursson, F. M., A. Danielsson and G. Stefansson. 1993. *On the Rational Utilization of the Icelandic Cod Stock.* Demersal Fish Committee, ICES Statutory Meeting. ICES CM 1993: G56.

Cushing, D. H. 1982. A simulacrum of the Iceland cod stock. *J. Cons. int. Explor. Mer.* 40(1):27-36.

deYoung, B. and G. A. Rose. 1993. On recruitment and distribution of Atlantic cod (Gadus morhua) off Newfoundland. *Canadian Journal of Fisheries and Aquatic Sciences* 50:2729-2741.

Dunne, E. B. 1990. Report of the Implementation of the Task Force on Northern Cod. Ottawa: Supply and Services Canada.

FRCC. 1993. *1994 Conservation Requirements for Atlantic Groundfish.* Report to the Minister of Fisheries and Oceans.

Garrod, D. J. 1988. North Atlantic cod: fisheries and management to 1986. Chapter 8 in *Fish Population Dynamics.* 2nd ed., edited by J. A. Gulland. New York: John Wiley & Sons.

ICES. 1992. Report of the Arctic Fisheries Working Group, 25 August - 3 September 1992. Copenhagen.

ICES. 1993. Report of the North-Western Working Group, 3-11 May. Copenhagen.

Jakobsen, Tore. 1992. Biological reference points for North-East Arctic cod and haddock. *ICES Journal of Marine Science* 49:155-166.

Jentoft, S. 1993. *Dangling Lines: The fisheries crisis and the future of coastal communities. The Norwegian experience.* ISER No. 50. MUN. St.John's.

Jorgensen, T. 1992. Long-term changes in growth of North-east Arctic cod (Gadus morhue) and some environmental influences. *ICES Journal of Marine Science* 49:263-277.

Lane, D. E. and B. Kaufmann. 1993. Bioeconomic Impacts of TAC Adjustment Strategies: A Model Applied to Northern Cod. Pages 387-402 in *Risk Evaluation and Biological Reference Points for Fisheries Management,* edited by S. J. Smith, J. J. Hunt, and D. Rivard. Ottawa: Canadian Special Publications in Fisheries and Aquatic Sciences 120.

Lane, D. E. and R. L. Stephenson. 1995. Fisheries management science: the framework to link biological, economic, and social objectives in fisheries management. *Aquatic Living Resources* 8:215-221.

NAFO 1992. Report of the Special Meeting, Scientific Council, 1-4 June.

Restrepo, V. R, J. W. Baird, C. A. Bishop, and J. M. Hoenig. 1990. *Quantifying uncertainty in ADAPT(VPA) outputs using simulation: An example based on the assessment of cod in divisions 2J+3KL.* NFO SCR Doc 90/103.

Rice, Jake C. and Geoffrey T. Evans. 1988. Tools for embracing uncertainty in the management of the cod fishery of NAFO divisions 2J+3KL. *J. Cons. int. Explor. Mer.* 45:73-81.

Rivard, D. and M. G. Foy. 1987. An analysis of errors in catch projections from Canadian Atlantic fish stocks. *Canadian Journal of Fisheries and Aquatic Sciences* 44:961-981.

Rosenburg, A. and S. Brault. 1991. Stock rebuilding strategies over different time scales. *NAFO Science Council Studies* 16:171-181.

Schnute, J. T. 1985. A general theory for analysis of catch and effort data. *Canadian Journal of Fisheries and Aquatic Sciences* 42:414-429.

Schnute, J. T. and R. Hilborn. 1993. Analysis of contradictory data sources in fish stock assessment. *Canadian Journal of Fisheries and Aquatic Sciences* 50:1916-1923.

Sinclair, A., ed. 1993. Report on the Assessments of Groundfish Stocks in the Canadian Northwest Atlantic, 4-14 May. *Canadian Technical Report on Fisheries and Aquatic Sciences* No. 1946e.

Tjelmeland, S. and B. Bogstad. 1993. The Barents Sea capelin stock collapse: a lesson to learn. Pages 127-139 in *Risk evaluation and biological reference points for fisheries management,* edited by S. J. Smith, J. J. Hunt, and D. Rivard. Ottawa: Canadian Special Publications in Fisheries and Aquatic Sciences 120.

Walters, C. J. 1986. *Adaptive Management.* MacMillan.

5

UNCERTAINTY IN FISHERIES MANAGEMENT

Tim Lauck
Department of Mathematics
University of British Columbia

INTRODUCTION

A global assessment of fisheries finds that many fish stocks are at low population levels worldwide. Recent collapses in the cod fishery and losses of large numbers of Pacific Salmon indicate that Canada cannot consider itself immune to such problems. The reasons given for collapse are often attributed to some "natural" cause by management or politicians whereas the historical assessment often finds the stock is predisposed to catastrophe by overharvesting (Ludwig, Hilborn, and Walters 1993). The major dilemma facing resource managers is the necessity to make correct policy choices while having insufficient, wrong or conflicting information. Errors in policy may compound, amplified by underlying dynamics. Even assuming perfect information, natural or imposed variation hampers the decision making process. Under ideal circumstances most of the experts can still be wrong. Worse yet, chosen policies may lead to completely unpredictable human responses. Still, it is important to recognize that decisions often must be made under precisely these circumstances.

The notion of hedging is not new. Evolutionary biologists have found that many organisms employ bet hedging strategies that promote their long-term survival in stochastic environments (Lewontin and Cohen 1969, Kisdi and Meszena 1993, Clark and Yoshimura 1993). Similarly, the importance of diversifying one's portfolio in investment has proved itself both in theory and in practice. In fact it is

probably fair to say that the application of these principles distinguishes a gambler from an investor. Malkiel (1990) provides a
readable introduction, Cover and Thomas (1991) use information
theory and Samuelson (1969) or Merton (1969) provide the founda-
tions using stochastic optimal control theory.

THE BOUNDARIES OF GENERAL DYNAMICS

Perrings (1991) has eloquently advocated the precautionary approach
to problems of uncertainty. At one point the use of a stochastic
minimax theory is proposed. Unfortunately, there seems to be little
actual application of this method. In this section, boundaries on the
intrinsic growth factor are developed for a somewhat general model. It
is found that a few assumptions are still needed to pin down the
arbitrary nature of a general distribution. From this development the
basic portfolio theory can be easily understood. Subsequently, the
assumptions, analogies and limitations of the portfolio approach to
measures of "natural capital" or other economic measures applied to a
single or multiple fisheries resource are discussed.

Let X represent a measure of "capital". Let R be a replacement
fraction for that capital in one period. The value R may be determined
by its own dynamics that may depend on a variety of factors both
deterministic and random. In one period the growth (decay) of "capital" is given by

$$X_{t+1} = RX_t \tag{1}$$

where t is an index into the discrete period (time). In multiple
periods

$$X_{t+1} = R_t R_{t-1}...R_1 R_0 X_0 \quad \text{or} \quad X_{t+1} = X_0 \prod_{i=0}^{t} R_i \tag{2}$$

Consider the possible values of R. For now this will be taken to be
the open set $(0,\infty)$. The assumption $R \neq 0$ is an oversimplification. This
is because in natural populations or economic situations extinction or
bankruptcy can occur. The assumption $R < \infty$ is not restrictive for real
situations. Simply to avoid technicalities in deriving the general
results given by equations (17-20) below the values of R will now be
further restricted to take on a finite number of discrete values

$$0 < R_1 \leq R_2 \leq \ldots \leq R_m < \infty \tag{3}$$

We now can view the dynamics above in two different ways, either as the evolution of the state (capital) or the evolution of a weighting system (distribution) on the values r_i. For example if $R_0 = 1.1$, $R_3 = 0.9$, $R_3 = 1.1$ and $X_0 = 1.0$ then the evolution of the state variable in time is $X_0 = 1.0$, $X_1 = 1.1$, $X_2 = 0.99$, $X_3 = 1.089$. The corresponding evolution of the weights on possible R values is $(1.1)^1(R_k)^0$, $(1.1)^1(0.9)^1(R_k)^0$ and $(1.1)^2(0.9)^1(R_k)^0$ where R_k stands for the remaining values of R which are all weighted 0. The last entry could also be written $((1.1)^{2/3}(0.9)^{1/3})^{t=3}$ which shows the structure of the distribution $(2/3,1/3)$ on the values 1.1 and 0.9. This distribution will continue to change in time as more values are observed.

Using the alternative dual view the dynamics of equation 2 may be written as

$$X_t = X_0 \prod_{i=1}^{m} R_i^{w_i} = X_0 \left(\prod_{i=1}^{m} R_i^{p_i} \right)^t \tag{4}$$

where $\sum_{i=1}^{m} w_i/t = \sum_{i=1}^{m} p_i = 1$ \hfill (5)

In other words each possible value of R will appear 0 or more times. The product as shown in equation (4) is a weighted geometric mean of the R values that have appeared up to time t. Now consider the following problem: if the mean m and variance v of the sequence of R values is known (these actually cannot be known without knowing the joint distribution perfectly), what are the upper and lower bounds for the geometric mean growth g? To answer this, consider maximizing and minimizing the geometric mean where the r_i may vary and the first two moments are known. The p_i are considered arbitrary but fixed.

$$\max_{Ri} \prod_{i=1}^{m} R_i^{p_i} \tag{6}$$

$$\text{subject to} \quad \sum_{i=1}^{m} p_i R_i = m \tag{7}$$

$$\sum_{i=1}^{m} p_i R_i^2 = m^2 + v \tag{8}$$

Taking the log of the objective and using Lagrange multipliers

$$\pounds(R_i, \lambda_i, \lambda_2) = \ln(\prod_{i=1}^{m} R_i^{p_i}) - \lambda_1 \Sigma p_i R_i - \lambda_2 \Sigma p_i R_i^2 \qquad (9)$$

$$\frac{\partial \pounds}{\partial R_i} = p_i(1/R_i - \lambda_1 - 2\lambda_2 R_i) = 0 \qquad (10)$$

For $p_i \neq 0$

$$R_i = \frac{\lambda_1 \pm \sqrt{\lambda_1^2 + 8\lambda_2}}{-4\lambda_2} \qquad (11)$$

Equation (11) implies that for an extrema the weights are only on two R values. Further since each R_i is strictly positive,

$$\lambda_1 > 0 \qquad (12)$$

$$\lambda_2 < 0 \qquad (13)$$

$$\lambda_1 - \sqrt{\lambda_1^2 + 8\lambda_2} > 0 \qquad (14)$$

The first two constraints on the lagrange multipliers in equations (12) and (13) indicate that increasing the mean or decreasing the variance while holding the other fixed will increase both maximum and minimum geometric mean provided the weights p_i on each R_i stay the same.

It is sufficient to solve the constraint equations for the two R values to find the extrema values. Equations (7) and (8) become

$$p R_1 + (1 - p)R_2 = m \qquad (15)$$

$$p R_1^2 + (1 - p)R_2^2 = m^2 + v \qquad (16)$$

Solving this equation yields two pairs of R values corresponding to the maximum g^* and minimum g_*. The representation for the distribution associated with g_* is

$$R_1 = m - \sqrt{v(1 - p)/p} \quad \text{with probability } p \qquad (17)$$

$$R_2 = m + \sqrt{vp/(1 - p)} \quad \text{with probability } 1\text{-}p \qquad (18)$$

The distribution for the maximum g^* is

$$R_1 = m + \sqrt{v(1-p)/p} \quad \text{with probability } p \qquad (19)$$

$$R_2 = m - \sqrt{vp/(1-p)} \quad \text{with probability } 1\text{-}p \qquad (20)$$

What happened to all the p_i if they were fixed? They were not fixed in the normal sense for a distribution because each weight was attached to its corresponding R_i. In comparing a non extremal distribution to an extremal one, it is found many p_i amalgamated in to p or $(1\text{-}p)$ when all the R_i became one of two values. Some readers may find the discrete treatment inadequate. Please refer to Krein and Nudelman (1977, chapter 4, theorem 1.1) to get started on a far more general and quite different treatment of these types of extrema problems. Using the general theory, the extrema results above also hold for arbitrary distributions.

The maximum (minimum) geometric mean is a decreasing (increasing) function of an increasing value p. The limiting values for the geometric mean are 0 and m regardless of any non zero variance. It appears that nothing is learned by adding the variance since these same boundaries would result if only the constraint on the mean were used in the optimization problem. However, the variance constraint has restricted the form of the distribution. To attain the extreme value m for example, a small amount of probability mass is pushed towards ∞ while most of the mass concentrates just below the mean value. Now add another condition: an upper and lower bound on the set of replacement multipliers R. When the set is restricted to $0 < A \le R \le B < \infty$ the extrema p value may be determined. The largest geometric mean possible corresponds to the smallest p possible which corresponds to R_1 (equation 19) as large as possible or

$$B = m + \sqrt{v(1-p)/p} \quad \text{and} \qquad (21)$$

$$p = v/(v + (B-m)^2). \qquad (22)$$

Substituting all these values into equation (6) and working similarly for the lower bound, the expressions for the most optimistic and pessimistic geometric mean growth given the assumptions are

$$g^* = \left(B^v(m - \tfrac{v}{B-m})^{(B-m)^2} \right)^{1/(v+(B-m)^2)} \qquad (23)$$

and $\qquad g_* = \left(A^v(m - \tfrac{v}{m-A})^{(m-A)^2} \right)^{1/(v+(m-A)^2)} \qquad (24)$

In the case of an added assumption of symmetry about the mean equation (23) becomes

$$g^* = \sqrt{m^2 - v} \qquad (25)$$

This result can also be obtained by squaring the first few terms of the familiar Taylor series expansion of the geometric mean

$$g \approx m - \tfrac{v}{2m} \qquad (26)$$

by dropping the v^2 term and taking the square root.

The results so far are summarized in figure 1. For arbitrary horizons and distributions meeting mean, variance and boundary constraints, boundaries on g lie between two curves. The curves are functions of the coefficient of variation and the boundary assumptions on each r_i. The following principles should be evident. If $g > 1$, growth is occurring so this condition would be desirable for a recovering population. Reducing variance while holding the mean constant or increasing the mean while holding the variance constant increases g^* and g_*. Continual use of mean performance in a deterministic model that is designed to "sustain" the population (capital) certainly results in $g < 1$ (extinction or bankruptcy). A more specific model may include density dependence, but its growth factors must be contained within this more general picture. Assumptions about density dependence would guide our beliefs about when $g > 1$ and when $g < 1$ for multiple time periods. If the time period is long enough, we might expect $g = 1$ or $g = 0$ if we include extinction.

Complete objectivity is a myth. Bayesian methods assume something about the prior distribution and assume something about the form of the model then update this information on the basis of incoming information. Often the idea is to learn more about the model by the incoming data and update model parameters (Walters 1986). The approach adopted here so far has required assumptions about boundaries on the growth multipliers. All models consistent with this

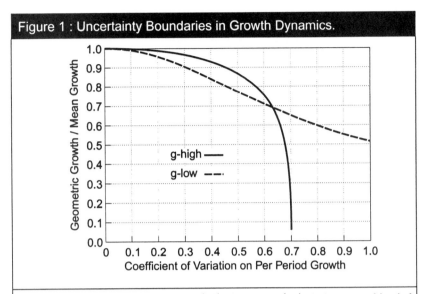

Figure 1 : Uncertainty Boundaries in Growth Dynamics.

This figure provides example upper (g^*) and lower (g_*) limits on multiperiod growth (g) given assumptions on the per period growth factor $R : A/m = a \leq R/m \leq b = B/m$. The upper limit is independent of the lower limit assumptions and vice-versa except where the curves intersect which are absolute limits on $g = g^* = g_*$ or coefficient of variation $(\eta = \sqrt{v}/m)$. As an example suppose we assume all $R/m < b = 1.5$ and the $\eta = 0.4$. One can be sure that any multiperiod growth factor is never above about $0.93m$. This means that if the mean growth multiplier is used the actual multiperiod equivalent for the growth factor will be at best about 7% regardless of any other modelling assumptions or the length of period considered. Imagine the effect of setting a policy for a supposed nice comfortable mean growth factor of 1.03. In five periods we could expect about $(0.93)^5 m \approx 0.7m$. Further if we believe all R stay above $(a = 0.2)m$ the multiperiod growth factor could be as low as about $0.83m$ where m is the mean. If we only make the boundary assumptions we can be sure the coefficient of variation η is between about 0 and 0.63 and the geometric growth mean is between about 0.7 and 1.0.

assumption will then fall somewhere in the bounded region of a type indicated by figure 1. If any assumptions about a coefficient of variation can also be given, this narrows the range of uncertainty in the growth rate. Additional assumptions about model dynamics are necessary such as density dependence or the form of environmental or demographic stochasticity to say more about the limits of uncertainty. If one of these models is developed it should fall within these boundaries. Any model which makes optimistic predictions outside the boundaries should not be used to construct policy.

THE PORTFOLIO PROBLEM

The principle of portfolio diversification or portfolio rebalancing can be easily derived from the principles developed. In a portfolio there are a number of financial instruments each producing their own relative returns m_i. Since each return is uncertain and not completely correlated, the idea is to hedge — not completely trust a belief in which particular stock will rise the fastest next period — and place some capital in a very safe asset, thus spreading investment capital across a number of different financial instruments. The hope is a reduction in the coefficient of variation while still maintaining a high mean growth. In a growing market these strategies have a number of optimality properties (see Cover and Thomas 1992). In a catastrophic market, safe assets may prevent bankruptcy.

Let a_{ij} represent the proportion of capital allocated to a given financial instrument during the ith period. Then in the above model

$$R_i = \sum_j a_{ij} m_j \tag{27}$$

The Markowitz method minimizes variance of all the possible R_i while maintaining a desired mean constant.

Note that in the sum in equation (27) there is generally always a safe asset that will grow at the inflation rate $m_1 = 1$. In doing the above optimization, one generally finds allocation over a number of financial assets and allocating some resources to safe assets is a wise plan. Using the minimax theory developed above we find that the optimization reduces the coefficient of variation, likely pushing the growth path between two more efficient boundaries (see figure 1) while maintaining the mean. This likely increases performance. Another method directly optimizes the geometric mean growth. Here the R_i are just as in the Markowitz method. Cover and Thomas derive optimality conditions and prove a number of optimality results for ergodic markets. The methods of stochastic optimal control theory or dynamic programming can extend these ideas to multiperiod problems with state dependency. The models can be complicated considerably when some assets may be frozen for a number of periods so that movement of capital is not as easy.

It is worth noting that steps are taken in advance to prevent catastrophe by holding safe assets and that there is a certain degree of humility involved in acknowledging that one cannot really predict the swings of the market or individual financial instruments. One reason for hedging is that it may optimize long term growth. But one can hedge even further than any optimization problem. It is always possible to put more money in a safe asset than is called for by any optimization problem. When hedging is used in this sense one is hedging beyond the model used to solve the optimization problem, anticipating perhaps more uncertainty than modeled or simply adopting a greater risk-averse stance. Constructing a portfolio requires some knowledge about the distribution of relative returns for each asset. This can be difficult to anticipate. The principle is still used in spite of the difficulty.

Now the use of this type of philosophy to fisheries management and economics is explored. First the use of a reserve to hedge against uncertainty in the control of overharvesting.

A BASIC FISHERIES MODEL

Concern about a stock is often amplified when the stock is in trouble. This is translated to a call for increased management action or attention. There may be a variety of social, economic and political problems associated with the fishery. Suppose that a wish list can be agreed upon. It might contain the following characteristics:

- An improving stock
- An improving harvest
- Hedge against short term economic disasters
- Hedge against management errors
- Hedge against environmental degradation

Assumptions:

- The fish stock has the potential to grow in size if left alone. While not precisely true when the stock reaches density dependent conditions, it is assumed here that the stock is at low levels and will take time to recover. Otherwise extraordinary measures might be necessary to save the stock and it should not be considered for harvesting.
- Management is effective most of the time but because of uncertainty related to imperfect control of harvest is not effective

all of the time. In other words, actual harvests may occasionally
exceed quotas to a significant degree.
- A reserve area can be established, where harvesting does not
  occur. This assumption may not be completely defensible.
  Poaching, migration, schooling and other behavior will have an
  impact.
- Reserve and managed stocks eventually mix uniformly. With a
  properly designed reserve the assumption may be a good
  approximation.

Questions:
- Can a reserve policy achieve the wish list objectives?
- How should reserves and managed (i.e. exploited) areas be
  apportioned?

Let:
   X_t : be the biomass at the beginning of season t,
   N : denote the natural unharvested replacement multiplier,
   H : indicate a random variable: fraction harvested,
   h : be the designated fraction to harvest and
   a : be the proportion of stock protected by a marine reserve with
   $\ln(g)$: the percentage growth rate of the stock given reserve, harvest-
          ing and natural growth.

Consider the dynamics shown in figure 2. First the current stock X_t
grows to the amount NX_t. Proportion a is set aside in a marine reserve
while $1-a$ is to be managed and exploited. This means that $aN\,X_t$ is
protected while $(1-a)NX_t$ is available for managed harvesting. Harvesting cannot be completely controlled and the basis for catch limits may
rely on faulty or uncertain information. Let the random variable H
from an unknown distribution model this uncertainty. Then the harvest
is the random quantity $(1-a)\,N\,X_t\,H$. The remaining biomass or escape-
ment $(1-a)\,N\,X_t\,(1-H)$ is assumed to mix (after harvesting) uniformly
with the portion in reserve $a\,N\,X_t$ yielding

$$X_{t+1} = X_t N(a + (1-a)(1-H)) \tag{28}$$

as the biomass before growth in the next season. The dynamics
continue in this way until some carrying capacity is reached. At this

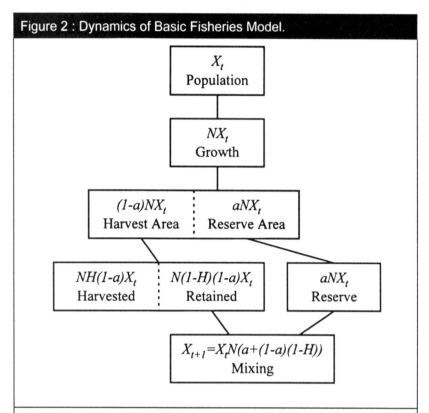

Figure 2 : Dynamics of Basic Fisheries Model.

The population grows to $X_t N$. Proportion a is held in reserve. A fraction H is harvested in the exploited region taking a total of $X_t NH(1-a)$. The remaining portion $X_t N(1-a)(1-H)$ mixes with the reserve population $X_t Na$ forming the population in the next generation. Uncertainty in harvest H is manifest by a failure to attain any desired control value h. For any biologically reasonable distribution with $E(H-h) \geq$ (uncertainty can be theoretically reduced to zero by setting $H = 1$ and $a = 1 - h$ while simultaneously improving the expected net growth in this period. The mixed strategy of allocating reserve and exploited areas "hedges" against overexploitation.

point wish list items 1 and 2 above cannot be met, so only recovery is considered in this model.

Analysis:

The dynamics up to time t are given by the following equation:

$$X_t = X_0 \prod_{i=1}^{t-1} N_i(a + ((1-a)(1-H_i)))$$ (29)

In general the multiplier and percentage growth rate are

$$g = \prod_{jk} (N_k(a + (1-a)(1-H_j)))^{p_{jk}} \tag{30}$$

$$\ln(g) = \sum_i p_{jk} \ln(N_k(a + (1-a)(1-H_j))) \tag{31}$$

$$\text{subject to } (1-a)E(H) \geq h \tag{32}$$

Equation (32) includes the potential for over harvesting by allowing a potential bias in harvesting. If management is not disturbed by a history of over harvesting, it might use the equality condition. Of course it is possible that $(1-a)E(H) \leq h$. Then management is attempting to adapt to over harvesting or apply more conservative measures. From the previous general development

$$R_i = N_i(a + (1-a)(1-H)). \tag{33}$$

Suppose the variability in the natural growth N_i is independent of the control efforts. Then

$$E[R_i] = E[N_i](a + (1-a) - (1-a)E[H]) \tag{34}$$

$$X_t = X_0 \prod_{i=1}^{t} N_i(a + ((1-a)(1-H_i))) \tag{35}$$

Now it can be shown that if the expected percent yield is fixed with $E[H] \geq h$ then increasing the reserve size and increasing h results in an improved growth rate for any reasonable distribution on H. A fixed percent yield is not necessarily "optimal" but is often justifiable in some prevailing political climates where many different parties may claim a share of the resource or the cost of a shutdown of industry may be costly. It is also for simplicity and to illustrate the mechanics of the hedging argument.

Since the control only influences the last product in equation (35) and the expected value constraint on H, equation (32) is entirely equivalent to an expected value constraint on R_i. We want to make all the factors $(a + (1-a)(1-H)))$ equal for the extrema — zero variance. This is theoretically achievable by the policy

$$H_i = 1 \text{ and} \tag{36}$$

$$a = 1 - h \tag{37}$$

The results are really common sense. Uncertainty in control is reduced to zero (theoretically) by the use of a large enough reserve. More interesting cases include poaching in the reserve area or density dependence. For poaching it is better not to use quite as large a reserve. Too much poaching is infeasible. The density dependent case can be solved using an algorithm similar to McNamara (1990).

CONCLUSION

In this paper an attempt has been made to explain the basics of portfolio theory and its relationship to the geometric mean growth. This gives a unified perspective on risk management and its relationship to population modeling. The boundary growth rates have been established and arbitrary population models may be tested for robustness. The basic growth model was introduced and it was found that establishment of reserves can improve productivity to a point where the growth rate is optimum. The model is highly abstract yet its implications cannot be completely dismissed. Further, the simplistic observation that any control policy may be mediated through a reserve strategy indicates the importance of considering the reserve in more general contexts. The reserve policy is likely also useful in multistage models as well. Here the protection of natural structure may be more important than previously thought.

Managers have a tendency to tamper with the age structure not really understanding if it has an evolutionary (survival) purpose. Beyond the simple model there are interesting problems in multiple fisheries to investigate. Obviously it is some advantage to be flexible economically, but these considerations must be balanced with the extraction. The portfolio approach may be useful for the allocation of effort and real capital as well as the maintenance of healthy populations.

REFERENCES

Brassard, Gilles and Paul Bratley. 1988. *Algorithmics, Theory and Practice*. Prentice Hall.

Clark, Colin W. 1990. *Mathematical Bioeconomics. The Optimal Management of Renewable Resources*, 2nd edition. New York: Wiley.

Clark, Colin W. and Gordon R. Munro.1975. The Economics of Fishing and Modern Capital Theory: A Simplified Approach. *Journal of Environmental Economics and Management* 2:92-106.

Clark, Colin W., Frank H. Clarke, and Gordon R. Munro. 1979. The Optimal Exploitation of Renewable Resource Stocks: Problems of Irreversible Investment. *Econometrica* 47:25-47.

Clark, Colin W. and Jin Yoshimura.1993. Optimization and ESS Analysis for Populations in Stochastic Environments. *Lecture Notes in Biomathematics* 98:26-62, edited by Jin Yoshimura and Colin W. Clark. Springer-Verlag.

Cover, Thomas M. and Joy A. Thomas. 1991. *Elements of Information Theory*. New York: Wiley.

Functowicz, Silvio O. and Jerome R. Ravetz. 1991. *A New Scientific Methodology for Global Environmental Issues*. New York: Columbia University Press.

Kamian, Morton I. and Nancy L. Schwartz. 1991. Dynamic Optimization, The Calculus of Variations and Optimal Control. In *Economics and Management*, 2nd edition. Amsterdam: North-Holland.

Kisdi, Eva and Geza Meszena. 1993. Density Dependent life history evolution in Fluctuating Environments. *Lecture Notes in Biomathematics* 98:26-62, edited by Jin Yoshimura and Colin W. Clark. Springer-Verlag.

Krein, M. G. and A. A. Nudelman. 1977. *The Markov moment problem and extremal problems: ideas and problems of P. L. Chebysev and A. A. Markov and their further development....* Translated by D. Louvish. Providence, RI: American Mathematical Society.

Lande, Russel, Steiner Eigen and Bernt-Erik Saether. 1995. Harvesting of fluctuating populations with risk of extinction. *American Naturalist* 145(5):728-745.

Lewontin, R. C. and D. Cohen. 1969. On population growth in a randomly varying environment. *Proceedings of the National Academy of Science USA* 62:1056-1060.

Ludwig, Donald, Ray Hilborn, and Carl Walters. 1993. Uncertainty, Resource Exploitation, and Conservation: Lessons from History. *Science* 260:17.

Malkiel, Burton G. 1990. *A Random Walk Down Wall Street: Including a Life-Cycle Guide to Pesonal Investing*. 5th edition. New York: Norton.

Mangel, Marc and Colin W. Clark. 1988. *Dynamic Modeling in Behavioral Ecology*. Princeton University Press.

McNamara, John M. 1991. Optimal Life Histories: A Generalisation of the Perron-Frobenius Theorem. *Theoretical Population Theory* 40:230-245.

Merton, Robert C. 1969. Lifetime portfolio selection under uncertainty: The continuous-time case. *Review of Economics and Statistics* 1:247-257.

―――. 1971. Optimum Consumption and Portfolio Rules in a Continuous Time Model. *Journal of Economic Theory* 3:373-413.

Puterman, Martin L. 1994. *Markov Decision Process*. New York: Wiley.

Perrings, Charles. 1991 *Reserved Rationality and the Precautionary principle: Technological Change, Time and Uncertainty in Environmental Decision Making. Ecological Economics. The Science and Management of Sustainability*. Columbia University Press.

Slastinikov, A. D. and E. L. Presman. 1984. Growth Rates and Optimal Paths in Stochastic Models of Expanding Economies. *IIASA 81 Stochastic Optimization*, edited V. I. Arkov, A. Shiraev and R. Wets. Springer-Verlag.

Samuelson, P. A. 1969. Lifetime portfolio selection by dynamic stochastic programming. *Review of Economics and Statistics* 1:236-239.

Walters, Carl. 1986. *Adaptive management of renewable resources*. New York: Macmillan.

6

LIMITED ENTRY FISHING PROGRAMS : THEORY AND CANADIAN PRACTICE

Diane P. Dupont
Department of Economics
Brock University

INTRODUCTION

Fisheries on both coasts of Canada are currently facing crises with respect to sudden and seemingly inexplicable reductions in the biomass of many commercially important species. It appears that scientists have vastly overestimated the expected returns of fish to many of Canada's key commercial fisheries, e.g., Pacific Salmon and Atlantic Northern Cod. The process of estimating the stock size of migratory fish species is subject to many uncertainties, not the least of which is the amount of fishing effort directed at the fishery. Given that these fisheries have been subject to limitations on the quantities of inputs used to take the harvests, these recent revelations suggest that these restrictions have been unsuccessful at preventing the near collapse of some of Canada's most important fisheries. This calls into question the usefulness of these management schemes in achieving the goal of biomass preservation. This paper examines both the theoretical and empirical reasons behind the failure of license limitation to satisfy the goal of stable harvests.

LIMITED ENTRY IN THEORY

In 1954 H. Scott Gordon wrote an article which influenced the direction of fisheries management policy in North America, Australia, and New Zealand for decades to come. His analysis explains how a self-reproducing fish stock can generate a resource rent, defined as the difference between the sustainable revenue and the total cost of harvest effort. In his model, the economically sustainable stock level is the one that maximizes this rent. He then argues that an unrestricted or open access fishery is unlikely to achieve this goal. The presence of a positive resource rent in such a fishery acts as an inducement for continual increases in the level of fishing effort until rents are driven to zero by the excessive harvesting costs of too many fishers. Equilibrium in this model is characterized by the total dissipation of resource rents, thereby putting an end to entry of new fishers, and a reduction in the fish stock below the economically sustainable size (also known as maximum economic yield or MEY). This equilibrium is suboptimal because the fishery could yield positive resource rents and maintain a larger biomass if harvesting effort could be contained.[1]

The basis for the divergence of the open access equilibrium from the socially optimal one is the lack of property rights in the fish stock. Since there is no security of tenure, it is not advantageous for a participant in an open access fishery to leave any fish in the sea. Each fisher continues to increase his efforts to catch a portion of the stock, so long as positive rents persist. He does not consider the impact of his activities, either on other fishers, or on the future availability of fish. Ultimately, the actions of all fishers combine to drive the fish stock below its optimal sustainable level. This is what Munro and Scott (1985) term a Class I form of rent dissipation. The major consequence of this economic overexploitation is that too few fish are left in the sea to contribute to future biomass growth. This implies higher harvesting costs in the future.

The obvious policy prescription emerging from Gordon's analysis is that the government (or regulator) of the fishery should place an overall quota on the allowable number of fish that can be caught during the fishing season, a so-called Total Allowable Catch (TAC). This permits a sustainable resource rent to emerge because, in theory, the policy guarantees that the biomass will evolve to the maximum economic yield level.[2] In practice, this policy can fail because of the

---

[1] Anthony Scott (1955) extended the Gordon model by examining the intertemporal dynamics of the fish stock. The basis conclusions of his model coincide with those of Gordon, however.

[2] This is less than maximum sustainable yield (MSY), the biological goal in many Canadian fisheries. MSY is calculated by assuming that harvesting costs are zero.

likelihood of the occurrence of a Class II form of rent dissipation. When the government restricts the total harvest of a fishery via a TAC, but does not have perfect control over the effort employed to catch the fish, the presence of above average returns (rents) in the fishery encourages the entry of additional effort. Entry once again continues until the total harvesting costs have risen to the level of total revenue. Complete rent dissipation is once again the fate of the fishery, however, the biomass is theoretically unaffected since the TAC policy is supposed to prevent it from falling to extinction levels.

Gordon's model, once again, provides a policy prescription for the Class II type of rent dissipation. It adopts the biologist's notion of fishing effort as the single input used by fishers in the capture of fish. As Rothschild (1972) points out, "... fishing effort is defined in terms of the catch: one unit of real or nominal effort is simply the numerical fraction of the average population that is caught." Rent dissipation occurs because the level of effort directed at the fishery is excessive. The theoretical solution is to limit directly the amount of effort directed at the fishery by permitting the minimum necessary effort needed to take the TAC. This is a limited entry or restricted access policy.

In practice, regulators have had difficulty in implementing such a policy. The difficulty arises because of the divergence between the theoretical construct called fishing effort and the reality of the bundle of inputs that comprise effort. Theoretically, effort is viewed as an index of fishing power. Using this definition, effort can be defined in standardized units per vessel, e.g., ton-hours of trawling, number of traps per year, etc., (Hannesson 1978; Roy, Schrank, and Tsoa 1980). This simplified view of effort as a single input at the fisher's disposal obscures the true nature of the fishing production function. The fisher uses many inputs such as vessels, labour, energy, and gear, to catch fish. When implementing a limited entry program, the real issue concerns which of the many inputs to restrict.

Ideally, the regulator should limit the overall use of a key input which has the crucial characteristic that it has few, if any, substitutes. If the underlying fishing production technology permits the substitution of unrestricted inputs for the restricted input, then fishers will use this avenue to improve their individual positions.[3] Limited

---

[3] This practice is often called "capital-stuffing", a term first coined by Bruce Rettig (1984).

entry does not remove the "race for the fish" mentality present in an open access fishery (Copes 1982) since competition still exists among the fishers, even though their numbers are reduced from an open access situation. Each of the remaining fishers tries to appropriate for himself the fish in the sea. To do so before one's competitors requires increasing one's fishing capability in whatever way permitted by the technology. As each fisher does this, the intentions of the regulation will be subverted. The result will be a Class II type of rent dissipation and ultimately this can cause the fishery resource rent to fall to zero.

LIMITED ENTRY IN PRACTICE

Canada has used limited entry for practically all of its commercially viable fisheries. Typically, the government issues a limited number of licenses. They are permits that convey fishing rights to a limited amount of some input. Inputs which have been licensed include vessels, fishers, and, gear (e.g., the number of traps, pots, or nets per vessel). In each instance, the government has begun the program by restricting only one input but has quickly moved to restrict additional inputs as fishers have increased the usage of unrestricted inputs.

This section presents a chronology of the license limitation programs used in each of 4 major fisheries in Canada : salmon and roe herring in British Columbia and lobster and groundfish in Atlantic Canada. The paper then evaluates the programs on the basis of several criteria. These are the effects of license limitation on the use of both restricted and unrestricted inputs, profitability, biomass and total harvest.

British Columbia Salmon Fishery

Prior to 1969 a TAC policy alone was used to control total harvests from year to year. Great concern was expressed regarding the excessive effort directed at the fishery, i.e., the number of vessels in the fleet was in excess of 6,100. In 1969 a limited entry licensing program was put into place. The licensed input was the vessel and licenses were given to existing fishers, a process called "grandfathering". Two types of licenses were issued: A type licenses conveyed permanent fishing rights, whereas B type licenses gave only temporary rights.[4]

---

[4] In this way, the regulator hoped to reduce the amount of effort. Ultimately, an appeal mechanism transformed some B licenses into A licenses.

During the early 1970's salmon prices rose. Because entry of new vessels was prohibited by the licensing program, this allowed resource rents to rise above zero. Responding to the new resource rents, fishers found a way to "increase" the restricted input, the vessel, by building bigger vessels because the license attached to the vessel did not restrict its size. In 1971 regulators placed further restrictions on input usage by introducing a ton for ton replacement rule. If an old vessel was replaced with a new one, the new vessel could have a net tonnage[5] no greater than that which it replaced. In this way, each license was limited to the net tonnage then present in the existing vessel.

Fishers responded to the increasing bite of the input restrictions in a predictable way. They retired two small vessels (e.g., gillnets) and their licenses in order to introduce a new, more powerful seine vessel with one license attached. This new vessel could be as large as the combined tonnage of the two retiring vessels. This practice of pyramiding meant that the effective catching potential of the new vessel was much enhanced relative to the smaller vessels it replaced. The government tried to make pyramiding more difficult by adding length restrictions to the ton for ton replacement rule in 1979. Finally, in 1980 the practice of pyramiding was made illegal. This effectively put a moratorium on the entry of new seine vessels into the fishery.

There have been fewer adjustments to the vessels in the last decade and very little new construction. However, trollers have improved the catching and keeping power of a vessel of fixed tonnage by adding on-board freezing equipment and using high-speed bow pickers (Department of Fisheries and Oceans, Pacific Region 1992). This was likely a response to area licensing regulations adopted in the early 1980s. These required trollers to choose between fishing locations inside and outside of the Strait of Georgia.

British Columbia Roe Herring Fishery

After facing a sudden large decline in the herring biomass in the 1960s, the government imposed a moratorium on fishing in 1967. By 1971 the herring had returned in sufficient numbers to warrant the resumption of a small experimental fishery, followed in 1973 by a much larger fishery. During this time, the roe herring fishery suddenly became extremely lucrative as the Japanese increased their demand for the

---

[5] Net tonnage is a rough measure of hold capacity.

product. Given the upward pressure on roe herring prices and mindful of the experience gained through licensing of the salmon fishery, the Department of Fisheries and Oceans moved quickly in 1974 to limit entry to the roe herring fishery by licensing established fishers.

At its onset, the goal was to create enough licenses to support 150 seine and 450 gillnet vessels (Pearse).[6] However, anyone who fished in 1974 was eligible to purchase an (annual) license for $2,000 (if the fisher used a seine vessel) and $200 (if the fisher used a gillnet vessel) and he could continue to purchase a license until January 1975.[7] In addition, the regulations allowed an existing licensee to purchase a second license, a provision of which most license holders took advantage. At the height of license ownership in the mid-1970s 270 licenses were purchased for seine vessels and 1,400 for gillnet vessels.

By licensing the fisher, the regulator hoped to see a natural attrition in the number of licenses as fishers retired or died, especially since licenses were technically not transferable to other individuals. However, lease arrangements and trust holdings of licenses were used to subvert this restriction.[8] Furthermore, the regulator assumed that control over the number of fishers meant control over the vessel (capital) used in the fishery since the licensee was required to designate annually the specific vessel that would be used during the upcoming fishing season. However, the fisher could change the designated vessel from year to year. Thus, while the total number of vessels participating in the fishery was limited, their catching power was not restricted. Licensees could and did lease or buy bigger and more powerful vessels as the fishery became more lucrative.

In response to the buoyant market for roe herring during the late 1970s fishers keenly went to the announced openings up and down the Pacific Coast. The presence of fishery rents encouraged fishers to increase the capacity and effectiveness of their gillnet punts through the addition of sonar, mechanical shakers and pullers, as well to improve their mobility and transportation speed. This led to virtually the entire fleet showing up at each fishery opening. There was so

---

[6] The choice of these numbers was presumably influenced by the number of vessels that participated in the 1973 fishery, i.e., 161 seiners and 223 gillnetters (Wilen 1981).

[7] Licensing of native Indian fishers continued until 1977. Such licenses were available for $10 per year.

[8] Finally, in 1979 the government formally suspended the "owner-operator" clause, which had proved ineffective at controlling effort.

much excess effort that openings that previously lasted hours would last minutes.[9]

In 1980, in an attempt to restrict the (still) excessive effort directed at the fishery, the government reduced the permitted net length of the gillnet vessel from 150 to 75 fathoms. (Since then, there have been additional restrictions on the length of the gillnet punt, the maximum gillnet mesh size, the number of nets per gillnet punt [one] and the maximum purse seine net length and mesh size.) During the 1980 fishing season, the regulator also introduced area licensing. The entire fishery was divided into areas and license holders were required to choose a single area for that year's fishing.[10] Their decisions were to be based upon the announced expected total allowable harvest for anticipated openings in each area.

In 1987 there was a further change to the provisions surrounding roe herring licensing. License holders could no longer lease their licenses to other fishers in return for a share of profits. This, of course, increased the opportunity cost to inactive[11] license holders and was, in part, an effort to encourage them to leave the fishery for good, thereby, lowering the potential effort that could be directed at the fishery.

Atlantic Lobster Fishery

This fishery is largely conducted inshore in Atlantic Canada by fishers using small boats of between 25 and 45 feet. Since 1914 traps have

---

[9] There was some attrition in the number of licenses, however, after the 1979 season. While the 1979 total harvest was unchanged from that of 1978, the fish were unevenly distributed across fishing grounds and some fishers were unlucky. For example, some areas had a total allowable catch limit that could be caught with one net set of a seine (Wilen 1981). At the end of that season some licensees dropped out of the fishery, leaving some 249 seine and 1,302 gillnet licenses outstanding.

[10] Currently, the entire fishery is divided into 5 areas for gillnet vessels and 5 areas for seine vessels.

[11] An issue of concern is the existence of inactive license holders. They chose not to participate during a fishing season, however, continue to have a future claim on the fishery by paying the annual license fee. They make a license buyback program less successful than would otherwise be the case. Suppose a buyback program is introduced in order to reduce the amount of effort directed at the fishery. Inactive licensees may be among the first to avail themselves of this method to retire from the fishery. Buyback of these licenses will not guarantee that actual fishing effort will be reduced. Since these fishers had already chosen not to fish, their effort was not counted in annual statistics.

been the only gear type legally permitted.[12] This fishery was the first in Canada to attempt a limited entry licensing program. In 1966 the regulator placed an upper limit on the number of traps which could be fished from each lobster vessel in one of the 8 Maritime fishing districts. In 1967 a second district was included in the regulations. Trap limits for each vessel were extended to all districts in 1968 (Scott and Tugwell 1981). Initially, trap limits per vessel were set higher than the actual number of traps used by fishers. This meant that the TAC could actually be taken with fewer than the maximum number of traps permitted in the fishery. This encouraged fishers who had been using fewer than the maximum number of traps allowed to increase the number of traps to the maximum allowed per vessel! As a result, the total number of traps increased by 5.6% over the period 1968-1972 (Scott and Tugwell 1981). The meant lower catches per trap and depressed incomes.

In addition to trap restrictions individual fishers were licensed using a 2-tier licensing system in 1967. Full-time fishers were granted transferable A licenses, whereas part-time fishers were granted non-transferable B licenses. These latter were intended to be temporary licenses. Their expiration was to bring about a reduction in the effort directed at the fishery.[13] In 1969 the regulations licensing and limiting the number of operators in the fishery were changed to introduce a limit to the number of vessels. Again, a distinction was made between A licenses (now attached to the vessel instead of the fisher) and B licenses. If a fisher with a B class license were to stop fishing, the license could never be renewed. If the fisher with the A license were to retire, he could sell his vessel and license.

In 1977 the licensing of vessels was revoked in favour of a return to the licensing of the fisher. The practice of distinguishing between A and B class licenses continued, as did the regulations regarding the maximum number of traps per vessel.

---

[12] In early attempt to limit harvesting effort resulted in the prohibition of trawling and diving.

[13] An exception was made for Newfoundland. In that province unlimited access to lobster fishing continued until 1976 (Department of Fisheries and Oceans 1985).

Atlantic Groundfishery

While the groundfishery is exploited by fishers in all Maritime provinces and Quebec, it has its greatest importance in the province of Newfoundland. Much of the discussion that follows concerns the management of the fishery in that province. Although the various species that comprise the groundfishery (e.g., Northern Cod, flatfish, haddock, etc.) are all currently subject to limited entry licensing, this management strategy was adopted in stages and did not become fully effective until 1977 for the offshore fishery (comprised roughly of vessels of 25 gross tons or more [Copes 1983]) and 1980 for the inshore fishery. In order to understand fully the experience with limited entry in this fishery, one must first look at the historical evolution of the fishery.

There was in fact a form of entry control in the fishery during the period of 1950 to the mid-1970s when offshore fishing vessels were not permitted to fish inshore. This restriction was effective and arose from the fact that there were two fisheries with separate fleets and separate administrations: the offshore and inshore fisheries. The offshore groundfish stocks were managed by the International Commission for the Northwest Atlantic Fisheries (ICNAF) and exploited by both Canadian and foreign fishing firms operating from large ocean going trawlers using mostly mobile gear, such as seines, and some fixed gear, such as gillnets and longlines. ICNAF set the annual TAC according to an MSY policy but permitted unrestricted access (Macdonald 1984). The inshore fishery was managed entirely by Canada. It consisted of fishers using small vessels under 65 feet in length that did not venture far from shore and used fixed gear like traps and gillnets. While the offshore fleet was not permitted to fish in the inshore, nonetheless the policy of unrestricted access in the offshore had an impact upon the inshore fishery. Because of the migration of the stocks from the offshore to the inshore, excessive offshore effort during the 1950s began to reduce the stock remaining for inshore fishers.

Prior to the 1970s it was not physically possible for the inshore fleet to reduce the total biomass below MSY, so it was Canada's policy to permit unlimited entry of fishers and vessels to that fishery. Not only was entry unrestricted, it was encouraged in two ways.[14] Firstly, the Federal government subsidized fishing activities with unemployment insurance (UI). Thus, it was possible for a seasonal fisher to collect UI, even though he was self- employed! Secondly, the provincial government of Newfoundland subsidized vessel purchases to 35% of the capital costs (Munro and McCorquodale 1981), in addition to providing subsidies for gear purchases. Furthermore, fuel purchases were made exempt from the provincial fuel tax.

Inshore harvests fell during the early 1970s. In response, regulatory effort was directed at the perceived problem, namely, the excessive capital in the offshore fishery. The government introduced the notion of limited entry in 1973 via the licensing of large, mostly offshore, groundfish vessels (i.e., those greater than 65 feet in length).[15] Mandatory licensing was extended to smaller vessels (e.g., otter trawlers under 65 feet) in 1976.

By 1974 the entire inshore groundfish harvest was equal to only 20% of the annual harvests in the 1950s. This crisis prompted the government to introduce mandatory licensing of all fishers in Newfoundland in 1974, however, it did not impose any limitations on entry. Instead, Canada requested and received from ICNAF a reduction in the foreign offshore harvest for 1975. The inshore fishery recovered and, since there were no barriers to entry in this fishery, the number of fishers grew.

In 1977 Canada took over the management of the entire fishery, both inshore and offshore, with the introduction of Extended Fisheries Jurisdiction (EFJ)[16] and introduced effective limited entry in the offshore fishery. In effect, only Canadian vessels were permitted to fish. Foreign fleets were allowed to take only fish that were surplus to Canada's needs. By 1977 there were only 80 licensed vessels in the Newfoundland trawler fleet, many of which were owned by a few large processing companies.[17] In addition, while Canada introduced a strict quota share (of the entire TAC) for the offshore fishery, there

---

[14] One of the major problems with the imposition of input controls has been the tendency of successive government administrations to use the fishery as an "employer of last resort" (Munro and McCorquodale 1981).

[15] In addition, a proposal to freeze the number at the 1973 level proved ineffective.

[16] This came out of the Third Law of the Sea Conference and gave Canada exclusive control of fisheries 200 nautical miles from its shore.

[17] In 1981 there were 135 such vessels in all of Atlantic Canada (Copes 1983).

was not an equivalent regulation regarding the overall size of the inshore harvest.

The combination of EFJ (with its promise of resource rents), along with no restrictions on entry in the inshore fishery and no overall inshore quota, encouraged even more participation in the inshore fishery. By the end of the decade there were 2098 vessels of between 20 and 65 length and more than 6000 vessels under 25 feet in Newfoundland alone (Munro and McCorquodale 1981).[18] Furthermore, over the period of 1973-1980 the number of fishers in three key management regions (2J, 3K, 3L) increased by 38.6% annually (from 6,821 fishers to 22,921)![19] At the same time, the overall inshore Northern Cod fish harvest (the mainstay of the inshore fishery) only went from 42.7 to 94.2 thousand tonnes (Munro and McCorquodale 1981).

With Canadian control there came a change in the method by which the TAC was determined. Canada adopted the $F_{0.1}$ goal which led to much lower annual TACs than the MSY goal pursued by ICNAF. Furthermore, these lower TACs had to be shared between the inshore and offshore fisheries. Canada had to contend with the fact that, because the offshore fleet was no longer largely foreign owned, competition between the offshore and inshore fleets for the stock was a zero-sum game insofar as Canada was concerned. A larger share of the TAC for the offshore fleet meant less for the inshore fleet. In 1980 Canada finally began to set an overall quota for the inshore fishery harvest in addition to the existing offshore quota.

It was not until 1980 that the Federal government effectively restricted entry into the inshore fishery by imposing a moratorium on the entry of all new vessels of any size using any type of gear (with the exception of certain parts of Newfoundland). Later in that year, it imposed a freeze on the issuing of new personal fishing licenses in the entire Atlantic. In 1981 the government adopted suggestions from the Levelton Report (1979) and established a new type of personal fishing license. A two-tier licensing system of fishers was adopted. Full-time fishers were given A licenses and part-time fishers were given B licenses. For example, in Newfoundland in 1981 there were 11,000 A

---

[18] For the entire Atlantic region there were 14,069 licensed vessels under 65 feet long in 1979 (Kirby 1982).

[19] While the number of fishers pursuing groundfish is marginally smaller, the annual growth rate of labour in the groundfishery for the same three regions was 38-39% (Munro and McCorquodale 1981)!

and 24,000 B licenses issued (Munro and McCorquodale 1981).[20] Of these, only some 1,200-1,300 fishers were engaged in the offshore fishery. The remainder, of course, participated in the inshore fishery (about 95%). While there were no attempts to reduce the number of B licenses explicitly, a B license could only be sold to a full-timer. At the time of transfer, all assets had to purchased. In addition, the new license holder was limited to the vessel length and capacity of the previous license holder. Thus, licenses were subject to a limited type of transferability. In this way, part-time fishers would be encouraged to retire from the fishery.

Since 1981 the regulator has sought new methods of control, including the adoption of an enterprise quota system for the offshore fishery[21] and the introduction of sectoral management for the inshore fishery.[22] Over the period of 1989-1992 there was a 33% decrease in the groundfish catch in Atlantic Canada (Task Force 1993). TACs to both the inshore and offshore fisheries have been reduced each year as the groundfish biomass — especially of the Northern Cod — has continued to fall. In July 1992 the Federal government announced a 2 year moratorium on the harvesting of Northern Cod in the face of a stock collapse.

EVALUATION OF LIMITED ENTRY PROGRAMS

Effects on Use of Restricted Inputs

Three of the limited entry programs have achieved moderate success. Both Pacific Coast fisheries and the Atlantic Lobster fishery have not only prevented an increase in the quantity of the restricted input — either the number of fishers or the number of vessels — but they have also managed to reduce the total quantity of the restricted input from

---

[20] For the entire Atlantic there were 24,269 A licenses and 24,165 B licenses (Kirby 1982).

[21] Four large vertically integrated fishing companies were each given a share of the TAC to be taken in the offshore fishery by company trawlers. Given the financial difficulties associated with reduced groundfish stocks during the 1980s only two such companies remain in operation.

[22] Each of the three sectors has been allocated a given share of the TAC. The purpose of this policy is to ensure an "even" distribution of fishing income across the various regions that comprise the entire Atlantic fishing area.

the pre-license limitation levels. This has been accomplished largely through buyback programs, aided in part by the cyclical nature of the fishery returns.

The Atlantic Lobster buyback program has been the most successful. In 1978 the Lobster Vessel Certificate Retirement Program came into effect for Nova Scotia and New Brunswick (Scott and Tugwell 1981). This was a program designed specifically to buy back the fisher's license, permitting him to fish, and not to buy back his vessel. The intention at the program's inception was to retire 1,060 A class licenses within 3 years. After 2½ years of operation the program had bought back and retired 1,027 licenses in New Brunswick and Nova Scotia. During the period 1980-1982 approximately 50% of the licenses were retired (Department of Fisheries and Oceans 1985).

Buyback in the British Columbia Salmon fishery took place in two stages. The initial stage was instituted in 1971. License fees were doubled in order to fund the purchase and retirement of vessels. The program was abandoned in 1974 after 362 vessels had been purchased at a cost of $6 million in 1971 dollars (Crowley, McEachern, and Jaspere 1990).[23] As fishery rents rose, their values became capitalized into the licenses. Officially, licenses were not transferable, however, in practice, the sale of the vessel included the sale of the license. Regulators could no longer afford to purchase licenses of retiring vessels. The second stage of the buyback program took place in 1981. Again, rising prices meant rising license values. The program saw 36 boats retired at a cost of $2.9 million in 1981 dollars (Crowley, McEachern, and Jaspere 1990).

Prior to license limitation, more than 6100 vessels fished for salmon. By 1982 this had fallen to 4,528 (Dupont 1991) and in 1990 only 4,508 vessels reported landings of salmon (Department of Fisheries and Oceans, Pacific Region 1992). However, there has been a change in the fleet composition in favour of bigger and more diversified operations. For example, the seine fleet (comprising the biggest vessels) has grown from 370 vessels in 1969 to 536 in 1990. The number of multipurpose, multigear (gillnet-troll) vessels first

---

[23] The majority of these vessels were gillnet and troll vessels. On average, catching ability of these vessel types is low relative to that of the seine vessel, the largest and most powerful of all vessel types in the fleet.

increased over the 1970s in response to gear restrictions, but it has fallen from 1,020 (1982) to 978 (1990).

There has been some rationalization in the British Columbia roe herring fishery, as well. For example, in the early years of licensing (1974) there were some 270 licenses that could be used on seine vessels and 1,400 that could used on gillnet vessels. By 1990, these numbers had fallen to 239 and 954. The larger decrease in gillnet vessels is the result of the 1990 implementation of a new regulation requiring fishers in the popular Strait of Georgia area to hold two gillnet fishing licenses (Chalmers 1991).

Unfortunately, limited entry management in the Atlantic ground-fishery has not even had the limited success of the other programs. In practice, entry has not really been strictly controlled. For example, the number of groundfish licenses in 1979 was 14,132 for the entire Atlantic area. This had increased to 15,671 in 1986 and to 16,565 in 1991 (Task Force 1993).[24] There are more offshore vessels now (90 in 1989) than in 1977, the first year of limited entry in that fishery (Department of Fisheries and Oceans 1989). They employ about 1,800 licensed fishers. While the number of inshore vessels has not changed much, the number of registered full time inshore groundfishers in Newfoundland has fallen marginally from 11,000 in 1981 to 10,365 in 1989.

Until the crisis in 1992 no attempt was made to rationalize the fishery either by easing fisher retirement or by attempting a reduction in the number of species licenses through a buyback scheme. The Government announced the Northern Cod Adjustment and Recovery Program (NCARP) in 1992 (Department of Fisheries and Oceans, Economic Policy and Analysis Branch 1992). Among the measures that are planned to rationalize the fishery are the Northern Cod Early Retirement Program (a program to ease retiring fishers out of the fishery) and the Northern Cod Licensing Retirement Program (a program to remove a large number of active fixed gear groundfish licenses).[25]

---

[24] To some extent these numbers are somewhat misleading since some of the ground-fish species were not subject to limited entry over the entire period. Furthermore, there have been periodic exemptions from licensing for certain types of gear, e.g., handrakes and handlines. Nonetheless, the existence of such exemptions and different rules regarding entry and license transferability in the various fisheries is indicative of a certain degree of confusion regarding the administration of the licensing program.

[25] For the 1993/94 fiscal year the Federal Government had approved $40 million to fund this program (Department of Fisheries and Oceans 1992/93).

Effects on Use of Unrestricted Inputs

While there has been limited success in terms of the ability of limited entry to control the amount of the restricted input component of overall fishing effort, none of the programs have been able to control effectively the amounts of the unrestricted inputs used by fishers. (Dupont 1991). In each of the four limited entry programs fishers have responded to input controls (e.g., restrictions on the number of vessels or their size or the number of fishers or traps) by increasing the use of unrestricted inputs.

Much of the input substitution activity of fishers has been directed towards purchases of electronic equipment, capital deepening through the acquisition of hydraulic traphaulers on lobster boats, and an increasing reliance upon vessel speed (and, fuel consumption) to ensure that one's vessel wins the race for the fish (Pearse 1982). For example, Fraser (1979) estimated that the amount of capital employed in the British Columbia salmon fishery increased by about 50% over the period 1969-1979. There have been no ancillary regulations in any fishery placed upon fishers with regard to the amount of fishfinding equipment (such as sonar, loran, and depth-sounders) used on a vessel, nor on the use of freezing equipment. There have been some attempts on the part of the regulator to restrict fuel consumption, through the use of area licensing, e.g., in both Pacific coast fisheries and to some extent in the Atlantic groundfishery. They have been reasonably successful at preventing rent dissipation through the excessive use of this input.

In each case, the catching power of the reduced fleet has been increased well beyond the number of fish available for capture. For example, the Scotia-Fundy active inshore groundfish fleet consisted of 2,300 longlines and gillnets and 400 draggers in 1989. This represented twice the capacity needed to take the available fish (Department of Fisheries and Oceans 1989).[26]

In addition to the input substituting activities within a given fishery, there have been spillover effects into other fisheries when one fishery is subject to limited entry and a second is not. Fishers have increasingly directed their inputs at new fisheries and this has led to excessive

---

[26] If one were to include the 1,000 inactive vessels, then there would be four times the fishing capacity needed!

effort levels directed at these fisheries. In response, the regulator has adopted limited entry for more and more species, e.g., in the Atlantic groundfishery. A second example of this type of behaviour comes from an examination of the British Columbia Salmon and Roe Herring fisheries. Many fishers participate in both fisheries because the latter takes place in March and April and the season for the former begins in May/June and lasts until September.[27] The presence of rents in one fishery has encouraged excessive capitalization in the second. For example, a herring gillnet punt needs speed in order to get to a fishery opening. These gillnet vessels have more fishing power than the vessels they replaced. When they are used in the salmon fishery, this means that more fishing power is directed at that fishery.

Effects on Profits

While data on profitability are few, it is possible to draw some conclusions through indirect observation. First, given that licensed fishers have earned resource rents or profits (or expectations of profits), they have had additional funds to spend on improving the catching ability of their vessels. This phenomenon has been observed in all fisheries. Second, with the possibility of the transfer of the license granting permission to fish, the resource rent will come to be capitalized in the license value, i.e., license values will reflect the capitalized value of potential future resource rent earnings from the fishery. Those programs which have adhered most strictly to limitations on entry, and have managed to reduce the number of licensed participants, have generated the largest profits.

During the 1970s a large number of salmon licenses were "traded"[28] as fishers responded to economic conditions and changing regulations. The value of the salmon license rose during this period to its all-time high of $7,000 (1979 dollars) per ton in 1979 (Department of Fisheries and Oceans, Pacific Region 1992). Since that time, license values have remained positive, but smaller since the fishery has had some lean years. For 1988, the cost of leasing a roe herring license on a

---

[27] For example, in 1988 146 salmon seine vessels fished herring using seine gear and 61 seine vessels used gillnet gear to fish herring. In addition, more than 330 vessels in the gillnet, troll, and gillnet-troll fleets also fished herring using gillnets (Department of Fisheries and Oceans, Pacific Region 1992).
[28] Although not officially transferable, licenses were sold with the sale of a vessel and, in this way, they exchanged hands.

long-term basis — 99 years — was $750,000 for a seine vessel and $90,000 for a gillnet vessel (in 1988 dollars).

While comparable data have not been found for the Atlantic Lobster fishery, anecdotal evidence suggests that Nova Scotia lobster fishers are the most profitable in the Atlantic region (Department of Fisheries and Oceans 1989). The Report of the Task Force on Incomes and Adjustment in the Atlantic Fishery (1993) found incomes of Newfoundland fishers to be lower than those in other Atlantic provinces. Clearly, groundfishing is not as profitable a venture as some other fisheries in Atlantic Canada.

Effects on Biomass and Harvests

All four fisheries have experienced the unpredictable behaviour of the spawning biomass and, hence, annual harvests have not been stable. This would have been the case, even in the absence of limited entry. The issue is whether limited entry programs that have not perfectly controlled effort can consistently lead to harvests that exceed the stated TAC and, therefore, lower the spawning biomass, possibly to some threshold of extinction level.

While the intended effect of a limited entry policy is not so much to control harvests as it is to control the effort used to take a given harvest (TAC), nevertheless an ineffective restricted access program affects the regulator's choice of TAC (and, ultimately, the biomass in future years). First, imperfectly controlled effort often translates into more fishing power on the fishing grounds, particularly in terms of engine speed. This makes it easier for fishers to travel from one ground to another quickly, thereby increasing the difficulty of monitoring by the regulator. In order to operationalize the TAC policy, the regulator must keep track of each fisher's catches and then signal either a continuation of an opening or a closing. A larger number of participants (or more effective fishing power) on a fishing ground may easily translate into a larger than desirable number of fish taken, since once caught, most species cannot be returned to the sea. With more fishers to monitor the regulator may have a harder time achieving the desirable harvest or TAC for a specific fishing ground. Second, the presence of group of fishers with a vested interest in the fishery creates a stronger lobby group that can bring pressure to bear on the regulator for an increase in the TAC. Too many years of acceding to fisher's demands may well have implications for future biomass levels.

The accumulated effects of a number of years of harvesting beyond the TAC is more detrimental in fisheries which exhibit depensatory (especially critical depensatory)[29] behaviour in the stock-recruitment relationship, e.g., herring (Clark 1976). If these fish are too heavily exploited the population can suddenly fall close to zero as happened in the herring fishery in the late 1960s prior to limited entry. It is a testimony to the British Columbia herring roe limited entry program that this has not reoccurred. In fact, the harvest levels have been fairly consistent over the past 10 years. For example, since 1983 the harvests have averaged 26,000 tonnes, but in 1990 there was a record high harvest of 33,846 tonnes. The salmon harvest has also had its ups and downs over the period, but the trend in the last 8 years has been toward increasing harvests. Finally, the Nova Scotia fishery has enjoyed increasing lobster landings over a similar period of time. In 1987 landings were 38,030 tonnes, rising to 41,827 tonnes in 1992 (Department of Fisheries and Oceans, Policy and Program Planning various years).

It is noteworthy that the limited entry programs previously identified as enjoying good harvests are the more successful of the ones that this paper has discussed. Notable in its absence is the Atlantic groundfishery. Landings have consistently fallen in this fishery over the last 10 years. For example, landings of cod were 458,051 tonnes in 1987, 308,325 tonnes in 1991 and 187,526 tonnes in 1992 prior to the moratorium (Department of Fisheries and Oceans, Policy and Program Planning various years). Many suggestions have been made as to the exact causes of the reduction in the cod biomass. It is beyond the scope of this paper to comment on them. However, the ineffectiveness of the limited entry program in the Atlantic groundfishery almost certainly played its part in the current crisis facing that fishery.

CONCLUSIONS

Canada's experience with limited entry has had mixed success. It appears to have functioned best either in newly established fisheries (e.g., roe herring), or when the regulator persists in closing the gaps

---

[29] Depensation in the stock-recruitment relationship means that the population growth rate increases at an increasing rate at low levels of the population. The corollary is a sudden drop in the growth rate as the population drops below a certain level. Critical depensation means that there may be some minimum viable population level which is greater than zero.

through which input substitution can take place and when the regulator buys back licenses in order to reduce the amount of the legally sanctioned effort. Recently, this type of management scheme has not found as much favour with regulators as it once did, perhaps, because of the practical difficulties in these conditions being met.

Currently, the focus in fisheries management policy has shifted toward the creation of "quasi-property" rights or individual transferable vessel quotas (ITVQs) for a number of ocean fisheries. This is a revolutionary approach to fisheries management since it cedes some limited right of ownership (in the form of a given share or quantity of fish) to each fisher. The adoption of ITVQs will mean the rationalization of an individual fisher's efforts at taking a given quantity of catch and in this way reduce the likelihood of Type II rent dissipation. However, there will still be a important role for the regulator to play in the determination of the annual TAC.

Based upon Canada's experience with limited entry one might conclude that the effectiveness of an ITVQ policy would be enhanced by delineating the ITVQ as a share of the annual TAC, not as a stated quantity of fish. Furthermore, strict penalties for over catching one's quota should be imposed upon malefactors. Finally, the most important lesson for ITVQs that can be gleaned from Canada's experience with limited entry is the following. Any policy which does not reduce the "race for the fish" mentality will still carry with it the incentive for each fisher to ensure that he has enough effort to capture the fish before his competitors do. This observation would argue in favour of defining the ITVQ over not only the species and the quantity of catch, but also with reference to a specific time period and geographical location.

REFERENCES

Chalmers, D. D. 1991. *Review of the 1989-1990 British Columbia Herring Fishery and Spawn Abundance.* Department of Fisheries and Oceans. Canadian Industry Report. Fisheries and Aquatic Sciences No. 207.

Clark, C. W. 1976. *Mathematical Bioeconomics.* New York: John Wiley and Sons.

Copes, P. 1982. Implementing Canada's Marine Fisheries Policy: Objectives, Hazards, Constraints. *Marine Policy* 6(2):219-232.

——— 1983. Fisheries Management on Canada's Atlantic Coast: Economic Factors and Socio-Political Constraints. *Canadian Journal of Regional Science* 1(1):1-32.

Crowley, R. W., B. McEachern, and R. Jaspere. 1990. *A Review of Federal Assistance to the Fishing Industry Since 1945.* Economic and Commercial Analysis Report No. 71. Canada Department of Fisheries and Oceans.

Department of Fisheries and Oceans. 1985. *Resource Prospects for Canada's Atlantic Fisheries 1985-1990.* Ottawa: Supply and Services Canada.

———. 1989. *Today's Atlantic Fisheries.* Ottawa: Supply and Services Canada.

———, Economic Policy and Analysis Division. 1992. *Structural Adjustment in the Northern Cod Fishery.* (mimeo). Ottawa: Supply and Services Canada.

Department of Fisheries and Oceans. 1992/93. *Atlantic Fisheries Restructuring Act.* Annual Report. Ottawa: Supply and Services Canada.

———, Pacific Region, Program Planning and Economics Branch. 1992. *Financial Performance of the British Columbia Salmon Fleet: 1986-1990.* Vancouver.

———, Policy and Program Planning. various years. *Canadian Fisheries Annual Statistical Review.* Ottawa: Supply and Services Canada.

Dupont, D. P. 1991. Testing for Input Substitution in a Regulated Fishery. *American Journal of Agricultural Economics* 73(1): 155-164.

Fraser, G. A. 1979. Limited Entry: Experience of the British Columbia Salmon Fishery. *Journal of Fisheries Research Board of Canada* 36:754-763.

Gordon, H. S. 1954. The Economic Theory of the Common Property Resource: The Fishery. *Journal of Political Economy* 62(1): 124-142.

Hannesson, R. 1978. *Economics of Fisheries.* Bergen, Norway: Universitetsforlaget.

Kirby, M. J. L. 1982. *Navigating Troubled Waters: A New Policy for Atlantic Fisheries.* Report of the Task Force on Atlantic Fisheries. Ottawa: Supply and Services Canada.

Levelton, C. R. 1979. *Toward An Atlantic Coast Commercial Fisheries Licensing System.* Report Prepared for the Department of Fisheries and Oceans.

Macdonald, R. D. S. 1984. Canadian Fisheries Policy and the Development of Atlantic Coast Groundfisheries Management. Pages 15-75 in *Atlantic Fisheries and Coastal Communities. Fisheries Decision-Making Case Studies*, edited by C. Lamson and A. Hanson.

Munro, G. R. and S. McCorquodale. 1981. The Northern Cod Fishery of Newfoundland. In *Public Regulation of Commercial Fisheries in Canada* Case Study No. 3. Ottawa: Economic Council of Canada.

Munro, G. R. and A. D. Scott. 1985. The Economics of Fisheries Management. Pages 623-676 in *Handbook of Natural Resource and Energy Economics*, volume II, edited by A. V. Kneese and J. L. Sweeney. Amsterdam: North-Holland.

Pearse, P. H. 1982. *Turning the Tide: A New Policy for Canada's Pacific Fisheries.* The Commission on Pacific Fisheries Policy. Final Report. Ottawa: Supply and Services Canada.

Rettig, B. 1984. License Limitation in the United States and Canada: An Assessment. *North American Journal of Fisheries Management* 4:231-248.

Rothschild, B. 1972. An Exposition on the Definition of Fishing Effort. *US Department of Commerce Fishing Bulletin* 70(3): 671-679.

Roy, N., W. Schrank, and E. Tsoa. 1982. The Newfoundland Groundfishery. *Canadian Public Policy* 8(2):222-238.

Scott, A. D. 1955. The Fishery: The Objectives of Sole Ownership. *Journal of Political Economy* 63(2):116-124.

Scott, A. D. and M. Tugwell. 1981. The Maritime Lobster Fishery. In *Public Regulation of Commercial Fisheries in Canada* Case Study No. 1. Ottawa: Economic Council of Canada.

Task Force on Incomes and Adjustment in the Atlantic Fishery. 1993. *Charting A New Course: Towards the Fishery of the Future.* Ottawa: Supply and Services Canada.

Wilen, J .E. 1981. The British Columbia Roe Herring Fishery. In *Public Regulation of Commercial Fisheries in Canada* Case Study No. 6. Ottawa: Economic Council of Canada.

7

INDIVIDUAL TRANSFERABLE QUOTAS AND CANADA'S ATLANTIC FISHERIES

R. Quentin Grafton
Department of Economics
University of Ottawa

INTRODUCTION

Fishery managers regulate fisheries to help ensure sustainability of the resource and to meet socioeconomic objectives. Input and effort controls have been the traditional method of regulation. While such approaches can be effective in preventing biological overfishing they have often proved ineffective in preventing economic overfishing.[1] Fisheries managed with input and effort controls have all too frequently been characterised by overcapitalization and excess competition among fishers that reduce the net return to fishers and the resource owners.[2]

The failure of input controls to control fishing effort and help ensure reasonable returns to fishers has stimulated fishery managers to use other forms of management. These management regimes have been based on the allocation and enforcement of property rights in the form of access and use rights in fisheries. One such instrument is individual transferable quotas (ITQs) which allocate a total allowable catch (TAC) among fishers in the form of individual harvesting rights.

---

[1] In the case of the Northern Cod fishery such regulations proved incapable of preventing either biological or economic overfishing.
[2] See, for example, Dupont (1990) for estimates of the costs of rent dissipation in the salmon fisheries of British Columbia where input and effort controls have been in place since the early 1970s.

ITQs, in contrast to input controls, operate on the principle that incentives rather than controls should be used to manage a fishery.

This paper examines the theory and practice of ITQs in various fisheries. Using the insights from these programs, the paper examines the consequences of expanding the use of ITQs in Canada's Atlantic fisheries.

THEORY OF ITQs

Fishers will harvest provided that expected returns exceed costs. In an open access fishery, fishers do not consider the costs they impose on others from harvesting a fish today (Warming 1911, Gordon 1954, Scott 1955).[3] Thus, in an open access fishery the total harvest will, in general, exceed the level that maximizes the net return from the fishery. ITQs, by ensuring that fishers must pay a price for harvesting an extra fish and providing them with a long-term interest in the resource can help change their behaviour and increase the net return from the resource.

Theoretically, if ITQs command a positive price fishers will take this into account when harvesting extra fish and, thus, can change the incentives faced by fishers. For example, a fisher wishing to increase her harvest under ITQ management must pay for the privilege of leasing or purchasing quota from another quota-holder. Similarly, fishers wishing to harvest only the quota they were initially assigned also face an implicit cost equal to the revenue foregone from not having sold or leased the quota to another. Thus, a share of the externality equal to the quota price is internalised by fishers with ITQs.

ITQs, however, will only maximise the net return from the fishery provided that there are no in-season stock externalities, such that the harvesting costs are invariant to the size and distribution of the biomass, and no congestion externalities, such that harvesting costs are invariant to the amount of fishing effort applied at a given location (Boyce 1992).[4] If ITQs do not, in general, lead to a first-best outcome

---

[3] An open access fishery may be defined as *res nullius* where there are no or ill-defined or unenforceable individual or communal rights with respect to use over the resource.

[4] Smith (1969) reviews the externalities prevalent in fishing.

they are, nevertheless, a desirable management tool if they result in a superior outcome to current practice.

In open access and most limited entry fisheries, each fisher is competing to catch some share of the total harvest. In this race for the fish, it may be profitable for an individual to invest in a faster vessel or in more sophisticated search gear so as to obtain a greater share of the catch. Such investment, although privately beneficial, does not increase the total harvest or total returns from the fishery, changes the distribution of returns among fishers, and increases total harvesting costs. In contrast in an ITQ fishery, where the quota are viewed as providing a durable and exclusive harvesting right, fishers may have a much greater chance of harvesting a given share of the TAC.[5] By ensuring that fishers only harvest their own quota, ITQs provide fishers with every incentive to minimise their costs because their gross revenue is more or less fixed by their quota-holdings.[6] In turn, this can help reduce overcapitalization and racing behaviour between fishers to "catch the fish before someone else".

ITQ management may also reduce the need for specific input controls and other types of regulations. It has even been proposed that the price of ITQs be used to set the TAC so as to maximise the net return from the fishery (Arnason 1990).[7] An example of an input control which, if removed, may increase the net returns of fishers is a limited fishing season. For example, allowing fishers to harvest year round instead of during a limited fishing season may enable fishers to land a higher quality product and increase safety at sea. Further, spreading the fishing season over a longer period can prevent sharp falls in prices brought about by a large increase in supply when fishing is restricted to only a few days. Allowing for transferability of the harvesting rights also permits more profitable fishers to harvest a greater share of the TAC. Such transfers should increase the total profits from the fishery and may change the structure of the industry as less profitable fishers exit through the selling or leasing of their quota to others.

---

[5] Scott (1989) reviews the notions of property rights and their characteristics with respect to the fishery.

[6] Fishers may, however, have the option of choosing the time to harvest which can affect the price and, hence, gross revenue.

[7] Heaps (1993) points out that setting a TAC using only the price of quotas will not, in general, be optimal if vessels are heterogeneous.

One other characteristic of ITQs is that they can provide fishers with an additional interest in the resource. This interest, represented by the value of the quota owned by individuals, may encourage more involvement in management by fishers. Cooperation among fishers in helping to manage the fishery, in collaboration with the owners of the resource, should improve both the management of the fishery and reduce the costs of regulation. Another form of cooperation, in the form of mutually beneficial agreements among fishers, may also be encouraged with ITQs through assigning quota on both a species and an area basis. When the gains from cooperative behaviour are sufficiently great and fishers can monitor the actions of others, one may observe the pooling of effort among fishers. For example, one fisher may specialise in search gear to find the fish and others in harvesting the fish with the returns shared according to some predetermined arrangement. In turn, this type of cooperative behaviour can reduce total fishing costs and the individual risk faced by fishers.[8] Scott (1993) has even suggested that ITQs, by "solving" the distribution question in the fishery, may even serve as a step towards achieving the goal of a joint fisher-ownership structure of the resource.

To ensure that the potential benefits of ITQs are realised, however, it is necessary that fishers view their quota as an exclusive and durable harvesting right. If it is the case that fishers who are not quota-holders are able to fish with impunity then the quota itself becomes valueless as a meaningful property right. A share of the externality imposed by harvesting is, therefore, not internalised and the race to fish still remains. The race for fish may also remain in so-called flash fisheries where the TAC is caught in a very short period of time even if there is adequate enforcement.[9]

ITQs, by restricting the harvest of fish that can be legally landed, also provide an incentive to maximise the return per quota unit. In turn, this encourages fishers to land a higher quality and valued product. It also has the effect of encouraging "high grading", whereby fishers dump at sea less desirable fish for which they have quota. Both quota-busting and high grading are potentially serious problems for

---

[8] An example of co-operative behaviour among fishers is provided by Wilen (1989) in a study of the British Columbia roe herring fishery.

[9] A flash fishery is one where the fishing season is very short for either biological or marketing reasons.

the sustainability of a fishery. These and other potential problems with ITQs are examined in detail by Copes (1986). In the following section, we examine the experiences of ITQ management and whether in practice ITQs have realised their theoretical potential.

EXPERIENCES WITH ITQs

ITQ programs have been implemented in a number of fisheries in several countries including Canada, Iceland, Australia, New Zealand, and the USA. These programs differ with respect to their restrictions on transferability, size of the fisheries, number of participants, and various other characteristics.

To evaluate the diverse experiences of these fisheries, it is necessary to use criteria to judge their successes and failures. The experiences of some but not all ITQ fisheries are evaluated according to the following criteria:

1. Changes in economic efficiency.
2. Changes in employment and harvesting shares of fishers.
3. Compliance with ITQs.
4. Cost recovery, management costs, and the capture of resource rents.

Changes in Economic Efficiency

There is evidence that ITQs have improved economic efficiency in a number of fisheries. In a survey of rights based management in Canada, Crowley and Palsson (1992) state that there have been efficiency gains with such regulations. Evidence of improvements in efficiency have also been documented in ITQ fisheries in Australia, New Zealand, and Iceland and have been characterised by reductions in fishing effort and an increase in profitability of fishers. These two issues are examined separately.

Reduction in Fishing Effort. One of the expected benefits of ITQs is that they can reduce the excess capital employed in the fishery. Depending upon the fishery, however, the removal of excess capital may involve an adjustment period of several years. For example, in fisheries where the earnings outside of the quota fishery are very low it will pay a vessel owner to keep fishing with an old vessel so long as the returns cover variable costs. In other fisheries where alternative

R. Quentin Grafton

Table 1 : Changes in Numbers of Vessels in Selected Canadian Rights Based Fisheries.		
Fishery	Number of Vessels Before Program	Number of Vessels in 1992
Herring (RTV)	16	11
Herring (4WX)	49	40
Offshore groundfish	139	115
Offshore scallop (4X, 5Ze)	73	61
Offshore lobster (4X, 5Ze)	8	8
Lake Erie	248	182 (1990)
Lake Winnipeg	800-1000	400-600
BC Sablefish	47	30
Sources : Cowan (1990), Crowley and Palsson (1992), Grafton (1992b)		

employment opportunities exist for displaced labour and capital, the structural change in the fishery brought about by ITQs may be quite rapid. A listing of the changes in vessel numbers in selected rights based fisheries in Canada is provided in Table 1. In most cases, the number of vessels employed in the fisheries declined with the intro-duction of ITQs.

The British Columbia (BC) Sablefish fishery is illustrative of the reductions in the number of vessels that can take place in the short run. In 1989, the year before individual vessel quotas (IVQs) were intro-duced into the fishery, there were 46 vessels harvesting the resource. In 1990, in the first year of IVQs there were only 30 vessels that actively fished for sablefish (Grafton 1995). The change in the harvesting pattern arose from transfers of fishing licences with quota among registered vessels in the fleet. This, in turn, resulted in a greater harvest and a higher profit per vessel. A similar adjustment also took place in the Lake Erie ITQ fishery. In 1983, the year before ITQs were introduced, there were some 248 vessels, in 1984 there were 242, and in 1988 there were only 182 vessels actively operating in the fishery (Cowan 1990). This represented a 27% decline over a four year period. It should be noted, however, that both the BC sablefish and Lake Erie ITQ programs have some of the least restrictive transferability provisions in Canadian fisheries.

In a review of Iceland's fisheries, Arnason (1986) notes that the number of vessels remained virtually unchanged in the first two years of the operation of ITQs. There was, however, a decline in the fishing effort measured as vessel tons/day at sea. On this criterion, aggregate fishing effort fell some 15% in the first year of the ITQ program in 1984 and then some 6% in the following year. It should be noted, however, that in the Iceland program vessels were allowed to opt for either quantity quotas or effort quotas. The effort quotas, which were removed in 1990, still provided an opportunity for fishers to compete among themselves and may have limited the reductions in fishing effort that would otherwise have taken place. Nevertheless, Arnason (1993) observed that although herring catches tripled over the period 1977-1990, fishing effort decreased by some 20% with the implementation of ITQs.

A more dramatic effect on the capital employed in a fishery is given with the introduction of an ITQ scheme into Australia's southern blue fin tuna fishery. In 1984, when ITQs were first introduced, there were some 143 quota-holders while by 1988 there were only 63 quota-holders (Muse and Schelle 1989). In contrast, in New Zealand there was actually an increase in the number of vessels in the year following the introduction of ITQs in its inshore fisheries (Clark, Major and Mollett 1988). It has been suggested, however, that the increase was attributable in large part to the purchase of squid-jigging vessels by New Zealand companies to take advantage of opportunities in the squid fishery (ibid.). The fact that vessel numbers did not immediately decline in New Zealand with ITQs may also be a reflection of the lengthy adjustment that arises in industries where the value of vessels and chances for employment in other activities is very low.[10]

Increased Profitability. Another benefit attributed to ITQs is that they can increase the profitability of those fishers allocated quota *gratis*. This may arise from reduced racing behaviour, improvement in the quality of the fish, and other factors. For those fishers entering the fishery at a later date and who must purchase quota from existing quota-holders, the price paid for quota should reflect the expected discounted profits from harvesting a given share of the resource. For these later participants, any resource rents from the fishery should be capitalised and reflected in the quota price.

Evidence of increased profitability with ITQs for the original quota-holders is available from a number of fisheries. Unfortunately, separating the increased profitability of fishers due to ITQs alone from

---

[10] Lindner, Campbell, and Bevin (1992) examine some of the issues with respect to transitions in the New Zealand fisheries brought about by ITQs.

other factors, such as improved market conditions or increases in the fish stock, is often not possible. In the case of Australia's southern blue fin tuna fishery, Geen and Nayar (1988) have simulated the impacts of ITQs and suggest that total net profits in the fishery would, at a steady state, be some A$6.7 million more with ITQs than with an open access situation. Substantial benefits attributable to ITQs are also found in the Icelandic demersal fisheries. According to Arnason (1986), the value of reduced fishing effort and improved quality of product was US$15 million in the first year of implementation of ITQs.

In New Zealand, there is qualitative evidence of increased profitability of fishers. In a survey of one group of fishers, Dewees (1989) notes that 23% of respondents claimed that ITQs have led to improved quality of product, 17% have switched to longlining gear, and some 10% of fishers have reduced their fishing effort. In a summary of the study, Dewees (1989) observed that these changes were aimed at maximising the price received by fishers and minimising their costs. In a survey of the ITQ programs in New Zealand, Macgillivray (1990) also credits the program with improving the financial performance of the industry. This view is supported by the industry itself (Sharp and Roberts 1991) in a submission by the New Zealand Fishing Industry Board (NZFIB) to the New Zealand Government Task Force on Fisheries Legislation. The NZFIB states that the ITQ system has been an effective means of moving towards optimal economic benefits while at the same time sustaining the resource. In particular, they single out the most obvious benefit resulting from ITQs is the reduction in the race for fish.

In Canada's rights based fisheries there is also evidence of increased profitability due to ITQs. In the BC sablefish fishery it was observed that the value of sablefish licences increased some four fold with the introduction of individual vessel quotas (IVQs) and the coupling of licences with quota (Grafton 1992b). Much of this change probably reflects a higher value placed upon quota which gives a more secure fishing privilege than licences alone. It may also reflect higher profits in the fishery with ITQs. In the sablefish and halibut fisheries of British Columbia there have also been big changes in the length of the fishing season. For example, before the introduction of IVQs in 1990 the sablefish fleet took only eight days to harvest the TAC. Under quota management, fishers are harvesting over several weeks and at different times of the year. This allows fishers to coordinate their harvests with market prices and has increased the quality of the fish landed. Both factors have helped fishers to receive a higher return for their product. An added benefit for fishers is improved safety because in the pre-quota regime, irrespective of the weather conditions, it was necessary to fish during the very short designated fishing season.

In a review of the enterprise allocation (EA) program of Canada's offshore groundfish fishery, Gardner (1988) has noted efficiency improvements in both the harvesting and processing sectors from the introduction of individual quotas. In particular, he notes that individual quotas have allowed for improvements in quality of the product through improved timing of the catch. This has led to improvements in processing with fewer production bottlenecks, lower inventories, and a higher proportion of higher valued products being produced.

Changes in Employment and Harvest Shares of Fishers

To reap the full benefits of individual quotas, transferability among fishers must be allowed. It is transferability of quota that allows fishers to retire labour and capital. Without the ability to sell quota to others fishers, less profitable fishers may choose to remain in the fishery preventing more profitable fishers from harvesting a greater share of the TAC.

Transfers of quota also have implications for fishery managers beyond economic efficiency. Concentration of quota may reduce the total employment in the fishery by reducing the number of vessels in the fishery. It may also create market power for fishers with large quota shares who may be able to manipulate quota and product prices to the detriment of others.[11] A related concern is that transferability of quota will remove the smaller owner-operator fishers and allow those with larger vessels and processing companies to dominate the fishery. Whether such an adjustment takes place, however, is entirely dependent on the characteristics of the fishery. For instance, a larger and faster vessel may have been at an advantage in a pre-ITQ fishery where fishers were competing for shares of the catch. The same vessel under an ITQ regime may not have a comparative advantage when fishing is spread more evenly throughout the year but is likely to impose higher fixed costs on its owners than older and smaller vessels.

---

[11] Anderson (1991) addresses the issue of market power in ITQs.

For example, in a study of the BC sablefish fishery, the generally smaller and older longline vessels were found to have a higher profit per unit of sablefish landed than trap vessels (Grafton 1995).

To address the concern over quota concentrations, a number of ITQ programs have imposed limits on the quota that can be owned by anyone individual or company. For example, in New Zealand these limits are 20% for the inshore and 35% for the offshore fisheries (Gibson 1989). Nevertheless, with these regulations the owned and leased quota-holdings of the ten largest companies in New Zealand increased from 58% of the total in the first year of the program to 66% in February 1988 (Muse and Schelle 1988). In other jurisdictions the concern is more with the concentrations of quota on a regional basis. For example, in Iceland transfer of quota from one region to another requires the authorisation of the Minister of Fisheries. In the first year of operation of ITQs in Iceland, there were considerable transfers of quota between regions (Arnason 1986). In the regional transfers, net losses in landings were experienced in the urban areas of the Capital and gains were observed in the smaller fishing villages.

Significant changes in the regional distribution of the harvest of Australia's southern blue fin tuna were also observed with the introduction of ITQs in 1984. For example, at the end of 1987 quota trading had led to the exit of New South Wales fishers from the fishery and reduced by over 50% the quota owned by Western Australia fishers. This has resulted in a concentration of quota in South Australia with the share of the TAC increasing from 66% in 1984 to 91% in 1987 (Geen and Nayar 1988). Over the same period there was also a change in the share of the catch harvested by gear-type with purse-seine vessels increasing their total share from 16% in 1984 to 42% in 1987.

Another issue in the transfer of quota is its effect on employment in the fishery. The evidence from Canada and other countries suggest that ITQs are likely to reduce employment in the harvesting sector. This is because as vessels are retired from the fishery the labour previously employed on these boats is not re-employed on the remaining vessels. For example, in the year following the introduction of ITQs into the Lake Erie fishery, the labour force fell some 22% (Cowan 1990). In addition, for those vessels remaining in the fishery, a decrease in the race for fish can mean vessel owners are able to substitute labour for extra time spent at sea.

An issue related to employment is the remuneration of fishing crew with ITQs. Under quota management, there is less uncertainty faced by vessel owners with respect to their catch and more emphasis on minimizing operating costs. In this scenario and with longer fishing seasons, if the crew does not perform at their best there still remains an opportunity to fulfill the quota at a later date. As a result, the incentive to pay crew a share of the total value of the harvest so as to elicit the crew's best efforts is reduced. There may, therefore, be a change to paying crew on a daily or hourly wage with the introduction of ITQs. For example, in the BC sablefish fishery some vessel owners have changed the method of paying crew with ITQs and pay a daily wage of $100/day instead of the traditional share of 50% of the gross revenue less operating costs. Such a change has led the British Columbia United Fishermen and Allied Workers Union to oppose the introduction of ITQs in Canada's Pacific fisheries.[12] Opposition by crew members and their representatives to ITQs is, however, not untypical in fisheries. A proposal made by Hannesson to address this opposition is to make the initial allocations of quota to fishers and crew collectively (Hannesson 1988).

Despite likely reductions in employment in the harvesting sector, ITQs may be beneficial to the processing sector. If fish are landed over a greater period of time the period of employment for processing workers should also increase. Further, spreading the landings over a longer period can enable processors to change the output to obtain a higher quality and higher priced product mix. Depending on the labour components in the different products, this may increase or decrease employment in the processing sector. In the case of Canada's Atlantic fishery, there is evidence that individual quotas in the EA program may have increased employment in the processing industry. According to Gardner (1988), the EA program increased the quantity of labour-intensive but higher valued products such as packs of fresh and frozen fillets. This, in turn, increased the labour hours per tonne of fish harvested from 30 hours in 1984 to 36 hours in 1987.

Compliance with ITQ Regulations

One of the fundamental requirements for a successful ITQ program is fisher compliance with the regulations. Where fishers are able to fish

---

[12] See Cruickshank (1991) page 32.

over quota or undertake other prohibited activities with impunity, an ITQ system will not provide the expected benefits and may even be detrimental to the sustainability of the fishery.

A number of schemes have been implemented for monitoring and observing the harvests and landings of fishers to ensure compliance with quota regulations. Often, the monitoring of the harvest at sea of fishers is not feasible in terms of management costs or practical where there are large numbers of small vessels. Instead, many ITQ jurisdictions have set up systems for monitoring the landings of fishers. For example, in New Zealand the change to ITQs in 1986 led to a significant change in the monitoring activities of fisheries officers. Instead of an emphasis on dockside monitoring, the fishery managers set up a scheme to monitor the "paper trail" of quota landings. This monitoring is focused around a catch landing log and a quota management report which must be submitted monthly to the regulator and lists the fish caught by species and area and the quota under which it was landed. In addition, fish processors are required to submit a monthly report that indicates the quantities purchased, the price, the species, and the quota identification. This paper record has shifted the focus of monitoring from traditional fishery officers to accountants and persons experienced in fraud investigation. The system has also been helped by the introduction of a goods and services tax (GST) which also ensures record keeping is consistent. The monitoring program is aided by the fact that over 85% of New Zealand's harvest is exported. Trade data, therefore, provide additional verification of the quantities landed and a small domestic market reduces the opportunity for "over the counter" sales that by-pass the quota management system.

Another important feature of the New Zealand program is the legislative power accorded to the Government of New Zealand. Under the 1986 amendment to the New Zealand Fisheries Act, powers were defined to enable authorities to confiscate quota and vessels of fishers contravening quota regulations. In imposing such penalties, the onus is on the fisher to prove that he is not in contravention of the regulations. In general, the monitoring of quota regulations in New Zealand has been viewed as a success with a very high compliance by major producers in the industry (Gibson 1989). The system is, however, not without its problems and quota-busting does take place despite the fact that there are severe penalties for contravening the regulations. For example, in 1989 a fishing company lost NZ$4 million of quota and boats following a conviction for deliberate overfishing (Macgillivray 1990). Another concern is that there has been considerable dumping of fish at sea. This dumping arises from fishers high grading and from discarding of fish for which they do not have quota. To help address the discard problem, New Zealand increased from 10% to 50% the proportion of the market price paid to fishers for those species for which they do not have quota. This change was implemented to encourage the fish to be landed once it is caught but not to provide an incentive for fishers to actively search for species which they do not have quota. The system also allows for overages whereby fishers are allowed to land up to 10% over their quota in a season but the extra landings are deducted from the quota for the following season.

A Canadian example of a relatively successful monitoring of ITQs is provided by the Lake Erie fishery. In the scheme, fishers and processors themselves pay for monitoring of landings with a levy of ½ cent per pound on each group. The system requires fishers to land their product and pack it in ice in designated weights at designated ports. A port monitor then weighs 20% of the total landings to verify that the weights are within 5% of the prescribed weight. The system appears to work effectively and has reduced the enforcement costs of the fishery regulator. Prosecutions have also decreased from 54 in 1980 to none in 1988 (Cowan 1990). A key component of the program is that weight and landing conditions have been incorporated into the fishing licence. Procedurally this allows the regulator to suspend a licence, with its corresponding quota, should a condition of the licence be violated although in practice such suspensions only occur after two warnings. Under the pre-ITQ system, a licence could be suspended only after a court trial.

Less successful monitoring has occurred in some of Canada's Atlantic fisheries. Canada's first ITQ scheme, the 4WX Herring fishery in the Bay of Fundy, has been in place in one form or another since 1976 and is noteworthy in its failure to adequately monitor the harvests of fishers at the beginning of the program. A detailed evaluation of this fishery in its early years is provided by Campbell (1981) and a recent review is given by Stephenson et al. (1993). In the original ITQ scheme, quota were not legally binding regulations but were rather self-imposed and informal arrangements agreed to by vessel owners in collaboration with a fisher organisation, the Atlantic Herring Fishermen's Marketing Cooperative (AHFMC). Under this scheme, fishers were not required to notify the regulator the weight of their catch and there was a limited legal framework to prosecute those contravening the regulations.[13] Not surprisingly, there was a break-down in observing quota limits such that by one account 50% of catches were not reported in some years (Mace 1985). Despite noncompliance by fishers, the monitoring costs for the fishery were substantial and represented about 2.5% of the total landed value. In addition, the ITQ program did not encompass other gear-types such that in the first two years of the program increased prices for herring and increased profits for purse-seiners increased the fishing effort of drift gill-netters in the fishery (Kearney 1986).

Another example of monitoring of ITQs in Atlantic Canada is provided by the western Newfoundland otter trawl cod fishery. The program was originally set up on an experimental basis in 1984. Transferability was initially not allowed and an appropriate system of monitoring the harvests of fishers was not implemented. It is not surprising, therefore, that the fishery was described as being "plagued by discarding and misreporting." (Crowley and Palsson 1992, 7). Recognising the importance of ensuring adequate monitoring to ensure the benefits of ITQs, fishers are currently funding their own monitoring program of harvest with a royalty on landings.

The EA program in Canada has also had some difficulties in its monitoring. A major criticism of EAs was that skippers were high grading to maximize their returns per quota unit and consequently discarding lesser valued fish at sea. Unfortunately, the extent of the problem is not quantifiable although it is likely that some vessels in the past did discard some of their harvest. To address the problem, the regulator subsequently instituted an observer program on 100% of the foreign and 50% of the domestic offshore trawler fleet. The costs of such monitoring are substantial but there is no direct charge that is applied to the domestic fleet. Such a solution to discards and high grading is, unfortunately, impossible in many other fisheries where the number of vessels is greater and the landed value per fishing trip is much less.

---

[13] Since 1985 fishers have been obliged to provide the regulator with catch weights.

Cost Recovery, Management Costs, and Rent Capture

An attributed benefit of ITQs is that they can reduce the costs of management and that some of the increased profitability of fishers can be collected for the purposes of cost recovery and rent capture. Unfortunately, evaluating ITQ programs on the basis of their management costs is particularly difficult as many of the costs of regulations are not properly apportioned across fisheries and what costs are documented are often not publicly available.

In the case of New Zealand a system of checks, such as landing and processing records, was established to monitor the ITQs while many of the previous regulations remained in place. This, coupled with an extensive public relations campaign by the government to persuade fishers to accept ITQs and an arbitration system that ultimately reviewed the quota appeals of some 1,500 fishers, undoubtedly increased management costs. In fact, in 1986/87 in the first year of ITQs in the New Zealand inshore fishery, management costs increased in nominal terms by 36% over the previous twelve months (Macgillvray 1990). In the New Zealand case, however, there has been a systematic claim on the resource rent by the owners of the resource to recoup the regulatory costs. Indeed, the industry itself acknowledges its "...willingness to contribute to the costs of fisheries management, where the benefits of that management fall to the industry." (Sharp and Roberts 1991, 86). The resource rents paid by fishers are determined on the basis of quota values, the expected net returns of fishers, and other factors deemed important by the regulator (Grafton 1992a). In 1988/89, the New Zealand Government collected some NZ\$20 million, a little less than 10% of the total landed value of fish caught by the New Zealand fleet. In total, with foreign fleet access fees and other charges the revenue generated from the fisheries was some NZ\$34 million in 1988/89 or an amount equal to total the operating budget of the regulator (Macgillivray 1990).

Elsewhere, the cost recovery and the capture of resource rents has a much lower priority. In recent ITQ programs in Canada provision has, however, been made for some cost recovery with a charge on the landings of fishers. For example, in the BC halibut fishery, fishers currently pay a nine cents/lb landing charge that fully funds a monitoring and observation program. In the BC sablefish fishery, a charge of six cents/lb is currently assessed to cover the full costs of management and monitoring in the fishery. Similarly in the Lake Erie ITQ program, the cost of monitoring landings is almost exclusively borne by fishers and processors in a landing charge per pound of fish delivered.[14] In Atlantic Canada, fishers are generally charged token access fees. For example, in the EA program access fees do not bear any relation to the value of the fishery and in 1988 generated some $2.1 million for the regulator (Gardner 1988).

ITQs AND CANADA'S ATLANTIC FISHERIES

Rights based management has existed in one form or another in Atlantic Canada since 1976 with the use of individual quotas in the 4WX herring fishery. As of 1994 there were 11 individual quota programs for shellfish, five for groundfish and two pelagic fisheries (see Table 2). In total, these programs account for more than 50% of the total landings by weight in Atlantic Canada.

The following are important issues with respect to the expansion of ITQs in Atlantic Canada and coordinating current programs with other regulations and objectives.

1. Initial quota allocation;
2. Transferability of quota;
3. Monitoring and enforcement , and;
4. Cost recovery

Quota Allocation

A major concern of fishers when quota are allocated *gratis* is how the total harvest is allocated. Past allocations have been based on historical catches with some consideration of vessel characteristics or allocated equally among all vessel owners. In Atlantic Canada there are competing interests for harvest shares on an individual basis, by fleet and by region. Disputes in allocation arise because the quota can represent a valuable asset and, thus, the initial assignment of rights may have a considerable affect on the wealth of fishers. The initial quota allocation should not, however, affect the potential benefits that arise from ITQs.

---

[14] The appropriate method of collecting rent may vary across fisheries and will depend upon the level of uncertainty in the fishery (Grafton 1995). A review of several methods of rent capture in the BC sablefish fishery is given in Grafton (1995).

Table 2 : Selected Individual Vessel/Enterprise Quota Programs in Atlantic Canada.	
Fishery Description	Date of Introduction
Atlantic Groundfish:	
Offshore (>100 ft)	1982
Midshore (65-100 ft)	1988
Mobile Gear Gulf/Quebec (vessels 45-64 ft)	1988
Mobile Gear Scotia/Fundy (vessels <65 ft)	1991
Mobile Gear Gulf/Quebec (vessels <45 ft)	1992
Atlantic Pelagic:	
Herring Purse Seine Gulf	1983
Herring Purse Seine Scotia/Fundy	1983
Source: Task Force on Incomes and Adjustment in the Atlantic Fishery (1993b).	

An important issue in any initial allocation is that it is perceived to be fair. If one recognizes historical rights in a fishery, a logical approach is to assign quota on the basis of past catches as was done in the individual vessel quota program in the Scotia fishery. A problem of assigning quota to vessel owners is that crew members may also believe they have an historical right in the fishery and that they should also receive quota. Assigning both crew and vessel rights would, however, be much more difficult to implement as records of catches do not include crew members. Further, monitoring quota would be problematic if transfers of quota were permitted from crew to other vessels. Another possible method of allocation is by fishing community where sub-allocations would then be made by the community itself. In the small out ports of Newfoundland such a scheme may be possible given the small size of the communities and the strong ties to the community by fishers.

Whatever allocation mechanism is chosen, it is important to avoid a delay between the announcement of the program and its implementation. This will reduce the possibility of "fishing for quota". To avoid high costs in allocation, it is also necessary to avoid an expensive and time consuming review process of the initial quota assignments. For example, in the Scotia-Fundy inshore dragger program some 80% of quota holders appealed their initial quota allocation. Should ITQs be expanded to include all inshore fishers in Atlantic Canada, appeals in such proportion would result in thousands of reviews. Thus, appeals should probably involve a charge to the fisher to avoid frivolous reviews. In addition, a minimum level of documentation should be specified before an appeal can take place.

Another issue in allocation is whether quota is specified in quantity units or as a proportion of the TAC. The current policy of assigning quota on a proportional basis should probably be continued given the instability of fish populations and that the fact that most species in Atlantic Canada are fully exploited. In the case of declines in the TAC, compensatory payments to fishers to reduce the TAC could be very large indeed with quantity quotas.

Transferability of Quota

Quota trading is the mechanism by which more profitable fishers can increase their harvest shares and by which excess capital can exit the fishery. Given the current excess capital in many of Atlantic Canada's fisheries, transferability should be allowed in any rights based program. A major concern of transferability, however, is that it may favour one fleet and/or region at the expense of another. This is of particular interest in Atlantic Canada where there is a conflict between the inshore and offshore fleets and mobile and fixed gear in terms of harvest shares. Further, transfers of quota from economically depressed regions of Atlantic Canada may also run counter to other objectives such as employment. Another concern is that transfers may result in the concentration of quota in the hands of a few companies who could then exercise market power at the expense of others.

If undesirable transfers on a regional basis are of concern to regulators then restrictions could be placed on transfers across regions. Thus, transfers within a defined locale would be permitted but transfers across regions may require the permission of the regulator, as is the case in Iceland. If it were considered that improvements in efficiency from a regional transfer outweighed the costs imposed on particular communities then the transfer would be permitted. If not, the trade would be prohibited.

A major concern of fishers in terms of ITQs is the issue of transfers across fleets. In the current rights based programs in Atlantic Canada's inshore quota is restricted to gear and/or vessel type. For example, quota owned by inshore draggers in the Scotia mobile fishery cannot be transferred to another gear type. Thus, an increase in quota to draggers with a fixed harvest means a decrease in the total harvest of fishers with other gear. In a comprehensive ITQ program, however,

Table 3 : Profile of Atlantic Canada's Fishing Industry, 1990.		
Province	Number of Fishers	# of Fish Plant Workers
Newfoundland	28,830	25,567
Nova Scotia	15,951	13,465
Prince Edward Island	5,546	2,382
New Brunswick	8,494	10,329
Total	64,246	57,579
Source: Task Force on Incomes and Adjustment in the Atlantic Fishery (1993a).		

those fishers able to land fish at least cost should be able to purchase quota from others whatever their gear type.

Monitoring and Enforcement

There must be adequate enforcement and monitoring of ITQs to ensure their potential benefits are realized. Where there is inadequate enforcement such that fishers can contravene regulations with impunity then there are no advantages and there may be considerable disadvantages to ITQs. A key to the success of ITQs in Atlantic Canada, therefore, is an effective monitoring and enforcement program to ensure the integrity of harvesting rights.

The history of rights based management in Atlantic Canada suggests that establishing an effective monitoring program is difficult. In recognition of the problems in the 4WX herring fishery and western Newfoundland otter trawl fishery, greater resources have been allocated to enforcement and greater penalties attached to the breaking of quota regulations. For example, in the mobile gear Gulf of St. Lawrence fishery the fines for infractions have increased 100 fold and the possibility exists for a termination of a fishing licence at the discretion of the Minister of Fisheries.

One of the major hurdles faced in enforcing quota regulations in Atlantic Canada is the large number of fishing vessels and ports where fish may be landed (see Table 3). An approach that would help monitoring would be to enlist the support of fishers themselves. Experience from the 4WX herring fishery suggests that fishers will not report illegal activities of others to the regulator. To encourage self-policing, a system of rewards could be instituted for information leading to a confirmed violation of quota regulations. If the reward were set at a sufficiently high enough level fishers and fish processing workers would have a strong incentive to report on the illegal activities of quota-holders. In addition, the current system of recording landings could be expanded to include fish transported across provincial boundaries and the USA-Canada border. Further, a system for analyzing this data and the records of processors and fishers to identify anomalies and inconsistencies in a timely manner would also be required.

An important aspect of monitoring and enforcement is that *all* fishers including part-timers would be included under the regulations if the use of ITQs is expanded in Atlantic Canada. If ITQs are not universally applied then the opportunity arises for fishers not regulated by quotas to increase their harvests and for quota-holders to market product over and above their allocations. Finally, any system of monitoring must be adequately funded to be effective and should include resources for random surveillance and dockside monitoring, data-entry and analysis, and investigation of reports of noncompliance of quota regulations.

Cost Recovery

The increase in profits brought about by ITQs less any increases in the costs of management may be defined as a management rent and is the surplus over and above that needed to keep fishers in their present activity and the costs of fisheries management. In most fisheries, the regulator has chosen to let the management rent be kept by the first generation of quota-holders so as to ensure industry support for the program. Such is the case with the current rights based programs in Atlantic Canada.

If ITQs were to be expanded in the inshore fisheries, at the very least the regulator should ensure that fishers cover the costs of fisheries management including monitoring and enforcement. Such is the objective of IVQ programs in the Pacific with the halibut and sablefish fisheries. The justification for such cost recovery is that the fishers themselves are substantial beneficiaries of ITQs and thus should pay the costs incurred in generating these benefits.

There are several potential methods for recovering the costs of management from fishers. The most common approach is a fixed charge per unit of product landed. Two methods that may be preferable include an *ad valorem* royalty and a charge based on the quota price and quota holdings.[15] Both a royalty and a quota charge would be relatively easy to administer and would offer a number of theoretical advantages.

CONCLUSION

Atlantic Canada in the mid 1990s is suffering from a major downturn in stocks and, indeed, a catastrophic decline in the Northern Cod biomass. Depressed incomes in the fishery are, however, nothing new in Atlantic Canada with the last major crisis in the early 1980s.[16] With or without a recovery in the stocks the Atlantic Canada fisheries need restructuring because traditional fisheries management coupled with government assistance programs have failed to address the fundamental problems of excess fishing capacity and low average incomes.

To address the current crisis, the Government of Canada is committed to short-term income support of fishers and processing workers, early retirement of fishers and professionalization of the fishery. For 1994/95 the federal income support in the Atlantic Canada fisheries is estimated to be $1.9 billion which is in addition to $900 million spent between July 1992 and May 1994 under the Northern Cod Adjustment and Recovery Program (Department of Fisheries and Oceans 1994). For the longer term, there is a program of early retirement to fishers 55 years of age and above whereby retirees surrender their fishing licence and right to fish for a lump sum payment. The stated objective of the program is to reduce harvesting capacity by 50%. In addition to early retirement, it is proposed to professionalize the fishery with certification and registration programs and to restrict access to the fishery only to trained and certified fishers. Coupled with the professionalization and retirements it is also proposed that authority for making harvest allocations will be decided by Industry Renewal Boards that would operate at "arm's length" from the government and industry.

Unfortunately, the history of licence retirement programs suggest that without controls on individual output the problems of excess capacity and competition in the race to fish will quickly return. If this

---

[15] See Grafton (1992a, 1992b and 1995).
[16] See Taskforce of Atlantic Fisheries (1982).

is the case then even with a stock recovery the fundamental malaise in Atlantic Canada's fisheries will not be remedied despite several billion dollars spent on income support and the proposed adjustment program. Instead, fishery managers should seriously consider expanding the use of ITQs in Atlantic Canada. Given adequate support to monitoring and enforcement, which would be at a fraction of the cost of the current income support programs, ITQs may help solve some of the fundamental problems faced by Atlantic fishers. By generating a higher return from the fishery some of the benefits of ITQs could also be used to help compensate potential losers such as displaced crew members. Ultimately, this is to the long-term advantage of Atlantic Canada and its fisheries.

REFERENCES

Anderson, L. G. 1991. A Note on Market Power in ITQ Fisheries. *Journal of Environmental Economics and Management* 21(3): 229-296.

Arnason, R. 1986. Management of the Icelandic Demersal Fisheries. In *Fishery Access Control Programs Worldwide*, edited by N. Mollett. Alaska Sea Grant Report No. 86-4. University of Alaska.

———. 1990. Minimum Information Management in Fisheries. *Canadian Journal of Economics* 23:630-653.

———. 1993. Iceland's ITQ System. *Marine Resource Economics* 8(3):201-218.

Boyce, J. R. 1992. Individual Transferable Quotas and Production Externalities in a Fishery. *Natural Resource Modelling* 6(4): 385-408.

Campbell, H. F. 1981. *The Public Regulation of Commercial Fisheries in Canada.* Case Study No. 5 the Bay of Fundy Herring Fishery, Economic Council of Canada Technical Report 20. Ottawa: Ministry of Supply and Services Canada.

Clark, I., P. J. Major, and N. Mollett. 1988. Development and Implementation of New Zealand's ITQ Management System. *Marine Resource Economics* 5(4):325-350.

Copes, P. 1986. A Critical Review of the Individual Quota as a Device in Fisheries Management. *Land Economics* 62(3):278-291.

Cowan, T. 1990. *Fisheries Management on Lake Erie.* Unpublished Report, Toronto: Canada Department of Fisheries and Oceans.

Crowley, R. W. and H. Palsson. 1992. Rights Based Fisheries Management in Canada. *Marine Resource Economics* 7:1-21.

Cruickshank, D. 1991. *A Commission of Inquiry into Licensing and Related Policies of the Department of Fisheries and Oceans.* Vancouver.

Department of Fisheries and Oceans, Canada. 1994. *Structural Adjustment in the Northern Cod Fishery.* Ottawa: Economic Policy and Analysis Division.

Dewees, C. M. 1989. Assessment of the Implementation of Individual Transferable Quotas in New Zealand's Inshore Fishery. *North American Journal of Fisheries Managament* 9(2):131-139.

Dupont, D. P. 1990. Rent Dissipation in Restricted Access Fisheries *Journal of Environmental Economics and Management* 19(1): 26-44.

Gardner, M. 1988. Enterprise Allocation System in the Offshore Groundfish Sector in Atlantic Canada. *Marine Resource Economics* 5(4):389-414.

Geen, G. and M. Nayar. 1988. Individual Transferable Quotas in the Southern Bluefin Tuna Fishery: An Economic Appraisal. *Marine Resource Economics* 5(4):365-388.

Gibson, A. 1989. ITQ Assessment – New Zealand. Vancouver: Canada Department of Fisheries and Oceans.

Gordon, H. S. 1954. Economic Theory of a Common Property Resource: The Fishery. *Journal of Political Economy* 62:124-142.

Grafton, R. Q. 1992a. Rent Capture in an Individual Transferable Quota Fishery. *Canadian Journal of Fisheries and Aquatic Sciences* 49(3):497-503.

———. 1992b. *Rent Capture in Rights Based Fisheries*. Ph.D. diss., Department of Economics, University of British Columbia, Vancouver.

———. 1994. A Note on Uncertainty and Rent Capture in an ITQ Fishery. *Journal of Environmental Economics and Management* 27(3):286-294.

———. 1995. Rent Capture in a Rights Based Fishery. *Journal of Environmental Economics and Management* 28(1):48-67.

Hannesson, R. 1988. Fishermen's Organisations and their Role in Fisheries Managament: Theoretical Considerations and Experiences from Industrialised Countries. Pages 1-27 in *Studies on the Role of Fishermen's Organisations in Fisheries Management*. Rome: UN FAO Fisheries Technical Paper No. 300.

Heaps, T. 1993. *A Note on Minimum Information Management in Fisheries*. Discussion Paper 93-13, Department of Economics, Simon Fraser Univeristy, Vancouver.

Kearney, J. F. 1983. *Common Tragedies: A Study of Resource Access in the Bay of Fundy Herring Fisheries*. M.E.S thesis, Institute for Resource and Environmental Studies, Dalhousie University, Halifax.

Kirby, M. J. L. 1982. *Navigating Troubled Waters: A New Policy for Atlantic Fisheries*. Report of the Task Force on Atlantic Fisheries. Ottawa: Supply and Services Canada.

Lindner, R. K., H. F. Campbell, and G. F. Bevin. 1992. Rent Generation During the Transition to a Managed Fishery: The Case of the New Zealand ITQ System. *Marine Resource Economics* 7(4): 229-248.

Macgillivray, P. B. 1990. *Assessment of New Zealand's Individual Transferable Quota Fisheries Management.* Economic and Commercial Analysis Report No. 75. Ottawa: Canadian Department of Fisheries and Oceans.

Mace, P. M. 1985. *Catch Rates and Total Removals in the 4WX Herring Purse Seine Fisheries.* Research Document 85/74. Canadian Atlantic Fisheries Scientific Advisory Committee.

Muse, B. and K. Schelle. 1988. *New Zealand's ITQ Program.* Report CFEC 88-3, Alaska Commercial Fisheries Entry Commisssion.

―――. 1989. *Individual Fisherman's Quotas: A Preliminary Review of Some Recent Programs.* Report CFEC 89-1, Alaska Commercial Fisheries Entry Commisssion.

Scott, A. T. 1955. The Fishery: The Objectives of Sole Ownership. *Journal of Political Economy* 63:116-124.

―――. 1989. Conceptual Origins of Rights Based Fishing. Pages 11-38 in *Rights Based Fishing*, edited by P. A. Neher, R. Arnason, and N. Mollett.

―――. 1993. Obstacles to Fishery Self-Government. *Marine Resource Economics* 8(3):187-200.

Sharp, D. C. and P. R. Roberts. 1991. *Task Force Review of Fisheries Legislation.* A submission prepared for the New Zealand Fishing Industry Board and presented to the New Zealand Government Task Force of Fisheries Legislation.

Smith, V. L. 1969. On Models of Commercial Fishing. *Journal of Political Economy* 77:181-198.

Stephenson, R. L., D. E. Lane, D. G. Aldous, and R. Nowak. 1993. Management of the 4WX Herring Fishery: An Evaluation of Recent Events. *Canadian Journal of Fisheries and Aquatic Sciences* 50: 2742-2756.

Task Force on Incomes and Adjustment in the Atlantic Fishery. 1993a. *Charting a New Course: Towards the Fishery of the Future.* Ottawa: Canada Department of Fisheries and Oceans.

Task Force on Incomes and Adjustment in the Atlantic Fishery. 1993b. *Fisheries Access: Licensing and Registrations - Policy and Statistical Review 1977-1992*. DFO/4948. Ottawa: Canada Department of Fisheries and Oceans.

Warming, J. 1911. Om Grundrente af Fiskegrunde. *Nationaløkonomisk Tidsskrift* 49: 499-505.

Wilen, J. E. 1989. Rent Generation in Limited Entry Fisheries. Pages 249-262 in *Rights Based Fishing*, edited by P. A. Neher, R. Arnason, and N. Mollett.

8

CANADIAN EXPERIENCE WITH INDIVIDUAL FISHING QUOTAS

Paul Macgillivray
Program Planning and Economics Department
Fisheries and Oceans Canada, Pacific Region

INTRODUCTION

Purpose

During the 1980s, individual quotas (IQs) and enterprise allocations (EAs) came into use in many fishing nations around the world, most notably New Zealand, Canada, Iceland and Australia. The common feature of these management programs was the allocation of output quotas to individuals or companies. However, the specific design of the output quota programs differed considerably from one country to another.

In Canada, IQ/EA programs were introduced gradually throughout the country and now operate in over 20 fisheries representing more than 35 per cent of total landed value. Generally, output quotas were introduced on an experimental basis with strict restrictions on transferability. However, in all cases where IQ/EA programs have been introduced, they have become entrenched as the management approach preferred by participants in the fishery.

The purpose of this paper is to review and assess some of Canada's experience with IQ/EA management. The paper focuses on the Pacific Halibut fishery which has been under IQ management since 1991.

Background

Generally, IQ/EA programs have been introduced in fisheries that were experiencing problems associated with the traditional fisheries management approach of input controls — e.g., chronic excess fishing capacity, pressure to over harvest, increasingly unsafe fishing practices, poor economic returns, and recurring financial crisis. Of course, these problems are linked to the common property nature of fisheries resources.

Economic theory suggests that output quotas can overcome the waste associated with the exploitation of common property resources. In practice, the performance of IQ/EA management depends on a number of factors such as the characteristics of the fishery, the design of the IQ/EA program and its implementation.

The next section of this paper focuses on the Pacific Halibut individual vessel quota (IVQ) program and factors contributing to its success. In the following section, several factors associated with less successful IQ/EA programs in Canada are identified. The report concludes with some observations on Canada's experience to date with IQ/EA management.

PACIFIC HALIBUT IVQ PROGRAM

Overview of the Pacific Halibut IVQ Program

From 1979 until 1990, management of the halibut fishery was based on three main elements:

- limited entry was introduced in 1979 (435 licences were issued);
- a total allowable catch (TAC) was established for the season, and;
- the fishery was closed once the TAC was taken.

In 1980, the season lasted 65 days and the catch was 5.7 million pounds. Over the next decade technological advances such as circle hooks, snap-on gear, and automatic baiting machines improved the efficiency of the fleet enormously. By 1990, the fishing season had been reduced to 6 days while landings increased to 8.5 million pounds. By comparison, in 1980, the halibut fleet took more than 10 times longer to catch about two thirds of the halibut caught in 1990.

Fisheries management in the 1980s resulted in excessive fishing capacity, very short seasons, unsafe fishing practices, large quantities of by-catch being wasted, poor product quality, supply gluts and low landed prices.

In 1991, IVQs were introduced on a two-year trial basis. The IVQ program was developed with extensive input from halibut industry advisors and licence holders. The main features of the IVQ program were:

- The fishery is open from March 1 to October 31.
- Initial individual quota allocations were calculated using a formula based on the licence holders' vessel length and historical catch. The resulting 435 individual vessel quotas were expressed as fixed percentages of the annual Total Allowable Catch (TAC).
- During the first two years of the IVQ program, quotas were not transferable. Beginning in 1993, each quota was divided into two equal shares and up to four shares could be fished on one vessel.
- There is a mandatory port monitoring program where fishermen must notify an observer before they leave for the fishing grounds and again 24 hours prior to landing. The observer then meets the vessel at the landing site, validates the weight of the halibut landed, and tracks each quota holder's total landings.
- Quota holders are required to pay all the incremental costs associated with the management, monitoring, and enforcement of the IVQ program. The cost recovery program also pays for some stock assessment and other research activities, at the discretion of the quota holders. Activities under the IVQ program, paid by halibut licence holders, totaled nearly $800 thousand in 1993/94.

Assessment of the IVQ Program

The halibut season was 214 days in 1991, compared to 6 days in 1990. Under IVQ management, fishermen altered their fishing patterns to increase net revenue. This included fishing to meet market demand and reducing costs.

The major impacts of the IVQ program fall under the following categories:

- biological management;
- economic efficiency;

- equity and distribution considerations, and;
- administration and enforcement.

Biological Management. Prior to IVQs, it was difficult for fisheries managers to estimate when the TAC was reached, often leading to over-harvesting and negative effects on the halibut resource. Since the introduction of IVQ management, the catch has been slightly lower than the TAC each year. This is a noteworthy change since 1991 was the first time that the annual catch did not exceed the TAC since limited entry was introduced in 1979.

It is estimated that waste in the halibut fishery, resulting from lost and abandoned gear and discarding undersized halibut, decreased by 50% with the introduction of IVQs.

Additional stock assessment research is possible since the licence/quota holders are now supplementing the cost of stock assessment. In 1993, licence/quota holders contributed $34 thousand to the International Pacific Halibut Commission (IPHC) for research projects.

Economic Efficiency. The economic performance of the halibut fishery improved significantly with the introduction of IVQs. Improved performance is attributable to both higher revenues and lower costs.

Landed prices have risen under IVQs as harvesters time their landings to match periods of high market demand and supply the high value fresh market. Landed prices in BC, compared to those in Alaska, increased by an estimated 50¢ /lb in 1991 and $1.00 /lb in 1992 as a result of the positive marketing aspects of IVQs. The price increase translated into a jump in revenues of $3.6 million for fishermen in 1991 and a decrease in harvesting costs of $440 thousand in 1991 (mostly because of decreased crew payments). Fleet rationalization has occurred under IVQs as quota stacking has resulted in fewer vessels fishing halibut — 350 in 1993 compared to 435 prior to IVQs.

Equity and Employment Considerations. Since the introduction of IVQs, the number of crew members employed has been reduced by nearly 300 (from 1,600 to 1,300). Individuals still employed, however, are working a longer season and earning higher incomes. Employment of shore workers has declined slightly. Under IVQs there has been a shift from frozen product to fresh halibut. Processing fresh halibut requires less shore based employment because there is no need for freezing and storage.

Before IVQ management, harvesters were under pressure to fish even in bad weather and to overload their vessels. Now working conditions have improved and a safer, more stable working environment exists.

Administration and Enforcement. The level of enforcement has increased under IVQs as licence/quota holders pay about $800,000 annually towards the cost of fisheries enforcement and port monitoring. Their contribution provides for enforcement in addition to previous levels.

A port monitoring program, completely paid for by licence holders, ensures that the landings reported are accurate and allows quota holders to determine the balance of their quota immediately after landing their catch.

Participant's Views

In December 1992, halibut licence holders were asked to vote on whether to continue the halibut IVQ program. Ninety-one percent (91%) of responding licence holders voted in favour of IVQs. Since then the trial program has been extended on an annual basis.

While there is a high degree of support for the IVQ program, it is not without criticism. The main complaints focus on the reduction in the number of individuals employed and the "windfall profits" accruing to halibut quota holders as the increased profitability of the fishery is translated into higher market values for quotas.

Summary

The following factors have contributed to the success of the Pacific halibut IVQ program:

- single species fishery with selective gear;
- well designed program (extensive input from participants in design, focus on efficiency);
- effective implementation (including costs covered by participants);
- high degree of support from participants in the operation of the fishery through an advisory committee.

FACTORS AFFECTING THE PERFORMANCE OF OTHER CANADIAN IQ/EA PROGRAMS

There are several Canadian IQ/EA programs that have not achieved the same degree of success as the Pacific halibut IVQ program. The following characteristics have influenced the performance of these programs:

- Some IQ/EA programs apply to multi-species fisheries (e.g., groundfish) where the fishing gear is not selective. When quotas are set for individual species it can result in significant problems with by-catch dumping especially.
- In some cases, IQ/EA programs have been poorly designed (e.g., no catch monitoring) resulting in an inability to properly manage the fishery.
- In some cases, IQ/EA programs have been poorly implemented.
- Lack of industry support — when participants have not been involved in the design of an IQ/EA program there is generally not the same willingness to support and pay for an effective program.

CONCLUSION

Canadian experience with IQ/EA management has been mixed. There are both successes and failures. While efficiency gains have been made in many IQ/EA fisheries, concerns have been expressed about the distribution impacts — e.g., crew members losing their jobs while quota holders get windfall profits.

Programs have evolved somewhat in isolation — i.e. there is no national policy that guides the design and implementation of IQ/EA programs. Programs have generally failed to capture resource rent and in many cases have not addressed cost recovery adequately.

9

APPROACHES TO THE ECONOMICS OF THE MANAGEMENT OF HIGH SEAS FISHERY RESOURCES

Gordon R. Munro
Department of Economics
University of British Columbia

INTRODUCTION

One of the many factors contributing to the fishery resource management disaster in the waters off Atlantic Canada is the existence of important groundfish stocks (e.g., Northern Cod) which extend beyond the boundary of Canada's Exclusive Economic Zone (EEZ) into the high seas. The high seas portions of such stocks are subject to exploitation by fleets of distant water fishing nations.

The term now commonly applied to this form of transboundary fishery resources is "straddling" fish stocks. Canada encounters the straddling fish stock problem in two segments of the Grand Bank of Newfoundland which extend beyond the 200 mile boundary of the EEZ. The segments, to be found in the eastern and southern extremities of the Grand Bank, are referred to as the Nose and Tail of the Bank respectively.

With the advent of Canadian Extended Fisheries Jurisdiction (EFJ) in 1977, Canada attempted to address its straddling fish stock problem by establishing in 1979 an international organization, the Northwest Atlantic Fisheries Organization (NAFO), to manage the high seas portions of such stocks. Along with Canada, relevant distant water fishing nations (e.g., the European Union and Russia) were members

161

were members of the Organization. Notable nonmembers in the early days of NAFO were Spain and Portugal.

Initially, NAFO appeared to work reasonably effectively in the management of the high seas portions of the straddling fish stocks. NAFO ensured that resource management policies in the Nose and Tail of the Bank were compatible with those being adopted by Canada within the EEZ (Munro 1992). Thus, Canada effectively dictated the management policy for the high seas portions of the relevant straddling stocks.

The management policy was not without difficulties however. Fisheries relations with the non-NAFO members, Spain and Portugal, remained strained. Moreover, the appearance in the relevant highs seas fisheries of non-NAFO, non-Iberian fishing vessels continued to be a source of constant irritation.

Canada's chief partner within NAFO was the European Union (EU). In 1985, this partnership began to disintegrate. To what extent this disintegration was linked to completion of negotiations for the accession of Spain and Portugal to the EU is not known. In any event, the EU announced that it no longer accepted Canada's management goals and now saw them as unduly conservationist (ibid.).

The consequence of the breakdown in the partnership was that the EU began exceeding the heretofore NAFO established quotas for the EU in the NAFO governed region. In 1986, for example, EU harvests in the NAFO (high seas) areas were over 470 per cent of the assigned EU quotas (ibid.). The pattern continued for several years, with Canada complaining bitterly about the destruction of groundfish stocks in the high seas adjacent to its Atlantic coast EEZ (Kaitala and Munro 1993). At the end of 1992, however, it appeared that exhaustion of the stocks had led to a restoration of peace. A Memorandum of Understanding was signed between Canada and the EU, marking the resumption of cooperation.

The aforementioned Memorandum of Understanding, hailed as a de facto "peace treaty" in 1992, proved to be no more than a temporary truce. A dispute developed between Canada and the European Union in general, and Spain in particular, over the exploitation of, what until recently had been regarded as an inferior species, turbot (Greenland halibut) on the Nose of the Bank. The dispute erupted into a full fledged "fish war" in February/March 1995, when Canada went so far as to arrest a Spanish trawler on the Nose of the Bank.

The difficulties experienced by Canada with straddling fish stocks off Atlantic Canada were not unique, but were rather part of a worldwide phenomenon (FAO of the UN 1993).[1] Many other examples of severe resource management problems arising with respect to straddling fish stocks exist. The pollock resources in the so called Doughnut Hole in the Bering Sea is a case in point. So serious did these problems become that the United Nations felt called upon to convene a major intergovernmental conference on the issue, the UN Conference on Straddling Fish Stocks and Highly Migratory Fish Stocks, referred to hereafter as the UN Fish Conference. At the time of writing, the Conference has held three substantive sessions and looks forward to two more.[2]

Economists have only recently turned their attention to the management of straddling fish stocks. This paper reports on the progress to date in developing the economics of the management of such resources, with special reference to Canada, and points to possible avenues of future research.

BACKGROUND

The so called straddling fish stocks were not always seen as constituting a significant resource management problem. On the contrary, when the UN Third Conference on the Law of the Sea held its concluding session in December 1982, straddling fish stocks were thought to be of minor importance. First, it was believed that 90 per cent of the world's marine harvest of fish would be accounted for by fishery resources encompassed by the established, or to be established, EEZs.

Secondly, it was believed that distant water fishing nations exploiting the high seas portion of a straddling stock would not be able to do

---

[1] The issue also involves so called "highly migratory fish stocks", which means, to all intents and purposes, tuna. The UN continues to make a sharp distinction between straddling and highly migratory fish stocks. It can be argued that the distinction is based far more on political and historical factors, than it is on biological factors (Kaitala and Munro 1993). What the issue does not involve, at this stage, are fishery resources wholly confined to the high seas. These resources continue to arouse only minor interest.

[2] The substantive sessions were held in July 1993, March 1994 and August 1994. Further sessions are anticipated in 1995.

so on a viable commercial basis, unless they were also granted access to the EEZ (Munro 1994). Thus, the coastal state, armed with strong bargaining power, could monitor and effectively influence the activities of the relevant distant water fishing nations in the adjacent high seas, as well as within the EEZ. Certainly, it appeared in the early days of NAFO that Canada, the one relevant coastal state, had overwhelming bargaining power (Kaitala and Munro 1993).

One consequence of the seeming unimportance of straddling fish stocks is to be seen in the Law of the Sea Convention, which emerged from the aforementioned UN Fish Conference (UN 1982). The section of the Convention (which has become international treaty law)[3] pertaining to high seas fishery resources in general (Articles 116-120) is a model of imprecision and vagueness. In particular, the rights, duties, and obligations of coastal states, and those of distant water fishing nations, with respect to the high seas portions of straddling fish stocks are exceedingly unclear (Miles and Burke 1989; Kaitala and Munro 1993).

One school of thought maintains that coastal states, while not having full jurisdiction over fishery resources in the high seas adjacent to the EEZ, do have rights, for purposes of stock conservation, which are superior to those of distant water fishing nations. This school of thought has found its most persuasive champions in Professors William Burke and Edward Miles of the University of Washington (Miles and Burke 1989). Not surprisingly, this school of thought is vigorously opposed by most (if not all) distant water fishing nations, which view the school of thought simply as a promotion of "creeping coastal state jurisdiction."

The lack of clarity over jurisdiction in the adjacent high seas is starkly evident in the aforementioned Canada-Spain fish war in the spring of 1995. The Canadian government, obviously highly sympathetic to the Miles-Burke point of view, undertook what it deemed to be justifiable police action in order to protect overexploited stocks, when it seized the Spanish trawler on the Nose of the Bank. Canada maintained that the trawler was engaged in "illegal" fishing, involving, inter alia, the harvesting of immature fish. The European Union responded by maintaining that Canada was in clear violation of inter-

---

[3] The Convention became international treaty law on 16 November 1994.

national law and that Canada's action was nothing less than piracy (The Economist, 18 March 1995, 46).

The Canadian Minister of Fisheries and Oceans was widely acclaimed throughout Canada for his firm measures. The Spanish trawler was duly released (on bail). The vessel and crew returned to the vessel's home port of Vigo, Spain. The members of the crew were welcomed in Vigo as returning heroes.

In any event, since the mid to late 1980s, the problem of managing the high seas portions of straddling fish stocks has ceased to be minor, and has by now become severe. Case after case of over exploitation of such high seas fishery resources has been revealed. Canada's ongoing difficulties with the European Union on the Grand Bank constitute but one example. Some go so far as to argue that the problem has come to constitute a threat to the Law of the Sea Convention itself (Kaitala and Munro 1993).

The FAO suggests several reasons for the transformation (FAO of the UN 1992). First, the distant water fishing nations have found that their access to the EEZs has come to be steadily eroded, often for reasons flying in the face of basic economic principles. Secondly, distant water fishing nations fleet capacity has shown surprisingly little decline over the past decade. As a consequence, increased pressure on high seas fishery stocks seemed inevitable.

Thirdly, and perhaps most importantly, the comfortable coastal state assumption that coastal states could effectively monitor distant water fishing nations activity in the high seas adjacent to the EEZ proved to be demonstrably false. Canada's post-1985 experience with NAFO provides testimony to this fact.

Coastal states, such as Canada could, of course, attempt to deal with troublesome stocks in the high seas adjacent to their EEZs through a unilateral extension of jurisdiction. Without question, there have been threats of such extension of jurisdiction. There are difficulties, however, with this solution. The 200 nautical mile boundary of the EEZ is often derided on the grounds that it makes little sense in biological, economic, or legal terms. Yet, the 200 mile limit represented a compromise hammered out in the UN Third Conference on the Law of the Sea between coastal states demanding an extension of their jurisdiction over fisheries and those (distant water fishing nations primarily) resisting any extension of jurisdiction. If coastal states were to begin violating this compromise, there would be the risk that the

Law of the Sea Convention could be seriously undermined. Secondly, extension of coastal state jurisdiction would mitigate the problem, but could not be expected to eliminate it entirely. Canada could, in all honesty, probably deal with its problem through a fairly modest extension of jurisdiction. The FAO, however, reports on stocks to be found in the EEZ and adjacent high seas which may extend as much as 900 miles offshore (ibid.). No one, at this stage, is seriously contemplating an extension of coastal state jurisdiction out to such distances.

It was the increasing severity of the problem of managing fishery resources in the high seas adjacent to the EEZ, and the concomitant threat of coastal state unilateral extension of jurisdiction, which caused the UN to take action and convene the UN Fish Conference. The Conference has now made progress sufficient to provide us with a framework within which to begin exploring the economics of the management of high seas fishery resources in the form of straddling stocks.

THE ECONOMICS OF THE MANAGEMENT OF HIGH SEAS FISHERY RESOURCES

A Preliminary Enquiry

If successful, the UN Fish Conference will produce a convention, or the equivalent thereof, to supplement or buttress the existing Law of the Sea Convention. The Conference has now brought forth a key document: *Draft Agreement for the Implementation of the United Nations Convention on the Law of the Sea of 10 December 1982 Relating to the Conservation and Management of Straddling Fish Stocks and Highly Migratory Fish Stocks*. The document will be referred to hereafter simply as the "Draft Agreement" (UN 1994).

In addition, a second document has arisen from the UN Fish Conference, which proves to be useful for our purposes. This is a draft convention, presented at the first substantive session of the conference (July 1993), and prepared by a group of coastal states, of which Canada was a leading member (UN 1993).

The Draft Agreement makes it very clear that the Conference will recommend that straddling fish stocks should be managed on a region by region basis, through regional organizations or the equivalent thereof (UN 1994, Article 8). The Northwest Atlantic Fisheries

Organization (NAFO) can be thought of as a prototype. The issue for economists thus becomes the nature of the optimal economic resource management programs for the to be established regional organizations.

We first recall that straddling fish stocks are, by definition, transboundary in nature. While the management of straddling fish stocks has not yet been studied in detail by economists, the management of another form of transboundary fishery resources has been extensively examined by economists. This other form of transboundary fishery resources consists of fishery resources which are "shared" by two or more coastal states. Pacific Salmon, shared by Canada and the United States, is an obvious example.

The management of shared fishery resources was recognized as an important issue well before the close of the UN Third Conference on the Law of the Sea. Economists began studying the issue seriously in the late 1970s. Consequently, the analysis is reasonably well developed (see, for example Munro 1990).

In light of these facts, a reasonable approach to analyzing the economic management of straddling fish stocks would be to commence by asking how far the analysis of the economic management of shared fishery resources will carry us. In studying the economic management of shared fishery resources, economists have asked basically two questions:

1. What are the consequences of non-cooperative management of the resources?
2. What is the nature of an optimal cooperative resource management regime?

Obviously, if the answer to (1) is that the consequences are trivial, one need not be unduly concerned with (2).

Let us commence with the question of non-cooperative management of a shared fishery resource. The approach taken by most economists to this question is to combine the standard dynamic economic model of the fishery with the theory of dynamic non-cooperative games.

Now let it be supposed that the relevant fishery resource is shared by two coastal states, Countries 1 and 2, that the resource can be modeled biologically by the famous Schaefer model, that the supplies of labour and capital services constituting fishing effort in the two countries are perfectly elastic, and that the demand for harvested fish is also perfectly elastic. Finally, let it be supposed that the two countries differ only in terms of their fishing effort costs. Let Country 1 be the low cost country and Country 2 the high cost country. We thus have:

$$\frac{dx}{dt} = F(x) - E_1 x - E_2 x \qquad (1)$$

where x is the biomass, $F(x)$ the natural growth function,[4] and E_1 and E_2 the rates of fishing effort for Countries 1 and 2 respectively.[5] The resource rent accruing to the ith country at a given moment in time is given by:

$$\pi_i = (px - c_i)E_i \qquad (2)$$

where p is the price of fish and c_i the unit cost of fishing effort.

If Country 1 had outright control of the resource, and was managing the resource in an optimal manner, its objective function would be given by:

$$\max J_1(x_0, E_1) = \int_0^\infty e^{-\delta t} \pi_1(t) dt \qquad (3)$$

where δ is the social rate of discount and where $x_0 = x(0)$. Optimal management would involve stabilizing the biomass at a level, which we shall denote as x_1^* (see Clark and Munro 1982). If, on the other hand, the authorities were to make no attempt to manage the resource, but rather were content to allow the common property aspects of the resource to go unchecked by permitting the fishery to operate on a strictly open access basis, the resource rent would be fully dissipated and the resource would be driven down to a level, x_1^∞, referred to as "bionomic equilibrium." We would have:

---

[4] It is assumed that the growth of the biomass is a function of the biomass itself. It is assumed further that there is an upper bound to the biomass, the so called carrying capacity which we shall denote by K. It is assumed that $F(0) = F(K) = 0$ and that $F(x) > 0$ for $x \in (0,K)$ (see Clark and Munro 1982).

[5] It is assumed that the so called harvest production functions for Countries 1 and 2 are simply:

$$h_1 = E_1 x$$
$$h_2 = E_2 x.$$

Thus dx/dt is equal to the natural growth rate minus the combined harvests of Countries 1 and 2. If for a given biomass level, x^t, we had $E_1 x^t + E_2 x^t = F(x^t)$, it would be said that the resource was being harvested on a sustained yield basis at $x = x^t$.

$$\pi_1 = (px_1^\infty - c_1)E_1 = 0 \tag{4}$$

It can be shown that x_1^* would be equal to x_1^∞, if and only if, $\delta = \infty$. If $\delta < \infty$, which is virtually certain to be the case, then it will be true that $x_1^* > x_1^\infty$. Bionomic equilibrium represents unequivocal over exploitation of the resource from society's point of view.

If Country 2, rather than Country 1, were to own the resource outright, there would be a corresponding optimal biomass level, x_2^* and bionomic equilibrium biomass level, x_2^∞. If the only difference between Country 1 and Country 2 is that $c_1 < c_2$, then it can be shown that:

$$x_1^* < x_2^*$$

$$x_1^\infty < x_2^\infty$$

We analyze the consequences of Countries 1 and 2 sharing the resource, and refusing to cooperate, within the framework of a Nash non-cooperative game (Nash 1951). If we can assume that $x_2^\infty < x_1^{*6}$ it can be shown that the non-cooperative strategies of the two countries will be characterized as follows (Clark 1980):

$$E_1^N(x) = \begin{cases} E_1^{max7} & x > \min(x_1^*, x_2^\infty) \\ F(x)/x, & x = \min(x_1^*, x_2^\infty) \\ 0, & x < \min(x_1^*, x_2^\infty) \end{cases} \tag{5}$$

$$E_1^N = \begin{cases} E_1^{max}, & x > x_2^\infty, \\ 0, & x > x_2^\infty \end{cases} \tag{6}$$

---

[6] If it were the case that $x_2^\infty > x_1^*$, cooperation would be unnecessary. Country 2 would be driven out of the fishery and the resource to all intents and purposes belong to Country 1. If that country followed an optimal management policy, the resource would be stabilized at x_1^*.

[7] It is assumed that there are upper bounds to both E_1 and E_2.

$E = F(x)/x$ implies that harvesting is taking place on a sustained yield basis.[8]

The solution to the non-cooperative game is that the resource would be driven down to $x = x_2^\infty$, which, given our assumption that $x_1^* > x_2^\infty$, is non-optimal from the perspective of both countries. Should it be the case that $c_1 = c_2$, the resource would be driven down to a common bioeconomic equilibrium level $x = x_1^\infty = x_2^\infty = x^\infty$. We are thus confronted with a Prisoner's Dilemma type of outcome. Hence, cooperation does indeed matter.

If we turn now and consider the non-cooperative management of a straddling fish stock, we find that the analysis used to examine the non-cooperative management of a shared fishery resource applies, essentially without modification. Let Country 1 and Country 2 now be the relevant coastal state and the one relevant distant water fishing nation, respectively. Refusal to cooperate leads to a straightforward Prisoner's Dilemma type of outcome and overexploitation of the resource (Kaitala and Munro forthcoming). If the number of relevant distant water fishing nations exceeds one, non-cooperative management still leads to the same decidedly non-optimal outcome (ibid).

The predictive power of the analysis of non-cooperative management of shared fish stocks and straddling fish stocks is high. The negotiators of the Canada-U.S. Pacific Salmon Treaty were, for example, driven forward by the threat that a fish war would break out if the negotiations were to break down (Munro and Stokes 1989). The history of NAFO, prior to 1992, was one of a moderately successful cooperative game degenerating into a competitive game with destructive consequences for the resources. The latest manifestation of this destructive competitive game was, of course, the Canada-Spain fish war. Indeed, it can be argued that the convening of the UN Fish Conference was, in part, a response to the growing evidence of the severe consequences of non-cooperative management of straddling fish stocks throughout the world.

In light of the consequences of non-cooperative management of shared or straddling fish stocks, the cooperative management of such resources clearly demands investigation. Economists approach the question of the optimal management of shared fishery resources

---

[8] I.e., $Ex = F(x)$. See footnote 5.

bringing to bear, not surprisingly, the theory of dynamic cooperative games.

Let the two coastal states once again be Countries 1 and 2. If we continue with the assumption that $c_1 < c_2$, then it can be shown that, in negotiating a cooperative management program, the joint owners of the resource will have to be concerned, not only with the division of the economic returns from the fishery, but also with the fact that the two countries will differ in terms of their management goals. As we have noted, it will be true that $x_1^* < x_2^*$. The low fishing effort cost country will be *less* conservationist than its joint resource owner (Munro 1979).

Let us commence by assuming that, if the two coastal states succeed in entering into a cooperative agreement, the agreement will be binding through time. The assumption greatly simplifies the analysis.[9] With this assumption in hand, we proceed by casting the problem within a cooperative game framework. We turn once again to Nash (1953).

Critical to the analysis is the concept of the threat point. The threat point consists of the set of economic returns (measured in present value terms), or payoffs, which the two coastal states, "players," could expect to receive if cooperation was non-existent. The threat point payoffs can be taken to be the payoffs arising from the solution to a non-cooperative game and can be characterized as: $J_1(x(0), E_1^N, E_2^N)$ and $J_2(x(0), E_1^N, E_2^N)$ respectively (Kaitala and Munro forthcoming). It is assumed that neither player will accede to a cooperative management agreement which offers the player a payoff less than its threat point payoff.

Conflicts in management goals can be a source of great difficulty in the negotiation of a cooperative management arrangement. The difficulty can, however, be mitigated if "side payments" (i.e., transfer payments) are feasible in the negotiations. Differences in management goals almost invariably mean that one co-owner places a higher value on the resource than the other. The existence of side payments will lead to an "optimal" cooperative arrangement, in which the management preferences of the co-owner placing the relatively high value on

---

[9] Cooperative non-binding fisheries management agreements have, however, been analyzed in detail. See, for example, Kaitala 1985; 1987.

the resource are adopted. That co-owner then compensates its fellow co-owner.

With the existence of side payments, the objective in establishing a cooperative resource management program is to select the one which will maximize the global net economic returns from the resource through time, measured, of course, in present value terms. Denote the present value of the global net economic returns from the resource, commencing with $x = x(0)$ and following the optimal harvest program through time, as $\omega(x(0))$, and let the shares under a cooperative agreement be denoted by: $\omega_1(x(0))$ and $\omega_2(x(0))$. We then have:

$$\omega(x(0)) = \omega_1(x(0)) + \omega_2(x(0)) \tag{7}$$

The shares are Pareto efficient, in that Country 1 can gain only at the expense of Country 2 and vice-versa.

Since each player must receive its threat point payoff for there to be a cooperative agreement, we can define the "cooperative surplus" as the difference between the global net economic returns from the resource and the sum of the threat point payoffs. Denote the cooperative surplus as $\Gamma(x(0))$. Thus we have:

$$\Gamma(x(0)) = \omega(x(0)) - \sum_{1,2} J_i(x(0), E_1^N, E_2^N) \tag{8}$$

The solution to the Nash cooperative game gives the result that the cooperative surplus will be divided equally between the players (Kaitala and Munro forthcoming). Each player is deemed to have made an equal contribution to the cooperative agreement. Thus, for example, the payoff to Country 1 arising from the solution of the cooperative game would be:

$$\omega_1(x(0)) = \Gamma(x(0))/2 + J_1(x(0), E_1^N, E_2^N) \tag{9}$$

In our particular example, the management preferences of Country 1, the low cost country, would prevail. Indeed, Country 1 would effectively buy out Country 2. Country 1 would make side payments to its co-resource owner.

In turning to the issue of the cooperative management of straddling fish stocks, we find that the analysis of the cooperative management of shared fish stocks will carry us only part way. At least two differences exist: the number of players and the constancy of the players through time. The typical economic model of cooperative management of a shared fishery resource assumes that there are but two players and that the players are unchanging over time. The assumptions are reasonable in the context of shared fishery resources (Kaitala and Munro 1993).

If, with respect to a straddling stock fishery, it were the case that there was a single coastal state facing one, and only one, distant water fishing nation which would be involved in the fishery indefinitely, and if one could be assured that all other distant water fishing nations would be barred from the fishery forever, the aforementioned analysis of the cooperative economic management of shared fish stocks could be applied without qualification (Kaitala and Munro forthcoming).

Let it be observed that the relevant distant water fishing nation would acquire de facto, if not de jure, property rights to the resource, which it would share with the coastal state. The de facto property rights would give the distant water fishing nation some assurance of receiving a stream of economic benefits through time from the fishery under cooperative management. The assurance could in turn be expected to enhance the prospects of establishing a stable cooperative management regime.

It is in fact not reasonable to assume that the typical straddling stock fishery will involve one coastal state facing a single distant water fishing nation. Rather it is much more likely that the straddling stock fishery will involve one or more coastal states facing several distant water fishing nations. The multiplicity of players complicates the analysis, since one has to be concerned with the emergence of sub-coalitions. This aspect of the problem has yet to be investigated in any detail (Kaitala and Munro forthcoming).

While the multiplicity of players is a significant factor distinguishing the straddling stock fishery case from the standard model of cooperative shared fish stock management, it is less important than the constancy of players through time. As we have already indicated, in the case of a shared fishery resource, the players (i.e., the coastal states sharing the resource) will, except under the most unusual circumstances, be constant, both in number and in nature, through time.

By way of contrast, the fleets of distant water fishing nations are, by definition, mobile. Hence, in the case of straddling stock fisheries, we must allow for the possibility that some distant water fishing nations currently engaged in the fishery will depart and we must allow for the possibility that distant water fishing nations not currently engaged in the fishery will enter in the future.

The exit of distant water fishing nations currently engaged in the fishery, although yet to be examined, should not cause great analytical difficulties. The entrance of distant water fishing nations not yet engaged in the fishery is an entirely different matter. Indeed it is the problem of "new entrants" which most clearly distinguishes the cooperative management of straddling fish stocks from that of the cooperative management of shared fish stocks.

Under the current interpretation of the Law of the Sea Convention, those states establishing a regional organization for the purpose of managing a straddling fish stock cannot bar would be new entrants outright (Kaitala and Munro 1993). What we might term the "charter members" of a regional organization can do is to bar any new entrant which refuses to abide by the management regime of the regional organization (UN 1994, Articles 8 and 32).

It should be obvious that the aforementioned constraint on would-be new entrants is not sufficient to ensure a stable cooperative management regime. Suppose that the charter members of a regional organization establish a cooperative management regime which brings with it the promise of a stream of resource rent from the straddling stock fishery. The promise of resource rent can be expected to attract new entrants which, while agreeing to abide by the established management regime, will demand a share of the resource rent. If the new entrants were at all significant in number, we could easily find that, for one charter member at least, the expected payoff from cooperative management could well fall below the charter members' threat point payoff. The situation is, let us note, not dissimilar to a strictly domestic fishery in which the authorities are successful in conserving the resource through global harvest quotas, but do nothing to control the fleet size, with the result that resource rent is dissipated in spite of the effective resource conservation. We conclude that, while no rigorous proof has been developed at this stage, one can assert with some confidence that, if the only constraint on new entrants was that they accept the regional organization's management regime, the prospects for effective cooperation could be completely undermined.

In searching for solutions to the new entrant problem, we turn to the aforementioned draft convention prepared by a group of coastal states, having Canada in the lead, which was presented at the first substantive session of the UN Fish Conference (UN 1993). This document presents three possible solutions, two of which have at least prima facie plausibility. While not denying the possibility of other solutions, we find it useful to commence with the draft convention solutions because we know that they were and are deemed feasible by the UN Fish Conference.

In any event, the two seemingly plausible solutions are (UN 1993):

1. Permit a new entrant access to the regional organization, but insist that it go through a waiting period before enjoying benefits from the fishery. Thus, the charter members would enjoy a period over which they would not have to share the benefits of cooperation.

2. The charter members declare the straddling stock fishery to be fully utilized, and announce that a prospective new entrant may participate in the fishery and become a member of the regional organization, only upon an existing member relinquishing its share, and hence membership, in the organization.

The interpretation we place on the first of the two solutions is that the new entrant, upon application, becomes a member of the regional organization, and thus a player in the game. Let it be supposed that the charter members of the regional organization consist of one coastal state and one distant water fishing nation only, which we shall denote as C and D_1. A new entrant now appears, which we shall denote as D_2, and which is accepted into the regional organization and under the terms specified under (1).

We now have a game consisting of three players. We shall suppose throughout that in establishing a cooperative arrangement side payments are feasible.

Turn now for guidance to Equations 7-9. The solution to the three player cooperative game will be such that D_2, as well as C and D_1, will receive a payoff equal to its threat point payoff plus 1/3 of what we have termed the "cooperative surplus." Since the payoffs are, of necessity, expressed in terms of present values, the fact that D_2 may have to wait before receiving its first return from the fishery is essentially irrelevant (Kaitala and Munro 1994). Hence, the first of the suggested solutions to the new entrant problem is an illusion.

The second suggested solution holds much more promise. It is difficult to think of a charter distant water fishing nation member willingly relinquishing its quota/membership for free. It is, however, quite possible to think of such a charter member *selling* its membership. Thus charter members upon contemplating a cooperative management arrangement can think of a stream of returns from the fishery which they can enjoy in perpetuity, or capitalize and sell off. The future returns will not be undermined by the appearance of new entrants. Consequently, the prospects for establishing a stable cooperative management regime are much more promising.

Research on the implications of what we might term "Individual Transferable Memberships" is in its early stages (see Kaitala and Munro forthcoming) so that there are, as yet, few concrete results to report. We can, however, provide the flavour of some of the complications that are likely to arise with the aid of a simple example (ibid.).

Let it be supposed that the charter members of the regional organization are once again C and D_1. Let it be supposed further that C and D_1 are identical except in terms of unit fishing effort costs: $c_C < c_{D_1}$. We continue to assume that, if a cooperative management arrangement is established, side payments will be brought into play. Thus the low cost country, C, will dominate the management policy.

A new entrant, D_2, appears. It is the case, we shall suppose, that: $c_C < c_{D_2} < c_{D_1}$. Assume further that $E_{D_1}^{\max} = E_{D_2}^{\max}$.

Given the differences in fishing effort costs between D_1 and D_2, a basis for D_1 to be willing to sell out its membership to D_2 may thus exist. Consider now the consequences for the coastal state C, if the transfer of membership were in fact to take place. Let us, in passing, simplify further by supposing that it is not possible to form sub-coalitions.

Since $c_{D_2} > c_C$, the global net economic returns from the resource under cooperation will remain unchanged. The threat point will, however, be quite different when D_2, as opposed to D_1, is the second partner. Note that $x_{D_2}^\infty < x_{D_1}^\infty$. This fact, combined with the fact that $c_{D_2} < c_{D_1}$ will lead to the result that:

$$J_{D_2}(x(0), E_C^N, E_{D_2}^N) > J_{D_1}(x(0), E_C^N, E_{D_1}^N) \qquad (10)$$

i.e., D_2's threat point payoff will exceed that of D_1.

Given that $x_{D_2}^\infty < x_{D_1}^\infty$ will also lead us to conclude that:

$$J_c(x(0), E_C^N, E_{D_2}^N) < J_c(x(0), E_C^N, E_{D_1}^N) \qquad (11)$$

While we cannot determine a priori whether the cooperative surplus will rise or fall as a consequence of D_2 replacing D_1, we can conclude that C would clearly be worse off with D_2 as its partner, as opposed to D_1. This then raises the possibility that, even though D_1 does not in fact leave the regional organization, it can "blackmail" C by threatening to sell out its membership. We are also left with the implication that D_2 will influence the negotiations, even though it does not gain membership in the regional organization (Kaitala and Munro forthcoming). How destabilizing the threat of blackmail will be is unknown at the time of writing.

CONCLUSIONS

A significant factor contributing to the fishery resource management catastrophe off Atlantic Canada is the existence of fishery resources straddling the boundary between Canada's EEZ and the remaining high seas. The problem of managing straddling fish stocks, far from being unique to Canada, however, has in recent years become a world wide phenomenon. The problem has become sufficiently severe to cause the UN to convene a major intergovernmental conference to address the issue.

The problem of managing straddling fish stocks has achieved prominence only within the last few years. At the close of the UN Third Conference on the Law of the Sea in 1982, the problem was deemed to be minor. As a consequence, economists have only recently turned their attention to the issue. This paper reports on progress to date and points to questions still to be explored.

Straddling fish stocks are by definition transboundary resources. There is a second form of transboundary fishery resources, the management of which has been studied extensively by economists. These are fishery resources which are shared by two or more coastal states. It is argued that it is appropriate to commence the study of the management of straddling fish stocks by seeing how far the analysis of the management of shared fishery resources will carry us.

With respect to the consequences of non-cooperative management, the analysis of shared fishery resources tells us all that we need to know. Non-cooperative management of either shared or straddling fish stocks leads straight to a Prisoner's Dilemma type of outcome, resulting in the possible destruction of the resource. Cooperation does indeed matter.

When we turn to cooperative management, we discover that the analysis of shared stock management provides at best an incomplete guide to the management of straddling stocks. This is due to the fact that there is a fundamental difference between the two situations. In the case of shared stocks, the participants, in the form of coastal states, are fixed and unchanging over time. In the case of straddling stocks, on the other hand, some of the participants are distant water fishing nations. We find, as a consequence, that some existing participants may leave the relevant fishery, while new participants may appear over time. This fact greatly increases the complexity of the analysis.

Research on the optimal cooperative economic management of straddling fish stocks is at a very early stage. Extensive further research is thus required for there to be a full understanding of the nature of such optimal resource management.

REFERENCES

Clark, Colin W. 1980. Restricted Access to Common-Property Fishery Resources: A Game-Theoretic Analysis. Pages 117-132 in *Dynamic Optimization and Mathematical Economics*, edited by P. Liu. New York: Plenum Press.

Clark, Colin W., and Gordon R. Munro. 1982. The Economics of Fishing and Modern Capital Theory: A Simplified Approach. Pages 31-54 in *Essays in the Economics of Renewable Resources*, edited by L.J. Mirman and D.F. Spulber. Amsterdam: North Holland.

The Economist. 18 March 1995.

Food and Agriculture Organization of the United Nations. 1992. *World Fisheries Situation*. Proceedings of the International Conference on Responsible Fishing. Rome : FAO.

———. 1993. *World Review of High Seas and Highly Migratory Fish Species and Straddling Stocks*. FAO Fisheries Circular No. 858. Rome: FAO.

Kaitala, Veijo T. 1985. *Game Theory Models of Dynamic Bargaining and Contracting in Fisheries Management*. In Report A11. Helsinki: Institute of Mathematical Systems, Helsinki University of Technology.

———. 1989. Nonuniqueness of No-Memory Feedback Equilibria in a Fishery Resource Game. *Automatica* 25:587-592.

Kaitala, Veijo T., and Gordon R. Munro. 1993. The Management of High Seas Fisheries. *Marine Resource Economics* 8:313--329.

———. 1994. *Conservation and Management of High Seas Fishery Resources: The Problem of New Entrants*. Paper prepared for workshop, Property Rights and the Performance of Natural Resources Systems. Beijer International Institute of Ecological Economics, Royal Swedish Academy of Sciences. August 1994. Stockholm, Sweden.

———. forthcoming. The Economic Management of High Seas Fishery Resources: Some Game Theoretic Aspects. In *Control and Game Theoretic Models of the Environment*, edited by C. Carraro and Jerzy A. Filar.

Miles, Edward L., and William T. Burke. 1989. Pressures on the United Nations Convention on the Law of the Sea of 1982 Arising from New Fisheries Conflicts: The Problem of Straddling Stocks. *Ocean Development and International Law* 20:343-357.

Munro, Gordon R. 1979. The Optimal Management of Transboundary Resources. *Canadian Journal of Economics* 12:355-376.

———. 1990. The Optimal Management of Transboundary Fisheries: Game Theoretic Considerations. *Natural Resource Modeling* 4:403-426.

———. 1992. Evolution of Canadian Fisheries Management Policy Under the New Law of the Sea: International Dimensions. Pages 284-310 in *Canadian Foreign Policy and International Economic Regimes*, edited by A. Clair Cutler and Mark W. Zacher. Vancouver: University of British Columbia Press.

———. 1994. The Management of High Seas Fishery Resources. Paper presented at the Seventh Conference of the International Institute of Fisheries Economics and Trade. Tapei.

Munro, Gordon R., and Robert L. Stokes. 1989. The Canada-United States Pacific Salmon Treaty. Pages 17-38 in *Canadian Oceans Policy: National Strategies and the New Law of the Sea*, edited by Donald McRae and Gordon Munro. Vancouver: University of British Columbia Press.

Nash, John F. 1951. Non-Cooperative Games. *Annals of Mathematics* 54:286-295.

———. 1953. Two Person Cooperative Games. *Econometrica* 21:128-140.

United Nations. 1982. *United Nations Conference on the Law of the Sea*. UN Document A Conference 61:122.

———. 1993. *United Nations Conference on Straddling Fish Stocks and Highly Migratory Fish Stocks*. In Draft Convention on the Conservation and Management of Straddling Fish Stocks on the High Seas and Highly Migratory Fish Stocks on the High Seas. UN Document A. Conference 164:L11.

———. 1994. Draft Agreement for the Implementation of the Provisions of the United Nations Convention on the Law of the Sea of 10 December 1982 Relating to the Conservation and Management of Straddling Fish Stocks and Highly Migratory Fish Stocks. UN Document A. Conference 164:22.

CONTRIBUTORS

Diane P. Dupont is an Associate Professor, Department of Economics, Brock University, St Catharine's, Ontario. Research interests: Uncertainty and Expectations Formation of Fishers, Travel Cost Methods of Evaluating the Value of Recreational Fishery, Contingent Valuation for Determining the Value of Environmental Quality Improvements, Fisher's Responses to their Regulatory Environment.

Daniel V. Gordon is an Associate Professor, Department of Economics, The University of Calgary, Calgary, Alberta and Professor II, Institute of Economics, The Norwegian School of Economics and Business Administration, Bergen, Norway. Research interests: Econometrics and Natural Resource Economics.

R. Quentin Grafton is an Assistant Professor, Department of Economics, University of Ottawa, Ottawa, Ontario. Research interests: Fisheries Economics, ITQ Management Schemes, Property Rights and Environmental Economics.

Daniel E. Lane is an Associate Professor, Faculty of Administration, University of Ottawa and Director, Faculty of Systems Science, University of Ottawa, Ottawa, Ontario. Research interests: Fisheries Management and Mathematical Modelling.

Tim Lauck is a doctoral student in the Department of Mathematics, The University of British Columbia, Vancouver, British Columbia. Research interests: Applied Mathematics and Natural Resource Modelling.

Paul Macgillivary is Chief, Economic and Commercial Analysis, Department of Fisheries and Oceans, Pacific Region,Vancouver, British Columbia. Research interests: Developing Strategies to Maximize the Economic Success of Pacific Fisheries and Habitat Resource Management.

Gordon R. Munro is a Professor, Department of Economics, University of British Columbia, Vancouver, British Columbia. Research interests: Fisheries Economics with a particular emphasis on Resource Management Issues arising from Extended Fisheries Jurisdiction.

Halldor P. Palsson is an economist with the Bureau of Competition Policy, Industry and Science Canada, Ottawa, Ontario. Research interests: Fisheries Management Policy and ITQ Quota Systems.

Noel Roy is a Professor, Department of Economics, Memorial University of Newfoundland, St John's, Newfoundland. Research interests: Fisheries Modelling and International Trade.

William E. Schrank is a Professor, Department of Economics, Memorial University of Newfoundland, St John's, Newfoundland. Research interests: Econometric Modelling of Fisheries, Fisheries Management and Political Economy of Canadian Fisheries Policy.

Eugene Tsoa is a Professor, Department of Economics, Memorial University of Newfoundland, St John's, Newfoundland. Research interests: Econometrics, Fisheries Economics and Natural Resource Economics.

INDEX

183

● Cap-Saint-Ignace
● Sainte-Marie (Beauce)
Québec, Canada
1996